Writing Systems
An Introduction to their Linguistic Analysis

During its long history the problem of reducing language to writing, and conversely that of interpreting written signs as language, has found a variety of solutions, which still exist in the form of different writing systems. Written by a leading expert, this new textbook provides an accessible introduction to the major writing systems of the world, from cuneiform to English spelling. Florian Coulmas presents detailed descriptions of the world's writing systems and explains their structural complexities as well as the intricate relationship between written and spoken language. The book also provides a clear and engaging account of the history of writing and its consequences for human thought and literate society.

This illustrated textbook includes questions for discussion at the end of each chapter, and an up-to-date explanation of theoretical issues. Clearly organized and engagingly written, it is the ideal textbook for use in courses on writing systems.

FLORIAN COULMAS is Professor of Japanese Studies at Gerhard Mercator University, Duisburg. He has published several works on writing and written language including *The Blackwell Encyclopedia of Writing Systems* (1996) and *The Writing Systems of the World* (1989).

CAMBRIDGE TEXTBOOKS IN LINGUISTICS

General editors: P. AUSTIN, J. BRESNAN, B. COMRIE,
W. DRESSLER, C. J. EWEN, R. LASS,
D. LIGHTFOOT, I. ROBERTS, S. ROMAINE,
N. V. SMITH

In this series

P. H. MATTHEWS *Morphology* Second edition
B. COMRIE *Aspect*
R. M. KEMPSON *Semantic Theory*
T. BYNON *Historical Linguistics*
J. ALLWOOD, L.-G. ANDERSON and Ö. DAHL *Logic in Linguistics*
D. B. FRY *The Physics of Speech*
R. A. HUDSON *Sociolinguistics* Second edition
A. J. ELLIOTT *Child Language*
P. H. MATTHEWS *Syntax*
A. RADFORD *Transformational Syntax*
L. BAUER *English Word-Formation*
S. C. LEVINSON *Pragmatics*
G. BROWN and G. YULE *Discourse Analysis*
R. HUDDLESTON *Introduction to the Grammar of English*
R. LASS *Phonology*
B. COMRIE *Tense*
W. KLEIN *Second Language Acquisition*
A. J. WOODS, P. FLETCHER and A. HUGHES *Statistics in Language Studies*
D. A. CRUSE *Lexical Semantics*
A. RADFORD *Transformational Grammar*
M. GARMAN *Psycholinguistics*
G. G. CORBETT *Gender*
H. J. GIEGERICH *English Phonology*
R. CANN *Formal Semantics*
P. J. HOPPER and E. C. TRAUGOTT *Grammaticalization*
J. LAVER *Principles of Phonetics*
F. R. PALMER *Grammatical Roles and Relations*
M. A. JONES *Foundations of French Syntax*
A. RADFORD *Syntactic Theory and the Structure of English: a Minimalist Approach*
R. D. VAN VALIN, JR, and R. J. LAPOLLA *Syntax: Structure, Meaning and Function*
A. DURANTI *Linguistic Anthropology*
A. CRUTTENDEN *Intonation* Second edition
J. K. CHAMBERS and P. TRUDGILL *Dialectology* Second edition
C. LYONS *Definiteness*
R. KAGER *Optimality Theory*
J. A. HOLM *An Introduction to Pidgins and Creoles*
C. G. CORBETT *Number*
C. J. EWEN and H. VAN DER HULST *The Phonological Structure of Words*
F. R. PALMER *Mood and Modality* Second edition
B. J. BLAKE *Case* Second edition
E. GUSSMAN *Phonology*
M. YIP *Tone*
W. CROFT *Typology and Universals* Second edition
F. COULMAS *Writing Systems: an introduction to their linguistic analysis*

Writing Systems
An Introduction to their Linguistic Analysis

FLORIAN COULMAS

PUBLISHED BY THE PRESS SYNDICATE OF THE UNIVERSITY OF CAMBRIDGE
The Pitt Building, Trumpington Street, Cambridge, United Kingdom

CAMBRIDGE UNIVERSITY PRESS
The Edinburgh Building, Cambridge CB2 2RU, UK
40 West 20th Street, New York, NY 10011-4211, USA
477 Williamstown Road, Port Melbourne, VIC 3207, Australia
Ruiz de Alarcón 13, 28014 Madrid, Spain
Dock House, The Waterfront, Cape Town 8001, South Africa

http://www.cambridge.org

© Florian Coulmas 2003

This book is in copyright. Subject to statutory exception
and to the provisions of relevant collective licensing agreements,
no reproduction of any part may take place without
the written permission of Cambridge University Press.

First published 2003

Printed in the United Kingdom at the University Press, Cambridge

Typefaces Times 10/13 pt and Formata   *System* LATEX 2_ε [TB]

A catalogue record for this book is available from the British Library

Library of Congress Cataloguing in Publication data

ISBN 0 521 78217 1 hardback
ISBN 0 521 78737 8 paperback

Writing . . . a mooring post for those who travel on mud

Contents

List of illustrations xi
List of tables xiv
Acknowledgements xvii
A note on fonts xviii
List of abbreviations and conventions xix

1	**What is writing?**	1
2	**The basic options: meaning and sound**	18
3	**Signs of words**	38
4	**Signs of syllables**	62
5	**Signs of segments**	89
6	**Consonants and vowels**	109
7	**Vowel incorporation**	131
8	**Analysis and interpretation**	151
9	**Mixed systems**	168
10	**History of writing**	190
11	**Psycholinguistics of writing**	210
12	**Sociolinguistics of writing**	223

Appendix: Universal Declaration of Human Rights, article 1 242

Bibliography 247
Index of names 259
Index of subjects 263

Illustrations

1.1	Chinese character *wú* 'nothing'	*page* 6
1.2	René Magritte 1929, 'The betrayal of images'	7
1.3	Saussure's model of the linguistic sign	12
2.1	Carved bones, approximately 35,000 years old	19
2.2	Quipu knots and their numerical values	20
2.3	Winter count of the Dakota	22
2.4	Frege's *Begriffsschrift*. Is it writing?	24
2.5	Example of Otto Neurath's *International Picture Language*	25
2.6	Hebrew letter *mem*, מ, as iconic depiction of tongue position according to van Helmont	27
2.7	Iconicity of Han'gŭl consonant letters	27
2.8	John Wilkins' physiological alphabet symbols	29
2.9	'Visible Speech', Alexander Melville Bell's 'Universal Alphabet'	30
3.1	Archaic Uruk tablet with pictographs	42
3.2	Archaic Uruk tablet containing calculations of rations of beer for a number of persons for consumption on the occasion of a festivity	44
3.3	Sumerian rebus sign of Jemdet Nasr period	46
3.4	Multifunctional Sumerian cuneiform signs	47
3.5	Sumerian example sentence	49
3.6	The Chinese character *shù* 'number' and its graphic composition	53
3.7	Variant forms of Chinese characters	54
3.8	Chinese example sentence	59
4.1	The structure of a simple syllable	63
4.2	The structure of a syllable in a tone language	65
4.3	Cherokee syllables, phonetic and graphic	72
4.4	Consonantal onset of Old Akkadian syllables is lost in Akkadian	77
4.5	Syllable analysis and mora analysis of Japanese *hon* 'book' and the word's kana notation	80
4.6	*Fanqie*, the 'turn and cut' method of showing the syllabic value of a Chinese character	86

xii *List of illustrations*

4.7	*Fanqie* and phonetic analysis of the syllable *hóng* 'insect'	87
5.1	The ideal model of phonemic writing	93
5.2	The letter *x* and some of its phonetic interpretations	95
5.3	Graphic representation of [ə] in English	96
5.4	Complex phoneme–grapheme correspondences	100
5.5	The Africa alphabet	102
5.6	The International Phonetic Alphabet (revised to 1993)	104
6.1	West Semitic languages	112
6.2	Lineage of ancient Semitic scripts	114
6.3	The Hebrew Gezer Calendar, tenth century BCE, in Phoenician script	120
6.4	Ionian Greek inscription of the early sixth century BCE without word boundaries	129
7.1	Scripts descended from Brāhmī	150
8.1	Amharic ləbəš 'cloak'	154
8.2	Han'gŭl calligraphy by Kwon Ji-sam, seventeenth century	158
8.3	A passage from *Hunmin Chŏng'ŭm haerye* explaining the vowel letters	162
8.4	Graphic composition of the syllable *kwŏn*	163
9.1	François Champollion's decipherment of royal names	171
9.2	François Champollion's first list of Egyptian phonetic signs	172
9.3	Logographic hieroglyphs	173
9.4	Polyvalence in Japanese writing	181
9.5	English <a> and its phonemes	186
9.6	English [ʃ] and its graphemes	187
10.0	Egyptian office. Mural relief in the tomb of official Ti in Saqqara (fifth dynasty)	191
10.1	Sandstone sphinx from the Middle Kingdom temple at Serabit el-Khadim with inscriptions in Egyptian hieroglyphs © Copyright The British Museum	194
10.2	Sign system to writing system: changing semiotic relationships	197
10.3	Schematic derivation of the Mongolian alphabet	206
12.1	Standard and dialects: some dialects are closer to the standard than others	228
12.2	Diglossia	231
12.3	Digraphia	234

12.4 Chinese characters, *mén* 'gate' and *wú* 'without', in full and reduced form ... 237
12.5 The General Rules of Kanandan, promulgated by the Internasionål Union for Kånådån (IUK) Toronto, On., Kånådå ... 239

Tables

3.1	Graphic development of cuneiform signs	*page* 45
3.2	Graphic development of four Chinese characters	51
3.3	Major Chinese script styles	51
3.4	*Liù shū*, 'the six writings'	52
3.5	Chinese compound characters, formed of semantic determinatives and the phonetic indicator *gong*	56
3.6	Chinese words of location	58
4.1	Some Manyōgana, Chinese characters used as phonetic symbols to write seventh-century Japanese	68
4.2	The Cherokee syllabary	70
4.3	The Cree syllabary	71
4.4	The Vai syllabary	73
4.5	Parallel development of Sumerian cuneiform sign and Chinese character adapted to other languages	75
4.6	Basic grid of cuneiform 'Syllabary A'. With permission from P. T. Daniels and W. Bright, *The World's Writing Systems*, Oxford University Press, 1996, p. 57.	76
4.7	Basic kana syllabaries	79
4.8	Middle Chinese final consonants are dropped in Old Japanese	80
4.9	Hiragana and katakana for palatalized onset syllables	81
4.10	The Cypriot syllabary	83
4.11	The Linear B syllabary	84
4.12	The standard Yi syllabary of 1980	85
5.1	Latin vowels and diphthongs	92
5.2	Latin consonants	92
5.3	Some ways of spelling /uː/ in English	99
5.4	Commonly used diacritics to enlarge the scope of the Latin alphabet	103
6.1	The Semitic root *qbr* 'to bury', imperative forms	111
6.2	The Aramaic alphabet	115

6.3	Scripts for Hebrew. Adapted from Avrin 1991: 126f.	117
6.4	The Hebrew alphabet	119
6.5	Tiberian pointing in relation to C letter ב *b* and ח *ḥ*	121
6.6	Hebrew vowels and their graphic indication	122
6.7	The Arabic alphabet	124
6.8	Greek vocalic reinterpretation of Phoenician consonant letters	128
7.1	Correspondences between Phoenician and Brāhmī signs	133
7.2	Brāhmī primary vowels	134
7.3	Brāhmī secondary vowels	134
7.4	Brāhmī *mātrās*, diacritic vowel signs on consonant letters *k* and *l*	135
7.5	Brāhmī *akṣaras*, consonants with inherent *a*	135
7.6	Devanagari plosives	137
7.7	Devanagari sonorants and fricatives	137
7.8	Devanagari vowel signs for Hindi	137
7.9	Devanagari conjunct consonants	138
7.10	Tamil consonant signs	141
7.11	Tamil vowel diacritics	142
7.12	Tamil independent vowel signs	142
7.13	Tamil Grantha letters for Sanskrit sounds	143
7.14	The Tibetan syllabic alphabet	144
7.15	Vowels of modern Tibetan	144
7.16	The Thai syllabic alphabet	146
7.17	Thai vowel diacritics	147
7.18	Thai tone diacritics	147
7.19	First page of K. F. Holle's 'Tabel van oud en nieuw-Indische alphabetten'	149
8.1	The Mangyan syllabic alphabet	153
8.2	The Ethiopic syllabic alphabet	155
8.3	Han'gŭl basic and derived consonant letters	160
8.4	Han'gŭl tense consonant letters	160
8.5	Combinations of consonants and vowels	164
8.6	Han'gŭl letters and their modern interpretations according to the South Korean Ministry of Education	166
9.1	Some common triconsonantal hieroglyphs	174
9.2	Some common biconsonantal hieroglyphs	174
9.3	The uniconsonantal hieroglyphs of the Egyptian 'alphabet'	175
9.4	Hieroglyphic determinatives	176
9.5	Kokuji, Japanese native characters	180

9.6	English consonants	185
9.7	English vowels and diphthongs	185
10.1	Proto-Sinaitic signs. From Sass 1988, Table 4.	195
10.2	The Etruscan and Latin alphabets	202
10.3	The Old Hebrew and Mongolian alphabets	205
10.4	Phoenician and Greek sibilant letters	207

Acknowledgements

I want to acknowledge my indebtedness to some of the scholars who have helped me in various ways, sharing their knowledge and friendship with me: Bill Bright, Danny Steinberg, Jean-Pierre Jaffré, Young-Key Kim-Renaud, Jan Assmann, Yuko Sugita, Giri Suzuki, Yoko Tamai, Minglang Zhou, Yoshimi Shimizu, Mahmoud Al-Khatib, Kim Hakhyon, Lun Du, Makoto Watanabe. In the fall of 2001, I had the good fortune to spend a sabbatical at the Centre of Asian and Pacific Studies of Seikei University, Tokyo. The library and administrative staff were as hospitable as they were helpful, especially Hiroshi Hasebe and Satoko Uno assisted me in many ways that helped the book along and made my stay at the Centre pleasant and gratifying.

A note on fonts

Technological advances in the electronic media have made it possible to produce fonts for a great variety of languages and scripts, ranging from decorative type for your personal correspondence to Egyptian hieroglyphs and other ancient writing systems. In this book I have by and large avoided using these fonts, at least for writing systems that ceased to be used long before even the printing press was invented. A font for a script that was used 3,500 years ago, such as Linear B in Greece and Crete, is anachronistic. Using it in a scholarly book amounts to a distortion and to underestimating the importance of media. Before print, all writing was by hand. True, some cuneiform inscriptions, Egyptian papyri, and Greek epitaphs look as sharp as copperplate, but the travail behind these chirographic documents cannot be compared with a mouse click. It is different with scripts that have been used continuously from antiquity until the present, such as Greek and Chinese. They have gone with the times and been adjusted accordingly. But the tradition of Hittite hieroglyphic and the Indus script broke off hundreds of years ago. Presenting these languages in the guise of a modern font is like letting Hannibal traverse the Alps in a tourist bus.

Abbreviations and conventions

BCE	Before common era
C	consonant
CA	Classical Arabic
CE	Common era
F	French
Gk	Greek
Gr	German
I	Italian
IPA	International Phonetic Alphabet
L	Latin
MC	Middle Chinese
OE	Old English
OJ	Old Japanese
Skrt	Sanskrit
V	vowel
< >	enclose graphemes
[ ]	narrow phonetic transcription
/ /	broad phonemic transcription

Italics in running text denote quoted forms and are used, rarely, for emphasis.

1
What is writing?

> The men who invented and perfected writing were great linguists and it was they who created linguistics.   Antoine Meillet

Writing has been with us for several thousand years, and nowadays is more important than ever. Having spread steadily over the centuries from clay tablets to computer chips, it is poised for further dramatic advances. Although hundreds of millions of people are still unable to read and write, humanity relies on writing to an unprecedented extent. It is quite possible that, today, more communication takes place in the written than in the oral mode. There is no objective measure, but if there were any doubts, the Internet explosion has laid to rest the idea that for the human race at large writing is only a 'minor' form of communication. It is not risky to call writing the single most consequential technology ever invented. The immensity of written record and the knowledge conserved in libraries, data banks, and multilayered information networks make it difficult to imagine an aspect of modern life unaffected by writing. 'Access', the catchword of the knowledge society, means access to written intelligence. Writing not only offers ways of reclaiming the past, but is a critical skill for shaping the future. In Stanley Kubrick's 1968 motion picture '2001: A Space Odyssey' a computer equipped with a perfect speech recognition programme, which is even able to lipread, threatens to overpower the human crew. This is still science fiction. In contrast, the ability of computers to operate in the written mode, to retrieve, process and organize written language in many ways surpasses unaided human faculties. Mastering the written word in its electronic guise has become essential.

The commanding relevance of writing for our life notwithstanding, it is anything but easy to provide a clear definition of what writing is. Partly this is because of the multiple meanings of English words and partly because of the long history of writing and its great importance. At least six meanings of 'writing' can be distinguished: (1) a system of recording language by means of visible or tactile marks; (2) the activity of putting such a system to use; (3) the result of such activity, a text; (4) the particular form of such a result, a script style such as block letter writing; (5) artistic composition; (6) a professional occupation. While in this book

2   *What is writing?*

my principal concern is with (1), the relationships with the other meanings are not accidental or unimportant. The various uses of 'writing' reveal the many aspects of society and culture touched upon by what cultural anthropologist Jack Goody has aptly called the technology of the mind. It can be studied from a great variety of angles in several different scientific fields. Philologists, historians, educationalists, perceptual and cognitive psychologists, cultural anthropologists, typographers, computer programmers, and linguists all have their own interest in writing based in their disciplines' specific understanding of how writing works, what functions it serves, and which methods can be applied to its investigation. What is more, of a technology that has evolved over thousands of years it cannot be taken for granted that it has not changed substantially. There is little reason to believe that writing means the same in different linguistic and cultural contexts. Rather, the meaning and validity both of past and contemporary theories of writing are contingent upon the historical and, perhaps, cultural circumstances within which they were conceived. Indeed, properties of writing systems may have an effect on how writing is conceived, and, conversely, conceptions of writing may influence the way certain signs are dealt with. Maya writing is a case in point. Anthropologist Michael Coe (1992) has shown how the refusal to recognize the Maya glyphs as writing long stood in the way of their linguistic decipherment, which, once accomplished, added a new facet to our understanding of the multiformity of writing. Every attempt at a single universal definition of writing runs the risk of being either ad hoc or anachronistic, or informed by cultural bias. To appreciate the difficulty it is useful to review some of the definitions that have been provided by writers who concerned themselves with the issue.

Aristotle

What is probably the most widely quoted definition of writing was given by Aristotle. The second part of his propositional logic, *Peri Hermeneias*, begins with some basic explanations about things, concepts and signs. Before discussing nouns and verbs as parts of sentences that can be true or false, Aristotle discusses how these linguistic entities relate to ideas and to things of the material world. He explains:

> Words spoken are symbols of affections or impressions of the soul; written words are symbols of words spoken. And just as letters are not the same for all men, sounds are not the same either, although the affections directly expressed by these indications are the same for everyone, as are the things of which these impressions are images.   (1938: 115)

Aristotle's main concern here was not with writing. Rather, his purpose was to alert his readers to the need to clarify the complicated relationships that obtain between things, ideas and words, as a prerequisite of developing logical thinking. He only dealt with writing because words manifested themselves in two different forms: as sounds produced by the human voice and as letters. Explaining the relationship between the two was a matter of systematic rigour and terminological orderliness, but of little importance for the rest of his treatise on proposition. Yet, this brief statement became hugely influential in Western thinking about writing.

Much has been written about it. His pronouncement that spoken words are symbols of affections or impressions of the soul – what we would call concepts or ideas – while written words are symbols of spoken words allows for interpretation. What is a symbol? Aristotle's term is *symbolon* which is usually translated as 'symbol' in English. Other translations of the Greek original have preferred the term 'sign', which is more general in meaning and thus makes it easier to accept that a relationship between nonperceptible entities (impressions of the soul) and perceptible entities (spoken words) should be of the same order as a relationship between perceptible entities of two different sorts (spoken words and written words). A variety of verbs such as *depict*, *designate*, *signify* or *stand for* have been used to give expression to the nature of the relationship between a *symbolon* and that which it symbolizes. The common element of all of them is the implicit assumption that this relationship is characterized by linearity and directionality, rather than being symmetric:

    things   affection of the soul   spoken word   written word

This formula can be given a temporal and an ontological interpretation. Things exist. You think about them, then you speak, then you write. The phenomenal world precedes cognition which precedes language which in turn precedes literacy.

The central element of Aristotle's definition is that it determines the function of writing as forming signs for other signs as their referents. Writing is not only preceded by, but also subordinate to, vocal speech. This assumption reflects the literacy practice of Greek antiquity. The notion that letters stand for sounds was firmly established, and that both individuals and societies used speech before writing was evident. Literacy had a place in society, but did not embrace large sections of society yet. It was not a form of life as it is now. Letters had not yet broken free of sounds. It followed that writing, at least Greek writing, was a secondary sign system serving the sole purpose of substituting for or representing the primary sign system, vocal speech. When writing was invented, such a linear representational relationship between speech and writing did not exist, but that was none of Aristotle's concern. Nor did he address the question of whether the relationship he had identified might change in the course of time as the consequences of literacy made themselves felt in society. His remark that 'letters are not the same for all men', although affections of the soul are, and the fact that it was part of a treatise on proposition suggest that he had a general statement in mind, and this is how it was understood by subsequent generations of scholars right to the present time. Writing is secondary to and dependent on speech and, therefore, deserves to be investigated only as a means of analysing speech. This is the gist of Aristotle's definition of writing, which became axiomatic in the Western tradition.

Liu Hsieh

It has been argued that Aristotle's definition is a direct result of the nature of the Greek alphabet, which is said to be the first full-blown phonetic writing system humanity developed. Thus, writing systems, rather than being conceptually neutral instruments, are thought to act on the way we think. In this connection an explanation of what writing is and whence it came that emerged within the context of Chinese literary culture is of some interest. It bears resemblance to Aristotle's, but upon closer inspection also differs in important respects. In his celebrated essay 'Carving of the Literary Dragon' writer and philosopher Liu Hsieh (465–522) states:

> When the mind is at work, speech is uttered. When speech is uttered, writing is produced.
> The Tao inspires writing and writing illuminates the Tao. What in mind is idea when expressed in speech is poetry. Isn't this what we are doing when dashing off writing to record reality?
> Writing originated when drawing of bird trace replaced string knitting.
> (1983: 13–17)

This definition shares a number of elements with Aristotle's. A mind at work is what Aristotle calls 'affections of the soul'. It produces speech that in turn generates writing. The Tao corresponds to nature, that is, things about which ideas are formed in the mind. However, Liu Hsieh's statement also contains an element that lacks a counterpart in Aristotle's definition. Writing is credited with a creative analytic potential: it illuminates the Tao. Moreover, the Tao inspires writing, apparently unmediated by speech. An idea in the mind is expressed in speech, but also in writing that is employed 'to record reality'. While Aristotle unambiguously places speech between ideas and written words, Liu Hsieh seems to concede the possibility that ideas are expressed poetically in speech or in writing, where the relationship between the two is not necessarily unidirectional. This does not imply that, unlike the Greek philosopher, the Chinese denied that writing was bound up with language, but from his account of the relationship between ideas, speech and writing it cannot be concluded that he conceived of writing as a mere substitute for speech.

Plato

Liu Hsieh and Aristotle speak of the same four elements: in modern parlance, objects, concepts, vocal signs and graphical signs, but the mapping relations between them suggested by their definitions are not identical. In the West, Aristotle's surrogationalist definition has been the basis of the bulk of scholarly dealings with writing ever since, although it was also recognized early on that writing does more and less than represent speech and can never replace it. More clearly than Aristotle, Plato sensed the unbridgeable chasm between discourse and text, between speech and speaker that writing brings about. He was concerned with the communicative function of writing and saw that it was the tool of artificial intelligence as opposed to empathetic dialogue-generated insight, but he was deeply sceptical of the new technology and the form of knowledge it made possible. In the *Phaedrus* dialogue he lets Socrates say, 'Written words are unnecessary, except to remind him who knows the matter about which they are written' (*Phaedrus* 275d). Writing, he reasoned, was just a memory aid, but could not substitute for speech, which was always bound to a speaker who could be asked for clarification. In contrast, written words were silent, they lacked the immediacy of speech, they were dead. In Plato's day, knowledge and knower were not separated, as is typically the case in fully literate societies.

Zen

Plato's critique of writing has been an undercurrent of Western thinking which, however, has strongly favoured the Aristotelian notion that writing is a representation of oral language. As a tool of enlightenment it has met with similar distrust in the Eastern tradition. For example, consider the common Zen slogan 'written words are useless' (Japanese: *furyū monji*), which protests the distance between message and author/reader and the reliance on objectified knowledge. Enlightenment is practice, consciousness in action, the Way; it cannot be captured in fixed signs. Notice, however, that there is no consistent Zen view on writing, just as there is no such thing in Plato. In both cases, scepticism is coupled with veneration. Plato put his misgivings about writing into writing. It was he who

Figure 1.1 *Chinese character* wú, *'nothing'*

preserved in his writing Socrates' philosophy for posterity. Excluding from his Republic poets who at the time were seen as reciters rather than creators of songs, he did more than anyone to usher in a literate culture grounded in analytic thinking. And much as Zen adherents denied the cognitive value of writing, they practised the art of writing. Calligraphy is one of the most highly valued and sublime arts inspired by Buddhism, *shodō* the Way of writing. Consider, for example, the Chinese character for 'nothing' (Chinese *wú*, Japanese *mu*) in figure 1.1 at which many a Zen master has tried his hand. The overwhelming presence of what means the absence of everything is striking and at least as amazing as René Magritte's painting 'The betrayal of images' (figure 1.2). It is hard to imagine that, in the absence of writing, the thingness of nothing would have become a philosophical problem. *Wú* is not nothing, it just means 'nothing', a relationship much like that between a pipe and a picture of a pipe. The visual nature of the sign does the trick.

It is perhaps not surprising that something that touches the human mind so deeply as does writing should evoke diverse and countervailing responses. There is something inherently contradictory about writing, the paradox of arresting the transitory. In this book I am not concerned with the philosophical aspects of this paradox or the artistic expressions it inspired, but we cannot ignore its consequences for linguistics. It is common practice in linguistics to ignore the paradoxical character of writing down language, of treating as achronic something whose very essence is its existence in real time. At best it is treated lightly as a necessary and legitimate abstraction. However, this proves nothing but the fact that linguistics, notwithstanding its claims to universality, is a Western science thoroughly rooted in the Aristotelian tradition. For the scientific study of language is confronted with this paradox from the very beginning. Before anyone thought of writing them down, words were evanescent, *verba volent*. Recording the ephemeral, providing the fleeting word with a permanent form ready to be inspected and reinspected is the first step of linguistic analysis, a step that, strictly speaking, is as impossible to take as it is impossible to give a straight answer to a *kōan*, an illogical riddle developed

Figure 1.2 *René Magritte 1929, 'The betrayal of images'*

by Zen masters as a technique to discredit the verbal side of the mind. 'How do you see things so clearly', a Zen master was asked. 'I close my eyes', he answered. This little episode warns of the danger of believing in one's own systems and categories, the categories, that is, that guide the seeing eye. Another *kōan* describes three monks watching a streamer flutter in the breeze. One of them comments, 'The streamer is moving', while the second objects, 'The wind is moving'. The third monk says, 'You are both wrong. It is your mind that is moving.'

To distinguish the categories that are inherent in the object of observation from those that are in the mind is a fundamental problem of linguistics, as of all empirical sciences. Writing suggests fixed categories and stability: words, syllables, letters. This would not be a problem if writing systems were the object of inquiry and analysed in their own right in order to discover the structural relationships between their constitutive elements. However, they are often studied for what they would reveal about the nature of language as well as the mental processes underlying it. The very existence of writing is taken as proof that language can be studied as if it were a stable object consisting of fixed parts. Even though it is recognized as 'only' a representation of speech, its categories are allowed to intrude into linguistic inquiry. In order to avoid confusion, it is of great importance, therefore, clearly to distinguish that which writing represents of language from what it imposes onto it. This is no easy task, as the following definition, which we find in an ancient Egyptian text, indicates.

Egypt

Egyptian hieroglyphs were understood as models of the totality of all things. An ancient Egyptian onomasticon, that is, a list of words ordered for subjects, is described in the introduction as 'the beginning of the teaching for clearing the mind, for instruction of the ignorant and for learning all things that exist: what Ptah created, what Thoth copied down' (Gardiner 1947: 1). It was things that were recorded, not words. In his introduction to the lists he edited, Gardiner (1947: III), therefore, remarks:

> Their title to be called Vocabularies could be upheld only if the lists could be shown to refer primarily to words, rather than to things, and that was clearly against the intention of the compilers.

That a direct relationship between things and written signs was assumed by the Egyptians is also suggested by a text about creation in which the hieroglyphs play a crucial role.

> And the whole multitude of hieroglyphs were created by what was thought in the heart and dictated by the tongue. And thus Ptah was content when he had created all things and all hieroglyphs.

'All things and all hieroglyphs', Egyptologist Jan Assmann explains, means the forms of nature and their rendition in writing. The heart envisages the forms, the tongue voices them as words, which, by demiurgical powers, attain a physical existence as things. Things are modelled as inner writing in the heart subsequently to be vocalized by the tongue and transformed into perceptible entities of the phenomenal world. 'There is a virtual congruency between the corpus of signs and the corpus of things' (Assmann 1991: 91). According to this view the signs precede the things, they are models rather than images. Creation is an act of articulation in the heart, which finds expression in written signs first and then in speech. Externalized writing is thus more properly viewed as a discovery than an invention.

This account puts Aristotle's linear order of the elements involved in writing on its head and, therefore, from an Aristotelian point of view, strikes us as bizarre. How is it to be understood? The pictorial clarity of Egyptian hieroglyphs is well known and offers an explanation. Does not the Egyptian understanding of writing differ from the Greek because of the iconic relationship between signs and objects so strikingly evident in Egyptian writing but lacking in Greek? This explanation, once again, implicitly assumes that properties of writing systems have repercussions on conceptions of what writing is. On this ground, the Egyptian idea of writing could be easily cast aside as irrelevant for a theory of writing proper, which consists in the representation of words, rather than things. Disturbingly, however, the Egyptians are not alone. Similar definitions of writing have been proposed within the Western tradition and about Western, that is, alphabetic writing.

Massias

After alphabetic literacy had shaped Western ideas of writing for more than two and a half millennia, in the nineteenth century, Nicolas de Massias published a book in Paris entitled *The Influence of Writing on Thought and on Language*. At the time, writing attracted much attention among European intellectuals because François Champollion's decipherment of the Rosetta Stone in 1822 had demonstrated to the world that Egyptian hieroglyphs could actually be read and thus constituted writing, though of an utterly different kind than alphabetic writing. Like many of his contemporaries, Massias thought that writing, especially phonetic writing, was closely linked with language. He thought of it not just as a means of representing language or of cultivating it, but as something much more essential, which permits language to fully develop:

> Here then is man, able by means of language, thought, spoken and written, to communicate with himself and with his present and absent similars. But these languages resolve themselves into a single one, which is limited, written speech. It is this necessity of writing which gives its name to grammar, osteology and framework of discourse. (Massias 1828: 5)
>
> The first writing, without which man could not speak to himself and which distinguishes him from animals is that which the mind has traced in itself by its own action. (p. 7)
>
> Phonographic writing is favorable to speech; it is speech; it makes up and breaks up the smallest elements of sound; and it sustains all movements and operations of the human spirit. (p. 96, quoted from Aronoff 1992: 72f.)

That writing is equated with speech sounds nebulous, but from the earlier quotes it is obvious that Massias does not speak metaphorically. Writing, for him, is at the heart of every language. Thought and spoken and written language are collapsed into one, written speech. As an ideal code it actively articulates rather than reproduces articulation performed in vocal speech.

In the Egyptian account of writing hieroglyphs are models of things created 'by what is thought in the heart'; in Massias' account language itself, its categories (grammar), structure (osteology) and framework of discourse are traced as writing in the mind. As we will see, the idea that writing is a blueprint for, rather than a representation of, speech is not as bizarre as it seems, although most linguists today would reject it out of hand.

Contemporary views

Although there is plenty of evidence that, in literate cultures, writing intrudes into the linguistic behaviour of people and that without writing many languages would not be what they are, the notion that writing is an active agent of language is unpalatable to many linguists for a number of reasons. One is that in modern linguistics languages are stripped of their historical dimension. Although the obvious fact that languages change in the course of time is acknowledged, the possibility that their nature may be affected by external factors such as writing is strictly denied, allegedly on the grounds that writing could not possibly have exercised any influence on the faculty of language because it is too recent an invention. The oldest records reach back a bit more than ten thousand years at best, while language must have evolved hundreds of thousands of years ago. Diachronic linguistics is essentially unhistorical, because, as a defining capacity of the human race, language is not supposed to change by virtue of a humanly contrived technology. There are no highly or less highly developed languages. This is a primitive of linguistics. Artifacts and technologies, such as writing, for example, are granted the potential to change the environment, but not humanity itself. Since language is conceived as an essential part of human nature, while writing is a mere technology, the effects of writing on language and by implication the complexities of their interrelationship remain largely unexplored.

Scholars in the language sciences who do believe that the invention or discovery of writing does make a difference, both with respect to what language is and how we think about it, are in a minority. Linguistic orthodoxy happily concurs with Ferdinand de Saussure's apodictic statement that made Aristotelian surrogationalism a cornerstone of modern linguistics:

> Language and writing are two distinct systems of signs; the second exists for the sole purpose of representing the first. The linguistic object is not both the written and the spoken forms of words; the spoken forms alone constitute the object.   (Saussure 1959: 23)

Following this prescriptive instruction, most introductory textbooks of linguistics simply exclude the problematic of writing or make do with a cursory review of a number of writing systems in the final chapter. Notice in passing that this is quite different in the Eastern tradition of the scientific study of language. The Encyclopedic Dictionary of Chinese Linguistics (Zhōngguó yǔyánxué dàcídiǎn 1991–2), for example, treats writing systems as its first topic at great length. A noble and widely accepted reason for ignoring writing or treating it lightly in the West is that all human languages are thought to be equal in the sense that they are expressions of the same inborn faculty of language. The concepts and theories of linguistics, therefore, have a universal appeal and should be applicable to all languages. Since the majority of the languages of the world are unwritten, it is only prudent to ignore writing when studying language. However, this argument is not as sound as it seems. For, if all languages are of a kind it follows that if some languages are writable all languages are, and since writing is undeniably not the same as language, it is a legitimate and interesting question how the two relate to each other. Two questions linguists should not sidestep are: 'What happens when a language is written down, (1) in terms of linguistic description, and (2) in terms of linguistic evolution?' As a matter of fact, linguists never study any language without recording speech and writing it down. This alone is a compelling reason for studying writing instead of assuming that writing, whose essential properties are so radically different from speech, can be ignored in the research process. Some of the differences are the following.

Speech	*Writing*
continuous	discrete
bound to utterance time	timeless
contextual	autonomous
evanescent	permanent
audible	visible
produced by voice	produced by hand

Each one of these contrasts warrants careful investigation because it is by no means self-evident how an audible sound continuum produced by the human voice, which can only be perceived at the time of utterance, relates to a discrete sequence of fixed visible marks produced by the human hand, which can be perceived at any time. One way out of the difficulty is to say that all of the above are external contingencies of language, which linguists are not really interested in. Linguistics is concerned with the abstract system of language, not with its physical manifestation through speaking, writing or signing. The unwelcome consequence of this line of thought is that vocal speech, too, would have to be expelled from the realm of linguistics and with it what many consider the heart of the science of language, phonetics and phonology.

Both the medium of sound and the physiological apparatus for modulating sound waves are deemed essential for the evolution of language. The human faculty of language cannot really be divorced from vocal speech. A soundless linguistics, therefore, most mainstream linguists would agree, is not just truncated, but an oxymoron. Relating sound to meaning is the very essence of language. Accordingly, a theory of language – a grammar – must specify rules for mapping semantic structures onto phonetic structures. Since Saussure, grammatical theory has undergone revolutionary changes, but the central concept of relating sound to meaning

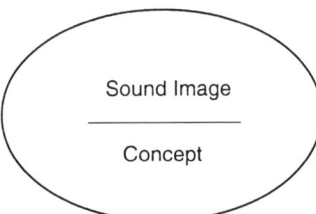

Figure 1.3 *Saussure's model of the linguistic sign*

in a structured way has remained the same. Saussure's model of the linguistic sign still captures the main point. Sound in language has three aspects, which he distinguishes: physical (sound waves), physiological (audition and phonation) and psychological, that is, sounds as abstract units, which he calls 'sound images' (*images acoustiques*).

> The linguistic sign unites a concept and a sound image. The latter is not the material sound, a purely physical thing, but the psychological imprint of the sound, the impression that it makes on our senses.   (Saussure 1959: 66)

'Image', 'imprint', 'impression' are the terms he uses to clarify what he means, plainly visual terms that he preferred to, or was not able to exchange for, others less reminiscent of writing. Saussure denounced the 'tyranny of the letter' and degraded writing as a distortion of speech. He may have fallen victim to this tyranny himself in unexpected ways. There has been little discussion about what exactly a sound image is. The cardinal question is what it is an image of, or of *what* sound it is an image. The sound shape of words varies from one speaker to another, and even one and the same speaker is unable to produce an exact copy of an earlier utterance. How then do we recognize sounds as 'the same'? Is there some kind of matrix or ideal sound that Saussure's sound image incorporates? Some scholars think that this is so, Frank Householder, for example. He speaks of a 'proto-written' variety underlying speech arguing that in a literate speech community speakers 'intuitively feel that speech is a rendition of writing, not vice versa' (Householder 1971: 253). In many cases this is undeniable. An ever increasing part of the vocabulary of written languages come into existence in writing. They can be given a phonetic interpretation, which, however, is decidedly secondary. What is more, thanks to the impact of literacy schooling, it is likely that most educated people's conception of language should be influenced by writing. A number of scholars have suggested that linguists are no exception and that 'sound image' and other important terms in linguistics are proof of that. They are derivative of writing.

Writing and linguistics

In 1982 Per Linell published a monograph with the telling title *The Written Language Bias in Linguistics* in which he presented elaborate arguments to the effect that

> Our conception of language is deeply influenced by a long tradition of analyzing only written language, and that modern linguistic theory, including psycholinguistics and sociolinguistics, approaches the structure and mechanism of spoken language with a conceptual apparatus, which – upon closer scrutiny – turns out to be more apt for written language in surprisingly many fundamental aspects   (Linell 1982: 1).

Ever since Saussure's above-quoted postulate, the primacy of speech is taken for granted in linguistics but belied by actual research and theory formation. Aronoff (1992) points out that, like Saussure, Edward Sapir, Noam Chomsky and Morris Halle appeal to alphabetic writing in developing their phonological theories. Faber (1992: 110) interprets the observation that many speakers cannot divide words into phonological segments 'unless they have received explicit instruction in such segmentation comparable to that involved in teaching an alphabetic writing system' as evidence that historically segmentation ability was a consequence of alphabetic writing, not a prerequisite. Various sounds such as diphthongs and prenasalized consonants, which in alphabetic writing are represented by sequences of letters, cannot realistically be conceived as isolated steady units. Segment-based phonology, Faber concludes, is an outgrowth of alphabetic writing and may not be suited to represent language as a mental system.

Other key concepts of linguistics have been linked to writing in a similar manner. Building on literacy and education research, David Olson (1994) stresses the point that the concept of the word as a distinct unit is a by-product of literacy acquisition. Morphology, the study of words and their parts, is deeply imbued with notions of literate 'word processing', such as 'lexical entry', for example. 'Lexicon' itself is such a term. A lexicon is a list of isolated words, a kind of usage that does not occur naturally in speech. The word is an artificial entity in another sense as well. It is basically the kind of unit that is listed in a dictionary and thus not necessarily the same in all languages. It stands to reason, therefore, that the lexicon as a part of grammar that supposedly we have stored in our heads and that grammarians investigate would not be a research object for grammar if it was not for the written model. The same is probably true of the unit on which syntax is centred, the sentence.

Many researchers who analyse unelicited real-life discourse have observed that in speech the sentence is unimportant and more often than not hard to identify. There is no cognitive, content, or intonation unit in spontaneous speech that corresponds to a grammatical sentence. At the same time, attempts at an unambiguous, uniform and universal definition of 'sentence' have been inconclusive. The sentence is a unit of written language, and 'a sequence of words between two full stops' is as good a definition as any. Further, sentences are said to have literal meanings. A question we may want to ask, without jest, is whether this also holds of unwritten languages. Is it just the language of writing from which we borrow a descriptive term suitable for the phenomenon, or is it the phenomenon itself that derives from written language? Olson (1994) has argued that the distinction between a speaker's meaning and literal meaning is a by-product of literacy. Static entities like the stock of words, sentences and written texts are alien to the spoken language where meaning is constituted in the act of speaking, bound to situation, speaker, context, the interaction history of speaker and listener, and so on. Take away all that and you get the literal meaning, true to the letter, that is. As Olson demonstrates at length, this terminology is not fortuitous but speaks of the fact that linguistics is grounded in written language. Since linguistics is concerned with 'natural language' while writing is an artifact, this is difficult to openly integrate into linguistic theory, which, as a result, is characterized by scriptism, which has been defined as

> the tendency of linguists to base their analyses on writing-induced concepts such as phoneme, word, literal meaning and sentence, while at the same time subscribing to the principle of the primacy of speech for linguistic inquiry.
> (Coulmas 1996: 455)

As Olson sees it, linguists are in this respect representative of literate society at large where writing provides the model for speech, rather than the other way around. We pronounce as we spell, we judge our utterances against the yardstick of written sentences and qualify as ellipsis, anacoluthia, reduction, false start and so on those which do not conform to these patterns. The literal meaning of a sentence is basic. Other meanings are taken to be derived from it. To a scholar who, like Olson, looks at language as something to be learned, such a conception, perhaps, comes quite naturally because it is the written form of language that is made the object of instruction, memorization and testing. As an institution, the school instils into the collective mind the primacy of writing. In contrast, those who prefer to look at language as a natural capacity tend to insist on the primacy of speech. These seemingly irreconcilable positions reflect the two sides of language, the acquired and the innate. Since no human being exists as a purely natural creature, both can be dissociated only in theory. This is the deeper meaning of Olson's notion that writing is a model of speech. Acknowledging the cultural and historical nature of humanity, it takes seriously the possibility that an artifact, writing, may act upon one of its most essential natural endowments, language.

In his conception of the relations between speech and writing, Olson has been influenced by Roy Harris (1986), one of the most outspoken critics of Aristotelian surrogationalism. Harris' project is to demonstrate that the development of written signs is independent of spoken language. Accordingly, his notion of writing is extremely comprehensive, encompassing both glottic, or language-based, notation systems and non-glottic systems such as musical and mathematical notations. Any analysis of glottic writing, he argues, should start from here rather than from the allegedly secondary character of writing as a representation of speech, however imperfect. Stressing the continuous nature of speech, he insists that 'there could be no complete isomorphism between any system of visible marks and any system of sounds' (Harris 2000: 189). It is quite unclear, therefore, what it means that written signs represent sounds. The relationship between speech and writing is fundamentally different from, for example, the representation of a city by a city map where an inch represents a mile in a straightforward and well-defined way. Hence it is necessary to rethink the conceptual model that has guided Western thinking about writing for so long. One alternative view is to conceptualize the relationship between speech and writing as one of interpretation. Rather than trying to depict sounds, written signs are given a phonetic interpretation. There is a historical justification for this view in that writing did not evolve as a means to record speech but as a system of communication.

I. J. Gelb, whose *A Study of Writing* was long the most widely cited work on writing, in a first attempt offered a very wide definition of writing as 'a system of human intercommunication by means of conventional visible marks' (1963: 12). Various kinds of visible marks seem to fall under this definition, because it says nothing about whether, how and to what extent language is involved. But Gelb, too, held a surrogationalist view of writing. While acknowledging that in history the representation of speech was not the origin or the initial purpose of writing, he sharpened his definition stating that 'fully developed writing became a device for expressing linguistic elements by means of visible marks' (1963: 13). Gelb's explanation that writing *became* a device for expressing language rather than having been such a device from its inception still seems to leave room for recognizing non-linguistic functions of writing. But since he considered its becoming such a device to be the first step of a goal-directed development it is hard, from his point of view, to see in the non-linguistic functions of writing anything but signs of immaturity. He saw writing evolve from a rather loose connection with language quasi-naturally towards an ever closer relationship, as the units of representation got smaller and fewer. The evolution, Gelb was convinced, could not but lead towards pure sound representation culminating in the Latin alphabet, the most perfect of all writing systems. This quasi-social Darwinist view has been criticized as 'the common Latin alphabet fetishism' (Battestini 1997: 285), because it makes writing systems that communicate information by other means not mediated through the representation of sounds appear deviant, deficient and underdeveloped.

Combining evolutionism with Aristotelian surrogationalism, Gelb tried to account for the multiformity of the world's writing systems in a uniform and theoretically founded way. However, by committing himself to the superiority of the Latin alphabet he not only opted for a very one-sided criterion for judging progress and the goodness of writing systems, he also made it difficult to appreciate other writing systems for their own merits. Gelb's scholarship was unrivalled in his day, and much of what he contributed to our understanding of scripts, especially of the ancient Near East, is still valid. But his theoretical approach should no longer satisfy the study of writing.

In this book, great importance is attached to Gelb's observation that writing *became* a means of expressing language, but his contention that an inevitable teleological evolution was thus initiated is where we part company. Recording information by graphical means is a basic function of writing that is never narrowed down entirely to the representation of sounds. Writing cannot and should not be reduced to speech. Saussure's above-quoted observation that 'language and writing are two distinct systems of signs' must always be kept in mind, but the second part of his definition, that writing exists for the sole purpose of representing speech, must be rejected, for writing follows its own logic which is not that of speech. From the above discussion about scriptism and the written language bias in linguistics it is clear that there are alternatives to the received opinion that writing is but an imperfect, distorted and hence misleading representation of speech, which deserve to be taken seriously. The relationships between speech and writing are undoubtedly highly complex, but if the medial, bio-mechanical and cognitive differences between them are acknowledged there is no reason to assume a perfect rendition of the former by the latter. If, as I will try to do in the chapters that follow, we free our grasp on writing from the Western preconception that writing should, really, be a faithful representation of speech, then there is little reason to blame writing for whatever discrepancies we discover in the analysis. No writing duplicates speech. Precisely for this reason a thorough understanding of writing is a necessary prerequisite to 'doing' linguistics, to reflect on what we as linguists are doing when we record speech for the purpose of analysis.

As will be demonstrated in the chapters that follow, a wide gap between spoken and written language is very common in the literate cultures of the world, and the fact that there are many functional and structural characteristics of writing that have no counterpart in speech is taken by their members as a matter of course rather than a deficiency of writing. Both historically and conceptually, writing has a certain autonomy. At the same time it would be unreasonable to ignore the importance of writing as a means of linguistic communication. With Harris I, therefore, avoid normative surrogationalist assumptions, but unlike Harris I reserve the term 'writing' to what he calls 'glottic writing'. Any definition of writing reflects both an understanding of, and a particular interest in, the object of inquiry. Since my concern here is mainly with the linguistic aspects of writing, only systems with an unmistakable linguistic interpretation are considered within the framework of this book. Precisely because writing is targeted here as a means of linguistic communication, due attention must be paid to the differences between the expressive potential of spoken and written language, which make it imperative to dispense with the reductionist assumption that writing does nothing but represent speech. Writing changes the way we think about language and the way we use it. By virtue of the fact that writing is based on an interaction of hand and eye, the writing systems of the world have many characteristics in common. Yet, they also differ in important respects due to their different histories and the diverse structural principles on which they are based. Before going into detailed examinations of individual writing systems, the next chapter gives an overview of the major types of writing systems and a number of attempts at their classification.

2
The basic options: meaning and sound

> I remember telling you about a plan for an extraordinary character which would be a means of painting not speech but thoughts like algebraic facts in mathematics. Putting one's discourse into this character one would make calculations and proofs rationally. I believe we could find a method to combine this with the ancient characters of the Chinese.
>
> Gottfried Wilhelm Leibniz 1701

> The language of this country is different from that of China, so that it is impossible (for us Koreans) to communicate by means of Chinese characters. [...] If there are sounds natural to Heaven and Earth, there should certainly be writing natural to Heaven and Earth. Thus ancient people made letters according to the sounds and through them the feeling of the myriad things were communicated.   King Sejong of Korea 1443

The diversity of the world's writing systems is enormous, but they can all be interpreted semantically and phonetically. The communication of meaning is the primary purpose of most writing, and in one way or another conventional relationships between graphic and phonic units are established to accomplish this. Meaning and sound are the two referential dimensions utilized by all writing systems. It has sometimes been assumed that writing could work by relying on one of them only. However, a graphic system that expresses meaning directly is as unrealistic as pure transcription, or 'visible speech'. As exemplified by the above quotes, both meaning-based writing, or semiography, and sound-based writing, or phonography, have been envisioned by influential thinkers who viewed the graphic expression of pure reason and pure sound, respectively, as ideals to be pursued in the design of writing systems. Notice that one and the same writing system, the Chinese, is adduced in support of their arguments by either side, though for opposite reasons. This indicates that real writing systems do not conform to ideals and that the true nature of a given writing system may not be easy to determine. Yet, the two ideals of semiography and phonography bring the main issues of the study of writing into focus. They are, therefore, reviewed here together with some other basic features of writing.

Visual perception

Writing is visible. It is a form of communication created by the hand and appealing to the eye. Students of writing are agreed on these two points across all theoretical differences. The dexterity of the human hand, visual perception and the ability of the central nervous system to maintain a feedback circuit by using a visual input for controlling delicate manual movements are basic to writing. Another characteristic of great importance is that writing consists of signs, that is, relatively durable marks that have an assigned external referent. Human beings produced graphic signs for many millennia before writing was invented. They drew pictures, cut notches into sticks, arranged pebbles in heaps and figures, tied knots in cords, scratched patterns onto rocks. Already the oldest pictures yet discovered, the cave paintings of Lascaux in south-western France dating back more than 30,000 years, exhibit unmistakable evidence of aesthetic sensibility. There is no way of knowing why they were produced and exactly what functions they were meant to fulfil. Perhaps the drawings corresponded to narratives or were in some other way connected with linguistic utterances, but nothing suggests that such a connection, if any, was systematic. What can be said, however, is that, being images of animals encountered by the palaeolithic artists, they were clearly signs.

The functions of other ancient graphic signs are easier to determine. For example, the main functions of notches carved into sticks or bones, known in Europe at least 35,000 years ago and still in use in medieval times (see figure 2.1), as also

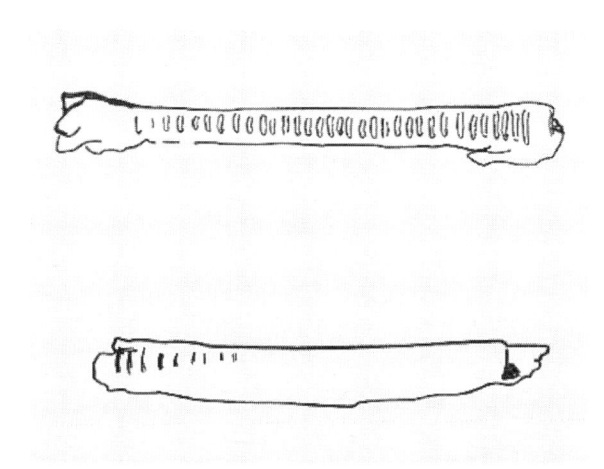

Figure 2.1 *Carved bones, approximately 35,000 years old. After Leroi-Gourhan 1964: 264*

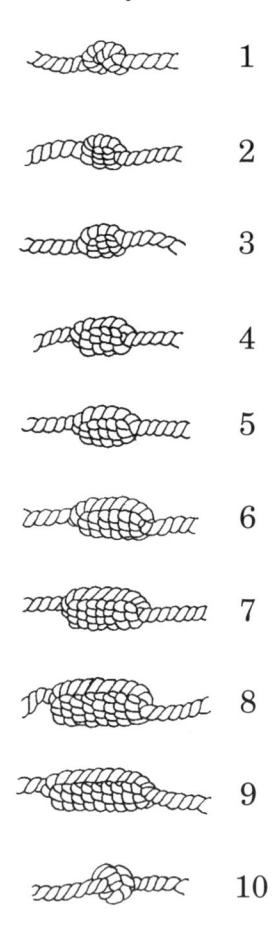

Figure 2.2 *Quipu knots and their numerical values*

of the knotted cords, or quipu, of Inca Peru (see figure 2.2), was memory support and social control. These systems are mnemonic devices, which embodied social obligations and conventionalized promises such as repayments of debts and warrants of goods to be delivered. The quipu were a recording system that enumerated different classes of objects and people. It has been reported by early Spanish sources that the cords also held non-quantitative information such as history, mythology and astronomy, although no conclusive evidence has been established in support of this assumption. Perhaps they were a means of communication for the initiated. If so, what is it that distinguishes quipu, tally sticks and other mnemonic devices from writing?

Auto-indexicality

No writing system is immediately comprehensible without instruction. In this sense writing, too, is a means of communication for the initiated. But there is a difference. Most scholars with a linguistic interest in the subject, such as, for example, Cohen (1958), Gelb (1963), Diringer (1968), Nakanishi (1980), Gaur (1985), Catach (1987), Coulmas (1989), DeFrancis (1989), Günther and Ludwig (1994, 1996), and Daniels and Bright (1996) recognize as writing graphic systems that, in addition to being codes learned by instruction, embody the principles of their learnability. By virtue of their graphic composition they reveal the procedures on the basis of which they must be used. In this sense writing is auto-indexical. Every written document not only embodies the message 'I am meant to be read' but also instructions, however indirect, as to how this can be done. In other words, the systematic make-up of writing contains a key to its own decipherment. Mnemonic devices such as quipu and tally sticks and many others lack this level of structural organization. Like both writing systems and pictures, they may indicate by their outward appearance that they are intended to be perceived as signs, but they do not incorporate any information about the procedure of their own interpretation. This must be communicated separately, as is usual also with writing, which is conventionally learned at school in accordance with established procedures. But where such procedures are unknown, for example because a tradition has been terminated, it is still possible to recover them by inspecting the written documents alone, as the great decipherers of Egyptian, Akkadian and Maya writing have demonstrated.

Conventionality

Pictures such as the cave paintings of Lascaux or the pictographs of North American Indians (Mallery 1972) may have had communicative functions, for instance by being associated with storytelling. Perhaps such an association, if any, was habitual, but it was not conventional. This difference is crucial. Habits establish a practice that is recognized by the members of a certain reference group as right or good or appropriate and that is transmitted from one generation to the next by demonstration and situated example. In contrast, conventions establish a code that assumes an independent existence. Codes are conventional procedures for using signs. They can be cracked, pictures cannot. They can be cracked because they encode information about themselves. The kind of relationship that holds between a code and its rules is not picturable, but it can be deduced from the

22   *The basic options: meaning and sound*

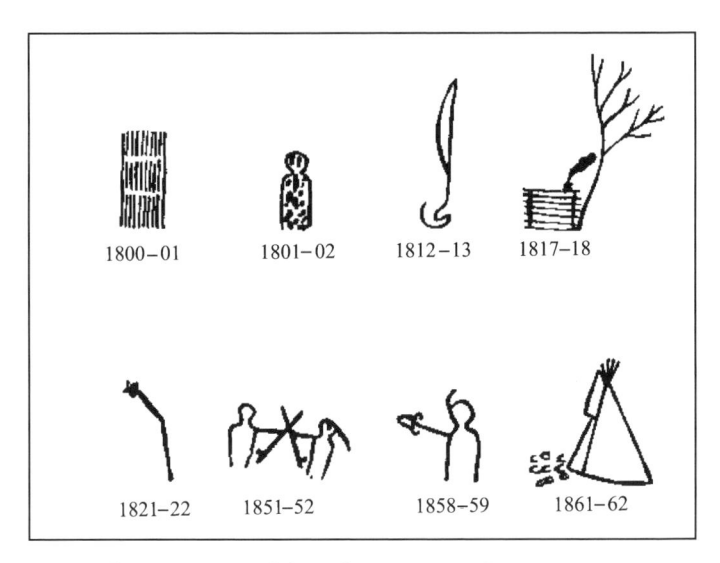

| 1800–01 | 1801–02 | 1812–13 | 1817–18 |
| 1821–22 | 1851–52 | 1858–59 | 1861–62 |

Figure 2.3 *Winter count of the Dakota. Pictographic signs serve as memory aids (Mallery 1893).*

graphic properties of its composite elements and their arrangement. Writing in the sense understood here is such a code. As we shall see, this implies that writing is bound up with language.

Taking auto-indexicality as the main criterion to distinguish writing from other graphic signs is a theoretical decision. Other criteria are conceivable. Semiotician and Africanist Battestini, for example, considers writing first and foremost as a means of conservation of the collective memory for which a great variety of visual marks, much like those of the Dakota winter count, are available. He argues against a narrow language-bound notion of writing. His reasons are threefold. One is the functional similarity of writing in the restricted sense with other graphic signs also serving the function of collective memory aids. Visible marks with an assigned meaning should all be analysed from the point of view of this functional similarity. His second reason refers to the medial difference between speech and writing, arguing that 'no system of graphic notation has ever been capable of effectively reducing speech. What is written is the trace of thought' (Battestini 1997: 32). Accordingly, he postulates 'that the function of writing, in the semiotic sense, is not to represent speech or language – as generally assumed in the West – but thoughts' (1997: 102). The ultimate reason why Battestini favours such a wide notion of writing is that he wants to include all graphic means of conserving and communicating thought, especially language-neutral systems he calls 'mythographic' of which there is an abundance in Africa, the continent whose peoples have commonly, and wrongly, been characterized as writingless. His purpose is to correct this perception and to expose its Eurocentric and demagogic foundations.

Battestini is certainly right to debunk the idea that writing defined in a particular and, as he puts it, restrictive sense can be used to evaluate civilizations. His is a powerful and convincing voice in the post-colonial discourse, and his 1997 work on Africa and writing is an important contribution towards a reappraisal of Africa's rich traditions, literal and nonliteral, and of the manifold semiotic means of conserving and communicating ideas. But he overshot the mark with his claim that a narrow definition of writing necessarily implies a denigrating view of civilizations that do not rely on writing systems that fall within its range.

The ideal of language neutrality

A wide semiotic conception of writing as advocated by Battestini, Harris and others gets support from another direction. That writing should not only be conceptualized but also developed as a mode of communication *sui generis* is an old dream. Do graphic sign systems hold the potential to overcome the obvious limitation of phonetic language of being comprehensible only by the members of a given speech community? Could writing be elaborated to become a universal code bypassing language? Leading European intellectuals of the Enlightenment such as Francis Bacon and Gottfried Wilhelm Leibniz were fascinated by the idea of a universal script as a logical instrument, an aid to memory, and a means of international communication. Bacon believed that Egyptian hieroglyphs, undeciphered at the time, referred to objects and could be used for transmitting knowledge so that 'countries and provinces, which understand not one another's language, can nevertheless read one another's writings because the characters are accepted more generally than the languages do extend' (Large 1985: 12).

In search of a means to transcend the limitations of language, Leibniz likewise looked at an extant writing system, the Chinese. In the seventeenth century, Jesuit missionaries returning from China described a kind of writing consisting of tens of thousands of characters directly expressing ideas. Based on such reports he tried to discover the principles underlying this script, which he thought might hold the key to the deepest philosophical problem, the relationship between reality and what we know about it. Logic and the theory of signs played a central role in his philosophy throughout his life. In his *Ars characteristica universalis* of 1666 he combined the two with logical atomism seeking to construct an *alphabetum cogitationum humanarum*, an alphabet of human thought. He was convinced that ideas could be visualized if only we could discover the fundamental concepts in all possible existence. The basic premise underlying this project is a cornerstone of Western thought: the world is exhaustively divisible into individuals. Although Leibniz's search for conceptual atoms became ever more elusive the more he worked on it, he held on to his belief that it was possible and that the Chinese writing system actually was an imperfect realization of a universal script that could directly express ideas and thus provided a model. Chinese characters he believed referred not to words but to things. This was a fundamental advantage because the *scriptura universalis* he envisioned would be a semantic script whose characters represent concepts independent of a particular language, but that could be pronounced in any language (Widmaier 1983: 33).

Leibniz did not succeed. The information he had about Chinese writing was fragmentary and misconceived. But his aspiration to construct a universal script of scientific thinking in which all true sentences could be formally deduced lived on long after him. Of the many attempts that explicitly followed in his footsteps Gottlob Frege's *Begriffsschrift*, or 'concept script', of 1879 is the most noteworthy. It was intended as a *lingua characteristica* as Leibniz had envisioned it. Concepts to Frege were unchangeable meanings, but while Leibniz saw the greatest and eventually insurmountable challenge in devising a catalogue of such semantic primitives, Frege's main concern was with propositions and their logical connections. His notation is completely different from conventional notations of sentential logic in that it exploits the two-dimensionality of the writing surface. The antecedent and the consequent of a conditional are written on separate lines connected by a vertical line. In contradistinction to common logical notations the *Begriffsschrift* has no symbols for alternation, conjunction and the existential quantifier. All of these relations are expressed by hierarchies of horizontal propositional lines and vertical connections as in figure 2.4.

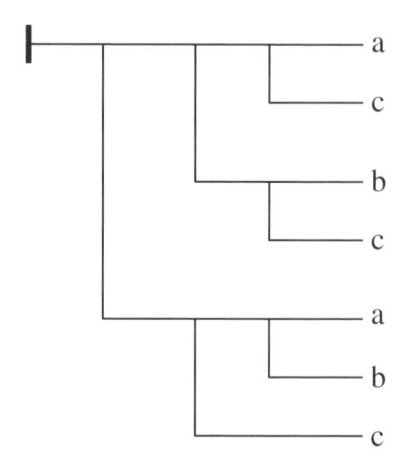

Figure 2.4 *Frege's* Begriffsschrift. *Is it writing?*

shoe

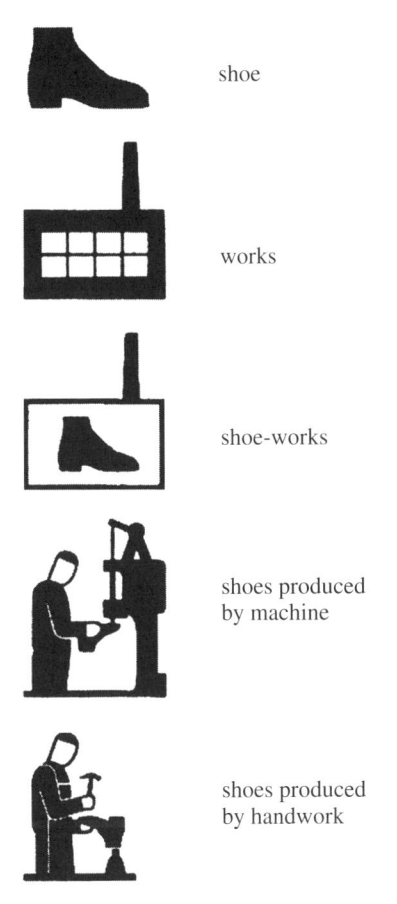

works

shoe-works

shoes produced
by machine

shoes produced
by handwork

Figure 2.5 *Example of Otto Neurath's* International Picture Language

A straight line symbolizes a sentence regardless of any claim to its truth. A vertical bar added at the left end indicates what we do when we assert the truth of a sentence. '⊢ a', then, is the assertion that **a** is the case. Using this as the base and adding just a couple of other graphic signs that need not concern us here, Frege produced a complete formalization of first-order logic. His notation is ingenious and uniquely adapted to two-dimensional visual expression of complex relationships between sentences, but is it writing?

After Frege many thinkers have devoted considerable effort to universal writing schemes. Logician and philosopher Otto Neurath designed an 'international picture language', paving the way for modern pictographic icons (see figure 2.5). The project of a universal character is periodically discussed in philosophical journals (e.g. Cohen 1954), while philosophers of language continue their quest for the 'language of thought' conceived as 'the smallest set of vocabulary items in terms of which the entire vocabulary can be defined' (Fodor 1978: 124). These are thought to be units of an 'internal code over which cognitive operations are defined' (Fodor 1978: 115). At the same time, the Chinese script has not lost its spell to inspire discussion of a world script (e.g. Nagel 1930), notwithstanding repeated explanations of its language-bound nature on the part of Sinologists. Anthropologist Jack Goody states that 'globalization' clearly requires some form of international communication

> ... While the Chinese script is a model, and while there would be some advantage in using a script already employed by a fifth of the world's population, a preferable alternative might be to attempt to construct a new, and possibly more logical, script, using existing icons but developing a new system altogether.[1]

The language in which this proposal is couched is modern, but the project is still the same as Leibniz's three hundred years ago.

The ideal of faithful transcription

The drive for a concept script according to what may be called the Leibnizian tradition was internationalist from the outset: one system for all of humanity. Internationalism was also the intention of a project that approached the problem of writing from the other end, sound, and again it was predicated on the same idea that the phenomenal world can be broken down into elementary parts. On the face of it, this project has been more successful than the search for semantic primitives. Early on, the description of speech sounds in terms of the physiological processes of articulation was recognized as the most promising path to a solution.

In 1667, Franciscus Mercurius van Helmont, a Dutch scientist and philosopher who believed in physical and mental atoms, or monads, and who may actually have influenced Leibniz, published a book entitled *Alphabeti vere naturalis hebraici brevissima dilineatio* in which he speculates that each Hebrew letter pictures the position of the articulatory organs as it is pronounced (see figure 2.6). Helmont was wrong about the Hebrew alphabet, but the idea that the physiology of articulation should be the basis for a scientific description and representation of speech sounds was pursued by many subsequent schemes, and preceded by at least one. The inventors of the Korean script, which was created because the Chinese script was ill-suited for the Korean language, claimed an iconic relationship between letters and sounds. Basic letter shapes were designed to imitate tongue positions during articulation (see figure 2.7). Such writing would be 'natural to Heaven and Earth',

---

[1] Jack Goody, 'A World Script – A Modest Proposal', 5 July 2000; unpublished ms.

Figure 2.6 *Hebrew letter* mem, מ, *as iconic depiction of tongue position according to van Helmont*

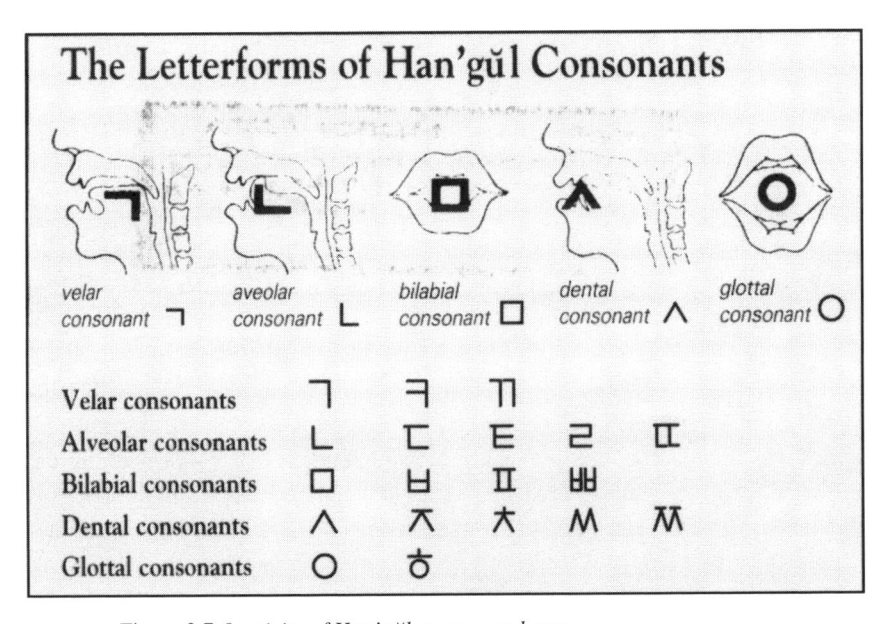

Figure 2.7 *Iconicity of Han'gŭl consonant letters*

as the introduction to the promulgation of the new script quoted at the beginning of this chapter put it. More will be said about the Korean script in chapter 8. Here it suffices to note that iconicity between graphical signs and positions of articulation organs has been regarded, for all we know independently in two parts of the world, as a formula to make speech visible. In the same spirit John Wilkins, an English bishop, in his *Essay towards a real character and a philosophical language* of 1668 developed a physiological alphabet whose 34 signs were meant to depict articulatory processes (Dudley and Tarnoczy 1950: 154), because 'there should be some kind of suitableness, or correspondency of the figures to the nature and kind of the Letters which they express' (see figure 2.8). Notice that Wilkins used the term 'Letter', as was common practice in his time, to refer to speech sounds, whereas 'figures' were graphic signs. A century later, Sir William Jones (1786), one of the founding fathers of modern comparative linguistics, believed that the signs of all scripts 'at first, probably, were only rude outlines of the different organs of speech'.

The different organs of speech were thus what had to be studied, and out of these and similar attempts to understand the physiological basis of speech production grew the science of phonetics in the West, which had been highly developed much earlier in the East and in South Asia. The development of signs suitable for the graphic symbolization of sounds was an important part of these attempts. In 1867, Alexander Melville Bell published a system he termed 'Visible Speech' consisting of the 'Universal Alphabet', a set of specially designed symbols of places of articulation, manners of articulation and phonation (figure 2.9). Since these symbols were not readily available in type, Bell provided a grid of roman letters and numbers to express the mechanism of articulation in common type. His portrayal of vocal action was intended to be so detailed as to include not only speech sounds but also paralinguistic sounds such as whispers, sobs and hisses, and even coughs and grunts. The Visible Speech letters are to be understood as graphic symbols as indicated in the diagrams, for consonants at the left side and vowels at the right side. For example, the consonant diagram shows three vocal cord positions, a bar for voicing, a circle for wide opening, and an X for closed glottis.

Bell's Visible Speech is immediately recognizable as a notation for specific purposes. Another approach was pursued by the International Phonetic Association, which was founded in 1886 in Paris. Following a suggestion by Otto Jespersen, the society devoted itself to devising an international phonetic alphabet (IPA) applicable to all languages, a first version of which was ready by 1888. The IPA was designed to meet practical needs of linguists and language teachers 'furnishing learners of foreign languages with phonetic transcriptions to assist them in acquiring the pronunciation, and working out romanic orthographies for languages written in other systems or for languages hitherto unwritten' (International Phonetic Association 1949: 1). The IPA presupposes that sounds can be counted and tries to approximate a bi-unique mapping relation of 'one sound, one letter', although the *Principles of the International Phonetic Association* warns that vowel

Figure 2.8 *John Wilkins' physiological alphabet symbols*

30 *The basic options: meaning and sound*

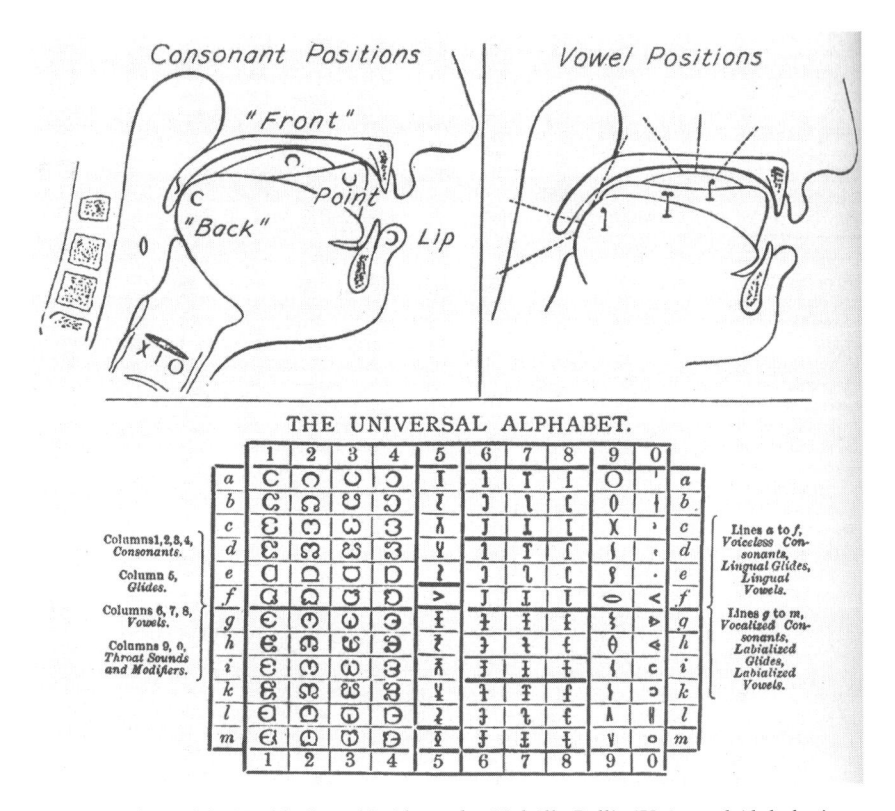

Figure 2.9 *'Visible Speech'*, Alexander Melville Bell's *'Universal Alphabet'*

symbols are 'necessarily elastic in their values'. It defines phonemes as families of related sounds and admits that it 'is not possible to design letters for the representation of all distinguishable shades of sound' (International Phonetic Association 1949: 4). As for graphic design, the IPA was deliberately based on the Latin alphabet, and additional letters – almost twice the number of its classical version – were fashioned to harmonize well with it. This has the obvious advantage of facilitating the learning and use of the IPA. But its closeness to the Latin alphabet also has the incalculable disadvantage of fostering a conceptual confusion of writing and transcription. Two faulty and misleading conjectures suggested by this confusion are (1) that the Latin alphabet and its Greek precursors were transcription systems and that whatever discrepancies between sounds and letters found in Greek and Latin texts are simply a result of sound change over time. (2) The other is that the Latin alphabet is a writing system whose structural characteristics are determined by the set of roman letters and that, therefore, all systems that make use of these letters belong to the same type.

As for (1), it is obvious that the Greek and Latin alphabets were meant to be interpreted in terms of Greek and Latin speech sounds, but this does not mean that Greek and Latin writing was transcription. Writing and transcription are functionally very different. Writing is for readers who have little need for minute phonetic information because they know the language that is written and, therefore, do not depend on such information for identifying meaningful units in the text. Rather, they are better served by a system that filters out unnecessary phonetic information and even omits phonological information for the sake of morphology and grammar. It is in this sense that 'a writing system is a grammar – a description of a language' (Scholes and Willis 1991: 230). Writing systems are conventionalized techniques of segmenting linguistic utterances in such a way that the resulting units can be interpreted as linguistic constructs such as words, morphemes, syllables, phonemes, as well as higher-level units such as clauses and sentences. In contrast, transcription, ideally, focusses on sound alone disregarding grammar. Transcription is a scientific procedure based on the insights of phonetics and phonology, which, in contradistinction to conventional orthographies, does not assume that the reader knows the language. While orthographies provide information about grammar and meaning by means of word spacing, capitalization, hyphenation, homophone differentiation and so on, it relies on phonetic information alone. A good transcription provides a graphic model that can be interpreted phonetically fairly accurately even without meaningful understanding. To the foreign language learner phonetic transcription is a supplement to written text, which tends to require more than superficial knowledge of the language in question to be given a correct phonetic interpretation. A written text, then, is functionally and structurally something completely different from a piece of transcribed speech. For this reason alone (and there are several others) it is wrong to regard the IPA as the ultimate perfection of the Latin alphabet. It is letters of the Latin alphabet put to new and distinctive use.

(2) Turning now to the second misunderstanding invited by the IPA, it must be emphasized that a set of symbols does not determine the nature of the writing system in which they are put to use. Consider, for an extreme and hence clear example, the Cherokee script (Table 4.2). The majority of its symbols look like Latin or Greek letters, the rest like modifications thereof. But the graphic similarity is deceptive. The symbols of the Cherokee script are interpreted as syllables quite unrelated to the range of sound values usually associated with alphabetic letters. Cherokee <A>, for example, is read as /go/ and <K> as /tso/. While the relationship between letters and their phonetic interpretations is different in the various writing systems that are historically derived from Latin, the main point at issue here is the same. The set of elementary graphic symbols must be carefully distinguished both from the interpretations they are given in isolation and from the operational

32 *The basic options: meaning and sound*

rules governing their use. To put it differently, the Latin alphabet is not a writing system in a generic sense. The rules governing its use in Latin and in English and other languages are drastically different, so much so that Latin and English writing should not be treated as writing systems of the same type. Hence, the expression 'Latin alphabet' is ambiguous. The two meanings at issue here can be paraphrased as

- the writing system of the Latin language; and
- a set of 26 letters serving the writing systems of a great number of languages.

In the latter sense it is also referred to as 'Roman' or 'roman'. The spelling with a small initial *r* is indicative of the general significance of this script which is no longer associated with a particular language or culture. Cherokee, English and the IPA make use of the same symbols, roman letters, but not only are their interpretations disparate, the functions they serve are unrelated. This difference tends to be overshadowed by the fact that the IPA looks like an extension of the Latin alphabet and thus like just another writing system, which it is not.

The confusions just discussed, it should be made clear, are not the fault of the IPA per se or the International Phonetic Association. They are simply suggested by graphic similarity. This is what happens when technical terms are couched in everyday language. The IPA is a technical instrument, but it resembles our ABC. Moreover, as a technical instrument it is subject to deliberate improvement and unnoticed change. The IPA is the most widely used system of phonetic transcription, but this should not be taken to mean, as unfortunately it sometimes is, that it incorporates the ultimate solution to the problem of rendering a continuous stream of sound into a discrete array of graphic signs. There is no ultimate solution. Since its inauguration the International Phonetic Association has changed its position on many topics and revised the IPA several times. Pullum and Ladusaw's (1986: xvii) observation that 'the tacit understandings about transcription represent not a firm common ground but one that shifts over time like any other cultural system' alerts us to the important point that transcription, as long as it makes use of discrete symbols,[2] is not a purely mechanical procedure. The transfiguration of audible into visible signs requires interpretation, which means that it is susceptible to cultural influence. It is bound to be imperfect because the medial difference between sight and sound stands in the way of isomorphic correspondence. It is not just that succession in time is not the same as extension

---

[2] These need not be letters. Notice that a transcription based on an exact description of sounds can be quite complex. What in IPA is represented as [n] corresponds to the following expression in a notation developed by Otto Jespersen: $\alpha_{,,}\beta 0^f \gamma_{,,} \delta 2 \varepsilon I \zeta 3$. Clearly, this expression is not to be interpreted as a sequence of features to be realized one after the other. For details on phonetic notation systems see MacMahon 1996.

in space, but a sequence of graphic symbols with a linear expansion, suggesting as it does temporal duration, may actually correspond to articulatory events that occur simultaneously rather than one after another. That transcription is possible at all is thanks, on one hand, to the fact that speech production is grounded in the physiology of articulation organs, and, on the other, to the exploitation of articulatory sound modulation and the formation of classes of sounds for communication. Transcription systematically maps onto these two levels. Very few writing systems do, although many writing systems are in a broad sense phonographic. But this is not a deficiency. Many important features of speech are ignored in writing, and vice versa. Many writing conventions are unrelated to speech, and many structural features of language that are recognized in writing go unnoticed in transcription.

Real writing

It seems clear then that 'painting speech' is no more what writing does than 'painting thoughts'. The ideal of faithful transcription is no closer to writing than the ideal of a language-independent universal character. Writing does not refer exclusively to either thought or sound, and it is quite misleading to consider pure semiography or pure phonography as ideals that real writing systems fail to reach. Real writing is compromise, it is historic, and it is pragmatic. There is no perfect fit between the linguistic constructs that are functional in speech and writing, because writing is static while speech is dynamic. All writing systems have phonetic and semantic interpretations, they differ in the importance attached to one or the other. In describing and analysing the distinctive properties of writing systems and the ways in which they relate to language these points must be borne in mind. The theoretical descriptions of the systems discussed in this book will proceed on the basis of the following assumptions.

  Writing and speech are distinct systems.
  They are related in a variety of complex ways.
  Speech and writing have both shared and distinct functions.
  The bio-mechanics of the production and reception of speech and writing are different.

Three analytic principles follow from these assumptions, which reflect the most important reasons for linguists to study writing. These are the principle of autonomy of the graphic system, the principle of interpretation, and the principle of historicity.

The principle of the autonomy of the graphic system

Like linguistic sound systems, writing systems are structured and can, accordingly, be analysed in terms of functional units and relationships. The distribution of these units is governed by restrictions limiting their linear arrangement in forming larger expressions. These restrictions can be understood as operating on the graphic level alone. In this sense every writing system is to be analysed as a system in its own right irrespective of other levels of linguistic structure to which its units and compound expressions may refer. What are the basic operational units of the system, and what are well-formed sequences of these units? These are the two fundamental questions to be investigated with regard to the principle of the autonomy of the graphic system.

The principle of interpretation

The autonomy of the graphic system notwithstanding, writing systems are structured in such a way that they map onto other levels of linguistic structure, those of phonetic, phonemic, morphophonemic and lexical representation in particular. These mapping relations are often highly complex, imprecise and not always transparent. Yet, not everything that appears to be irregular is unmotivated. It is here that the linguist has a task to unravel the intricate relationships holding between linguistic structures, on one hand, and graphic structures, on the other. To the extent that this is possible, the rules underlying the linguistic interpretation of writing must be made explicit, while non-regular interpretations must be accounted for as well. The basic questions to be pursued with regard to the principle of interpretation are these: On what level of linguistic structure are the units of a writing system interpreted and how do they reflect structural features of the language(s) they provide with a written form?

The principle of historicity

Although all extant writing systems are much younger than the human faculty of language, they carry a great deal of historical information, which makes them the richest source of information about language change in time. Both writing systems and the languages they represent change in the course of time. Moreover, it cannot be taken for granted that writing is a neutral tool that does not affect the object it represents. Rather, it may intervene in its historical development. A thorough understanding of the structural principles underlying the various writing systems is, therefore, indispensable if written documents are to serve as data for historical linguistics. Because established writing systems have a strong tendency to resist change, the spoken and written forms of a language usually progress in an asynchronous manner, which, in the long run, adds to the complexity of the mapping relations between both. Further, most original writing systems have been transferred to other languages. Sometimes such a transfer resulted in a change of type of the writing system. How are writing systems adjusted to the languages they represent, and how does writing a language affect its development? These are the key questions that the principle of the historicity of writing systems calls to investigate.

A note on terminology and notation

To avoid confusion it is necessary carefully to distinguish between references to symbols, their semantic and phonetic interpretations as well as between the systems to which these symbols belong. Some notational and terminological conventions help to ensure clarity. To begin with terminology, the term **writing system** as used in this book has two distinct meanings. It refers to the writing system of an individual language and to an abstract type of writing system. In the first sense, there are as many writing systems as there are written languages, but in the second sense the number is limited to a few types, such as logographic or word writing systems, syllabic writing systems, phonetic writing systems, or variant forms thereof. The term **script** is reserved for the graphic form of the units of a writing system. Thus, for example, 'The Croatian and Serbian writing systems are very similar, but they employ different scripts, Roman and Cyrillic, respectively.' Some scripts are thought by their speakers to be intrinsically related to their language, while others are perceived as serving a variety of languages. The Korean, Yi and Cambodian scripts are examples of the former, and Roman, Arabic and Devanagari exemplify the latter. The terms **writing system** and **script** are distinguished from **orthography**, which refers to the standardized variety of a given, language-specific writing system. The term **spelling** is used interchangeably: 'American and British orthography or spelling conventions differ in some details.' As for the term **alphabet**, it is difficult to restrict its use to a single sense. First of all it refers to a great variety of Semitic writings and their various Greek and Latin descendants. Another meaning is as the signary of a written language, that is, the inventory of basic signs of any writing system, for example, 'the Tibetan alphabet consists of 30 letters'. In this sentence the term **letter** is used in a very loose sense. In a more restricted sense it refers to the basic symbols of Semitic-derived writing systems, including the Latin alphabet. In the most general sense that encompasses the basic functional units of all writing systems I will use the term **sign** with or without further qualification, as the case may be, and the complete inventory of the basic signs of a given writing system is its **signary**.

Since roman letters serve multiple functions, brackets are used to forestall ambiguity. Whenever a roman or roman-derived letter is referred to in its own right, it is put in angled brackets, for example to discuss its graphic composition: 'French <ç> is composed of a regular <c> and a subscript hook <͕> called cedilla. In French it is interpreted as [s].' Square brackets, as in the previous sentence, are used for narrow phonetic transcription, while slashes are used for wide phonemic transcription. Thus,

<s> 'es, the nineteenth letter of the English alphabet'
[s] 'voiceless alveolar fricative'
/s/ 'the phoneme es'

The term **grapheme** refers to the abstract type of a letter and its position in a given writing system,[3] much like **phoneme**, the term on which it is modelled, understood as a group of similar speech sounds. When we refer in the running text to non-roman letters such as Hebrew aleph, א, and Greek psi, Ψ, or to the signs of typologically different writing systems such as the Chinese character 字 (zì), no brackets are used, because it will always be clear from the context whether it is the graphic shape, the phonetic interpretation, or the semantic interpretation that is at issue. Round brackets as in the previous sentence are sometimes used to enclose transliterations, in this case, the standard roman rendition of the Chinese character in Pinyin orthography. Transliteration, not to be confused with transcription, is the conversion of the graphemes of one writing system into those of another writing system. For example, 'In accordance with two different conventions, Japanese しち can be transliterated as (shichi) or (siti).'

Transliteration has not always been clearly distinguished from transcription. Writing systems of the same type, for example the Latin and Cyrillic alphabets, pose no conceptual difficulties, but transliteration conventions for typologically different writing systems are problematic. For example, the various Romanization systems for Chinese, Japanese and Korean include elements of transcription, because the question of how a given character shall be represented alphabetically is not kept apart from that of which alphabetic letters shall be assigned to the reading of that character. But these are different questions. For the scientific study of texts and for cataloguing and reference systems various transliteration schemes have been designed, and in some fields competing systems are in use. For instance, theologians and linguists use different systems for transliterating Hebrew texts in Roman letters.

---

[3] See Kohrt 1986 for a review of the history of this term.

Questions for discussion

(1) The ideals of pure semiography and pure phonography constitute opposite approaches to the problem of writing. How do you explain that they are both based on universalistic assumptions?
(2) What did Leibniz expect of Chinese characters?
(3) What did the Koreans experience with Chinese characters?
(4) What are the main differences between writing and transcription?

3

Signs of words

All words of necessary or common use were spoken before they were written; and while they were unfixed by any visible signs, must have been spoken with great diversity.   Samuel Johnson

It would be necessary to search for the reason for dividing language into words – for in spite of the difficulty of defining it, the word is a unit that strikes the mind, something central in the mechanism of language.
Ferdinand de Saussure

Theoretical words

Words are the typical units of lexicology and lexicography. This seems obvious enough, but there has been a great deal of scholarly discussion about the status of the word in language structure. Some linguists avoid the term altogether giving preference to the morpheme as the smallest and basic grammatical unit. For, while in everyday speech we can live with expressions that have vague and multiple meanings, scientific terms should be unambiguous and, ideally, universally applicable. The word fails on both counts. 'Word' is a highly ambiguous term and hard to define in a way valid for all languages. Words are units at the boundary between morphology and syntax serving important functions as carriers of both semantic (Sampson 1979) and syntactic (Di Sciullo and Williams 1987) information and as such are subject to typological variation. In some languages words seem to be more clearly delimited and more stable than in others. The structural make-up of words depends on typological characteristics of languages. In isolating languages such as Chinese and Vietnamese words are invariant in the sense that they do not undergo regular formal alterations that serve grammatical functions. In inflecting languages the internal structure of words is changed to express grammatical relationships, for example by the use of inflectional endings. For instance, the ending -*psi* of Latin *scripsi* 'I have written' expresses that the verb is in the first person singular, present perfect, active and indicative. This raises the question of whether other inflectional forms and the infinitive of the verb *scribere* 'to write' should be regarded as the same word or as different words. Similarly, agglutinating languages build up words out of units expressing grammatical relations. 'I was made to write' is rendered a single word in Japanese. Hyphens are inserted here between the stem, *kak-* and the agglutinated grammatical units indicating causative, passive and past tense, respectively: *kak-(a)-se-rare-ta*. None of the elements are words that can stand alone. Even more complex words are found in polysynthetic languages such as Inuit and Yupik. In these languages it is difficult to distinguish words from other linguistic entities such as clauses and sentences.

In spite of these difficulties, lexicologists are more or less agreed on the units of their inquiry, although they may differ in some detail of how to distinguish words from other linguistic units. Words are meaningful and they are grammatically autonomous. It is true that there are semantic units below the word level – for example verb stems in agglutinating languages – as well as minimal constituents consisting of more than one word – for example idioms such as *round the bend*. However, typically the word is the smallest unit that can stand alone as a complete utterance and that can be inserted, extracted and moved around the sentence without destroying its grammaticality. Positional mobility then is an important characteristic of words, which among other things allows them to be taken out of context and arranged in lists. In ordinary language the meaning of a word is governed by the context, but in a list there is no syntagmatic context. A word in a list has a general meaning of and by itself that cannot be specified by the context. This is what we call lexical meaning. Lists are what lexicographers deal with.

Dictionaries are basically word lists supplemented by information of various kinds, especially pronunciation, meaning and equivalents in other languages. Dictionary makers treat words as natural units. Obviously, they have to make reasoned decisions as to which entities to include, but theoretical rigour not being their chief concern they can be flexible and pragmatic. Yet, their decisions have profound consequences because, while they consider words as given, it is dictionaries that in literate societies are referred to in case of doubt: a word is a linguistic unit listed in a dictionary. This statement has an air of tautology, but it is far from meaningless. The remarks by both Johnson and Saussure quoted at the beginning of this chapter point to the important fact that words are intuitively given units but hard to pinpoint. Once fixed by visible signs, they acquire a corporeal existence. It should be borne in mind that first and foremost words are lexical units or lemmata, that is, analytic units of the written language. A popular encyclopedic dictionary of linguistics defines the orthographic word as 'the unit bounded by spaces in the written language' and the phonological word as 'the corresponding unit for speech' (Crystal 1992: 420).

A definition such as this is useful as it does not try to hide its makeshift character. Clearly, there is nothing universal about word separation. In some languages but not in others written words are recognizable units in accordance with this criterion, and it is not difficult to find examples of how inconsistently it is applied in a given language. *Almost* would appear to be one orthographic word, *all right* are two, and *all-out* is neither fish nor fowl. Word spacing, moreover, is not only different in different languages but also contingent upon historical developments. For instance, early writers of Greek and Latin did not separate words, while medieval scribes did. The Roman cursive script 'runs all the letters together as if the separate words had no significance...Even short words are arbitrarily bisected when the end of the line is reached' (Clanchy 1993: 130). Word separation in medieval Latin was developed by Irish and Anglo-Saxon monks. Clanchy (ibid.) explains why: 'Their unfamiliarity with Latin made it essential for them to distinguish the words of the sacred scripture from each other.' What the monks did then was to interpret an array of written signs in such a way that it was broken down into meaningful words. Word spacing superimposed a structure on the text to facilitate processing, an analytic structure not needed by those well versed in the language in question.

For present purposes it is appropriate to make do with a simple and pragmatic notion of the word, because where words are recognized in writing this is not the result of a theoretically founded analysis of speech, but an interpretation. We will assume that the word is a unit 'that strikes the mind' in the sense Saussure alluded to, but we will also assume that its status as a clearly delimited unit of a given language is a result rather than a prerequisite of writing. If words were not created by writing, the need to distinguish between words and other linguistic units was. When they first came into existence in this sense, words were units that could be associated with written signs, not the other way round. That is, writing systems such as the Chinese and Sumerian in which the word plays an important role as a unit are not based on prior explicit linguistic knowledge. It would be quite mistaken to assume that the Sumerians and Chinese who developed Sumerian and Chinese writing targeted words, which they isolated analytically in order to write them down. Rather, written signs came to be interpreted as words which, as a result, were recognized as the operational units of the ensuing writing systems. To these we now turn.

Logographic writing

Graphemic or orthographic words are recognizable in many writing systems, in some more than in others. One way of classifying writing systems is by the level of linguistic analysis to which their basic functional units relate. Writing systems whose basic functional units are interpreted as words are known as 'logographic' or 'word writing' systems. Alternatively, the term 'ideographic' is also commonly used. However, it is doubtful that there ever was a writing system that expressed ideas, as this term would seem to suggest. In the previous chapter we saw that all attempts at construing a universal character or concept script have failed. In the threefold relation between objects, concepts and words it has not been possible to design a writing system that operates on the level of concepts regardless of language. Those who speak of ideographic writing do not necessarily contend that idea writing is possible. What they want to emphasize is rather that the signs of the systems they are concerned with are to be interpreted primarily not in terms of sound but of meaning. Yet, since the term 'ideographic' is prone to lead to misunderstandings, 'logographic' is preferred here, although this term, too, requires some qualification, as will become apparent in the following discussion of two major logographic writing systems, which are also two of the most ancient, the Sumerian and the Chinese.

Sumerian writing

Graphic structure

At the beginning of Sumerian writing were pictures of objects. The iconic quality of many early signs is evident. Animals or their distinctive body parts, such as horned heads, tools, vessels and plants are clearly discernible on the most archaic clay tablets, the typical surface on which writing in Mesopotamia developed. Clay is uniquely suitable for preserving records as it is virtually indestructible. When it has been baked it can be kept for many centuries without decaying. A disadvantage is that it is heavy, but at a time when the main purpose of writing was not pocketbooks but inventories and other economic records that were to be kept in one place, the weight of the tablets did not matter much. Just 15 per cent of the archaic documents of the late Uruk and Jemdet Nasr periods (ca 3300–2900 BCE) when the system took shape are not economic (Nissen, Damerow and Englund 1990; Michalowski 1996: 36).

If a little lump of moist clay is flattened, lines can be drawn easily on the plastic surface. However, the material actually lends itself more comfortably to imprinting and stamping than to drawing. This is testified by the earliest Sumerian number signs, spheres and cones impressed into clay tablets. These are non-pictorial, purely symbolic signs, which derive from clay tokens or 'count stones' used in Mesopotamia as early as 8000 BCE as a primitive accounting system. As Schmandt-Besserat (1992) has convincingly demonstrated, these tokens constitute another source of Sumerian writing, in addition to pictures. Most of them are geometrical forms, circles, half circles, triangles, rectangles, and so on. Special numerical signs are attested on the earliest documents from Uruk, now Warka,

42   *Signs of words*

Figure 3.1 Archaic Uruk tablet with pictographs

a city in southern Iraq, which because of its rich yield in excavated documents is considered the place where Sumerian writing originated. The drawing of an archaic Uruk tablet in figure 3.1 represents the oldest stage of Sumerian writing, approximately 3200 BCE. On the reverse side a bull's head and a cow's head are written under two lines of numerical signs, spheres representing ten and cones representing one. On the obverse side the cone-shaped numerical sign is combined with a variety of other signs divided into a series of compartments or 'cases' separated by straight lines, each of which contains an array of signs that can be interpreted as enumerations, as in a ledger, which is what these inscriptions were.

The layout of cases on early tablets was not fixed, and the signs, while more or less conventionalized in form, displayed considerable variation. The primary referents of the signs are physical objects. The line drawing of a bull's head refers to a bull or, perhaps, generically to cattle. The general form of the sign is significant, but the composition of the line drawing is not standardized. It is still the pictorial value that counts. But the more the scribes write the more they develop routines to produce the pictograms and in the process turn to impressing instead of scratching lines into the clay. Drawn lines are replaced by stylus impressions resulting in the characteristic wedge shapes that gave the Sumerian script its modern name: cuneiform, from Latin *cuneus* 'wedge'. In conjunction with this change in the writing technique the orientation of the signs also changes, as the hand-held tablets are rotated ninety degrees counterclockwise. Two design features follow from these technical aspects of writing on clay. Curved lines are replaced by series of short strokes, and the pictorial quality of the signs is lost.

These technical developments have repercussions on the structure of the signs and the way they are processed. Recognition of the signs is no longer based on similarity but on discrimination, as pictorial likeness is gradually replaced by the necessity to distinguish one sign from another. Differentiation thus becomes the principal design feature of the signs. For example, that the sign of a bull resembles a bull is now less important than that it differs from the sign of a cow. Hence the number and direction of wedges of which a given sign is composed are standardized. Signs come to be characterized as configurations of fixed numbers of strokes arranged in a fixed order. Moreover, the wedges are limited to a few categories and directions: vertical, horizontal, and oblique in south-easterly and north-easterly directions. In addition the full-blown system contains a triangular wedge made with the tip of the stylus. Of these elementary strokes all signs are composed.

The relationship between signs and objects is superseded by multiple relationships between signs and other signs as the scribes' chief concern. The signs thus become part of a graphic *system* characterized by negative differentiation. The underlying principle is that the many signs are to be kept from becoming confused with one another, much like the units of a language. The creation of new signs follows the same principle when lines are added to existing signs or one sign is adjoined to another. Contrast with all other signs becomes a defining feature of every sign.

The signary

Cuneiform was used over a period of about three thousand years, Sumerian being the dominant written language in Mesopotamia for some thirteen hundred years until about 1900 BCE. During this time, the signary of cuneiform signs

44   *Signs of words*

Figure 3.2 *Archaic Uruk tablet containing calculations of rations of beer for a number of persons for consumption on the occasion of a festivity. Source: Nissen, Damerow and Englund (1990). Photo copyright M. Nissen.*

Table 3.1. *Graphic development of cuneiform signs*

	original image	90° turn	ca 2500	ca 2000	Babylonian	Assyrian	sound shape	meaning
1							an, il	sky
2							ki, ke	land
3							lu	human
4							munus	female
5							kur, mat	mountain
6							sag, šag	head
7							ka, inim	mouth
8							nig, ša	bread
9							ku	food
10							a	water
11							nag	drink
12							du	foot
13							na	fish
14							gu, gud	bull
15							ab, lid	cow
16							še	grain

in common use varied regionally and across different kinds of text. The total number of attested independently occurring signs has been estimated at between 900 (Krebernik and Nissen 1994: 276) and over 1,000 (Cooper 1996: 41). Since syntagmatic combinations of individual signs are sometimes hard to distinguish clearly from compound signs, as over time compounds coalesced into complex signs, it is not possible to cite an exact number. Examples of complex signs that were formed by combining already existing signs are the signs for food and drink, nos. 9 and 11 in table 3.1, which were composed by adding respectively signs 8 'bread' and 10 'water' to sign 6 'head'. Not all cases of combinations of simple signs are equally clear, but the order of magnitude of the entire signary is not in doubt.

46 *Signs of words*

Linguistic structure

A conventional association of signs with Sumerian words was gradually established resulting from the fact that the graphic signs had the same referents as the names of the depicted objects. A pictorial sign of a fish could refer to the word 'fish' just as well as to a fish. It is not known at which point scribes began to be aware of the relational difference between a sign and an object and a sign and the name of an object. Probably these two relationships were not clearly differentiated in the scribes' minds for some time. The fact that the oldest signs all had concrete referents, while abstract or non-referential meanings were added later by metaphorical extension, supports this assumption. First there was the sign of a star which looked like a star. Then it was semantically expanded by metonymy to mean 'sky' and eventually also 'god'. That the signs were given linguistic interpretations at an early stage is, however, evidenced by the many word lists used for scribal training. Interpretations as Sumerian word signs stabilize from ca 3200 BCE. At this point, linguistic rather than object reference is unmistakable, but the written language of the early documents is very restricted. There are no sign sequences that can be interpreted as expressions larger than individual words.

When writing is used in earnest for record keeping and communication a point is soon reached where pure word signs can no longer satisfy the scribes' needs. The expressive power of a system that has to make do with 1,000 signs is very limited. For comparison, an average high school student's vocabulary comprises an estimated 20,000 words and comprehensive dictionaries list as many as 300,000 words. Inevitably, therefore, signs are employed for multiple functions, which is a characteristic feature of the fully developed system.

Sumerian, the original language of cuneiform writing, has a fair number of homonyms, a feature that the scribes exploited to overcome the limitations of

Figure 3.3 *Sumerian rebus sign of Jemdet Nasr period. The sign in the upper left corner of the tablet is a pictograph of gi 'reed' here used for the homophonous word gi 'to reimburse' (Vaiman 1974: 18).*

{ logogram 'land', 'country' mātu
{ determinative for names of mountains
{ phonetic kur, mat, sat

{ logogram 'wood' gis
{ determinative for names of wooden objects
{ phonetic iz

{ logogram 'sky' an
{ determinative for names of deities
{ phonetic an

Figure 3.4 *Multifunctional Sumerian cuneiform signs*

the system. Loss of the pictorial quality of the signs facilitated their transfer to semantically unrelated words. This is commonly known as rebus writing. For example a pictogram of an unknown tool *ba* was used to write *ba* 'to distribute'. *Su* 'body' was used as a rebus for *su* 'to replace', *sar* or *šar* 'plant' for *sar* 'to write'. Near homonyms were also included in the process of transfer. The sign for 'arrow', *ti*, was used for writing *ti(l)* 'life'. In this manner many signs acquired multiple unrelated meanings, the common sound shape being the link. It is here that the phonetic interpretation of cuneiform signs originates.

As the result of another process of transfer, the signs also acquired multiple readings. The expressive power of many word signs was enlarged by metonymy. For instance, the sign for 'mouth', *ka*, was given the additional readings *inim* 'word' and *dug* 'to speak'. Similarly, the sign for 'plough', *apin*, was given a second reading, *uru* 'to plough'. Being logograms, the signs refer to these words in their entirety, that is, the graphic complexity of the signs is not related to the internal structure of the words. As long as there is a one-to-one relation between signs and words a logographic system with its large signary is unwieldy, perhaps, but manageable. When the signs get associated with multiple readings and meanings it is in danger of becoming dysfunctional. To some extent the context helps to determine the intended meaning, but since homonymic and polysemous signs proliferated, reading became a guessing game.

The solution was disambiguation by means of supplementary signs. Two kinds of indicators were introduced. Existing word signs for generic terms such as 'wood', 'stone', 'god', 'plant', 'city', 'land' and so on were placed in front of polysemous word signs in order to specify their meaning where necessary. The signs for 'man' and 'woman' served the same function as markers of male and female personal names. The sign for 'plough' prefixed by that for 'wood' thus was to be interpreted as the tool rather than the activity, while the sign for 'man' instead of 'wood' could either mean 'man plough' or 'ploughman', eventually yielding a new complex sign with the latter meaning. These signs have no phonetic interpretation, their function being to indicate a semantic category. They are known as 'determinatives' or 'semantic classifiers'.

Another method of determining the reading and hence the meaning of a sign is by means of phonetic complements. For instance, the logogram for 'mouth', *ka*, was combined with a sign commonly read *dug* to indicate the intended reading *dug* 'to speak'. This practice greatly augmented the expressive power of the system, but at the same time added to its complexity, because the signs that were used as phonetic complements, like those used as determinatives, were not graphically distinct from logograms. The result was pervasive multifunctionality of signs as exemplified in figure 3.3. Only experienced scribes well versed in the Sumerian language could easily decide whether the logogram for 'land' was used in that function, or as a determinative for placenames, or as a phonetic indicator *kur* or *sat*.

Once additional levels of linguistic information were introduced and logograms were put into context to form syntagmatic expressions rather than itemized lists, phonetic indicators became indispensable. Typological properties of Sumerian as an agglutinative language were a major factor in this development. In agglutinative languages grammatical relations are expressed by means of bound function morphemes that have no independent existence. When immutable word signs are lined up to express relations between objects, activities and events, a way must be found to interpret the grammatical form of each logogram. Determinatives that indicate semantic categories are not suitable for this purpose. The only workable solution is found in phonetic indicators that can complement the lexical information given by the logograms indicating the phonetic form, which can be given a grammatical interpretation. The resulting writing style is rather convoluted. For example, the expression 'they have given him', which is one word in Sumerian, is composed of six elements, five phonetic indicators grouped around the basic verb form *sum* 'to give' as follows: *mu-na-an-sum-mu-uš*. How exactly this was phonetically interpreted is uncertain, but it is clear that the writing is highly pleonastic. The phonetic *-mu-* which is added to the verbal base *-sum-* duplicates its final consonant as well as the initial vowel of the subsequent phonetic *-uš*. Similarly, the phonetic *-an-* duplicates the final sound of the preceding *-na-*. The actual reading of the word was probably something like /munansumuš/ where -/na/- expresses third person singular object and -/n/- ... -/uš/ third person plural present perfect subject.

This device was a major step towards an unequivocal linguistic interpretation of Sumerian writing. While earlier logograms must be seen as what has been called 'nuclear writing' because it omits grammatical information, the necessity to provide explicit clues for the grammatical form of words meant that ever more signs

na   ru   a   bi   i   pad

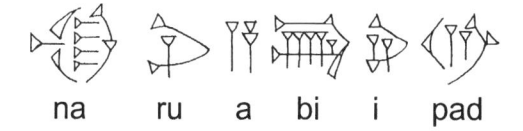

he destroyed the monument

Figure 3.5 *Sumerian example sentence*

were assigned non-lexical interpretations as phonetic indicators. Nuclear writing meant that a logogram could be given any of a number of possible specific interpretations. To write real Sumerian words meant narrowing these interpretations down to one. The agglutinative nature of Sumerian words was conducive to the process of transforming Sumerian writing into a medium that matched linguistic structures. That Sumerian scribes realized that writing moved closer to the spoken language is attested by the proverb *dub-sar šu ka-ta sa-a e-ne-am dub-sar-ra-am*, 'a scribe whose hand matches the mouth, he is indeed a scribe' (Green 1981: 359).

Like lists, nuclear writing is asyntactic and has no direction. Linguistic interpretation requires that writing proper should have a direction. Around the middle of the second millennium BCE the direction of the cuneiform script assumes a fixed format from left to right in horizontal lines. The increase of phonetic indicators in Sumerian texts notwithstanding, logograms remained the core of Sumerian writing. They were interpreted primarily for their meaning as evidenced by the fact that they were given lexical interpretations in another language, Akkadian, a Semitic language unrelated to Sumerian. When its speakers became dominant in Mesopotamia after about 2800, Sumerian was pushed back and eventually disappeared as a spoken language but continued to be employed for written communication. Attempts at writing Akkadian with the Sumerian writing system began with associating logograms with the Akkadian equivalents of the Sumerian words. For example, the sign for Sumerian *lugal* 'king' was given the Akkadian interpretation *šarru* 'king', adding yet another layer of complexity to the already polyvalent signs. Again phonetic indicators were employed to show that the logograms were to be interpreted as Akkadian rather than Sumerian words. Inflections, too, required phonetic indicators. An additional problem was that the sound patterns of Akkadian and Sumerian were different and that, therefore, Sumerian phonetic indicators were insufficient for Akkadian. New phonetic indicators had to be created. Eventually, this led to a transformation of the system and a reinterpretation of signs of words as signs of syllables. Before discussing this process and the ensuing system in more detail in the next chapter, we will now turn to another major logographic writing system, the Chinese.

Chinese writing

Graphic structure

Chinese characters, like Sumerian signs, grew out of drawings of natural objects. Their origin is still a matter of contention. Until recently, oracle-bone inscriptions, *jiǎgǔwén*, discovered in a massive find in Ānáyang, Hénán province, were generally thought to be the oldest specimens of Chinese writing. However, pottery wine vessels unearthed in Jŭxiàn, Shāndōng province, since the 1980s may have pushed back the history of the Chinese script by as many as 2,000 years. According to archaeologist Wang Shuming of the Shandong Institute of Relics and Archaeology, several of the drawings on the pottery could be identified as archaic forms of Chinese characters. Whether and how these relate to the oracle-bone characters is still uncertain. So far, there is no archaeological evidence that could bridge the great spatial and temporal distance between the finds of Jŭxiàn and Ānáyang. It is, therefore, the oracle-bone characters with which the bulk of research about Chinese writing begins. They made their appearance during the earliest period of attested Chinese history, the Shāng dynasty (ca 1750–1040 BCE).

Having been incised on ox scapulas and tortoise shells, the oracle-bone characters are angular and pointed. The characters of the bronze script, which also stem from the late Shāng period, are more rounded and more pictographic than the oracle-bone characters. They were carved into clay moulds used in casting bronze vessels. Both the bone and bronze characters are unmistakably writing. The earliest bronze characters were clan names, while the bone characters were used in divination. Writing implements and surfaces determined the different script styles from which others evolved. As writing came to be done more frequently, other writing implements came into common use, especially the brush. Over the centuries several different script forms developed. The most commonly distinguished are summarized in table 3.3. With the Clerical script, *lìshū*, of the second century CE Chinese characters had basically their modern stylized form. It is angular, perpendicular rather than slanted, and linear with no circles or twisted lines. Each character, no matter how complex, is assigned the same space. A running text is a succession of equidimensional squares, typically arranged in vertical columns from top to bottom running from right to left.

By the time the Clerical script had been commissioned as the proper script for redacting official documents, the principles of character formation had been systematized as the need to establish some kind of order in, and understanding of, the writing system became ever more urgent. During the Han dynasty about 120 CE, Xŭ Shèn, the compiler of the first major lexicon, the *Shuō wén jiě zì* comprising about 9,500 characters, distinguished six principles of formation and use called

Table 3.2. *Graphic development of four Chinese characters*

Oracle-bone script	Bronze script	Greater seal script	Lesser seal script	Clerical script	Cursive script	Running script	Standard script
							女
							心
							馬
							魚

Table 3.3. *Major Chinese script styles*

Period	Chinese term	Pinyin	English
13th–11th centuries BCE	甲骨文	jiaguwen	oracle-bone script
13th–4th centuries BCE	金文	jinwen	bronze script
8th century BCE	大篆	dazhuan	greater seal script
3rd century BCE	小篆	xiaozhuan	lesser seal script
2nd century CE	隸書	lishu	clerical script
since 4th century CE	草書 行書 楷書	caoshu xingshu kaishu	cursive script running script standard script

liù shū 'the six writings' (table 3.4). The first category (in developmental terms, though not in terms of the conventional order in the chart) are simple pictograms, *xiàngxíng*, directly derived from drawings of objects. In their modern stylized form the iconic quality of these signs is much reduced or lost entirely, but their pictorial origin can be reconstructed. Next, there are indicators, *zhǐshì*, also known as simple ideographs. These are characters indicating abstract notions such as 'above' and

Table 3.4. Liù shū, 'the six writings'

Category	Oracle-Bone	Modern	Meaning	Sound
Indicator	⌣⌣、⌢=	上、下	above, below	shàng, xià
Pictogram	ᶜ ᶜ, ⌀ ⌀	耳、目	above, below	ěr, mù
Meaning compound	⊟⊟ ⊅ ⊅ ⊟⊅	日+月 明	sun + moon bright	rì, yuè míng
Phonetic loan	朩	來	ear of corn to come	lái
Semantic-phonetic compound		米+唐 糖	cereal sugar	táng
Mutually interpretive	𢆉	樂	music → pleasure	yuè → lè

'below'. Numerals to four are also formed in accordance with this principle. Indicators or pictograms may be joined to form meaning compounds, *huì-yì*, the third category. These characters consist of components put together because of their meanings. For example, 信 'honest', *xìn*, consists of 人 'man', *rén*, and 言 'word', *yán*, a man whose word you can trust. Similarly, the character 明 for 'bright', *míng*, is composed of those for 'sun' 日 and 'moon' 月. Phonetic loans, *jiǎjiè*, follow the rebus principle. A character is transferred to a semantically unrelated word, which in archaic Chinese was homophonous or nearly homophonous. Thus, 足 *zú* 'foot' was transferred to write *zú* 'to suffice'. The fifth category of form-sound compounds, *xíngshēng*, typically consists of two elements, a semantic classifier or radical, which shows the general area of the meaning, and a phonetic, which hints at the pronunciation. The character 糖 is composed of the phonetic 唐 *táng* otherwise used for a proper name and the semantic classifier 米, 'cereal'. Finally, the category of redirected characters, *zhuǎnzhù*, is understood differently by different scholars, its original definition having been very ambiguous. It refers to characters which combine sound and meaning in unexpected ways. For example, the character 樂 *yuè* 'music' is also read *lè* 'pleasure'.

The *liù shū* are a description of the structure and function of characters intended as a classification system that would assign each and every character to one and only one category. But it was never that neat: categories did overlap and especially the final two left plenty of room for interpretation and uncertainty. Handed down through the centuries though it was, the system was not quite satisfactory

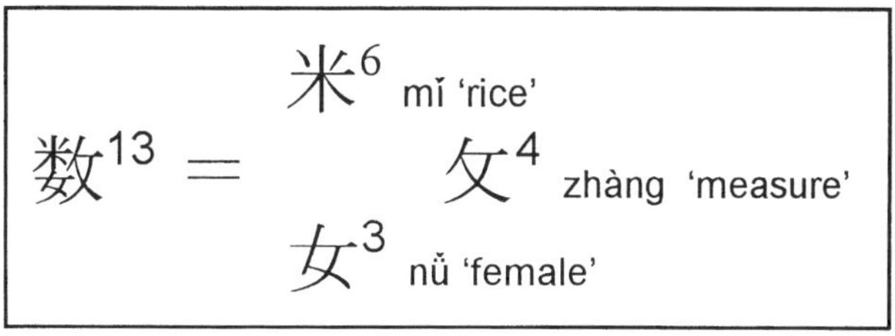

```
         米⁶ mǐ 'rice'
数¹³ =    攵⁴ zhàng 'measure'
         女³ nǚ 'female'
```

Figure 3.6 *The Chinese character* shù *'number' and its graphic composition. Index numbers show number of strokes.*

as a classification and, therefore, of limited use at best. The first three categories continue to play a role in teaching Chinese characters, pictographic qualities being exploited to support memorization. This potential is, however, soon exhausted. More important is the general principle of double articulation at the graphic level.

Double articulation, also called 'duality of structure', is a defining property of human language. It means that there are two levels of patterning: on one, language is being divided into meaningful units, and on the other, into meaningless phonological segments. Chinese characters have an internal structure conforming to the principle of double articulation. Each character, a meaningful unit, is composed of a fixed number of meaningless strokes. It is particularly noteworthy that, as in speech, many elementary components can function in either capacity. In English, for instance, [eɪ] can be analysed both as a phonological segment, for example the initial sound of *able*, and a morphological unit, for example a bound morpheme as in *a-symmetric*, or a word, the indefinite article *a*. Intuitively we feel that the [eɪ] of *able* is not the same as the indefinite article *a*, although it sounds the same. Similarly, many graphic elements of Chinese characters serve a double function as independent characters and parts of other characters. A single horizontal stroke can be the numeral one or an element that combines with others to form another character. As another example consider 数 *shù* 'number'. The character is composed of three elements that also occur as characters in their own right: 米 *mǐ* 'rice', 女 *nǚ* 'female' and 攵 *zhàng* 'measure'. The meanings and sounds associated with these characters are unrelated to the meaning and sound of 数 shù 'number'.

Duality of structure in Chinese characters is unrelated to duality of structure in the Chinese language; that is, while characters map onto morphemes and words, there is no systematic mapping relation between strokes and segments. In light of the fact that Chinese characters are occasionally compared to a lingua franca (Hashimoto 1987), that is, not a writing system but a language in its own right, it is very significant that in the graphic make-up of Chinese characters the same fundamental principle is put to use that underlies human language. This suggests

54 *Signs of words*

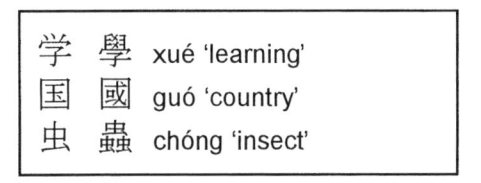

学	學	xué 'learning'
国	國	guó 'country'
虫	蟲	chóng 'insect'

Figure 3.7 *Variant forms of Chinese characters*

that, without actually reproducing the structural organization of speech, Chinese characters exploit the same coding strategy in the visual mode. The complexity and large number of Chinese characters is thus made manageable.

The signary

The Chinese signary consists of a huge number of characters. Already the appendix to the *Shuō wén jiě zì* dictionary has identified complex characters as an open set that could grow indefinitely. Since this is what actually has happened, the number of Chinese characters can only be estimated. Regular dictionaries list as many as 10,000 characters, but the total number is much higher. The Kāngxī Dictionary of 1717 CE comprises 47,035 characters. Morohashi's (1984–6) authoritative thirteen-volume Chinese-Japanese character dictionary lists 50,294 characters. In what seems to be the most comprehensive list to date, Huang and Huang (1989) have collected 74,000 characters, of which some 25,000 are variants. This still leaves about 49,000 standard characters. This is an aggregate figure produced by the tradition of Chinese lexicography, which has kept adding characters, but has never eliminated any.

Statistical studies have demonstrated that no texts have ever contained anything near this large number of different characters. Throughout Chinese history no more than about 6,000 characters have been in common use at any one time. The 'List of modern Chinese characters for everyday use' (*Xiàndài hànyǔ tōngyòng zìbiǎo*), published in 1988 by the Committee for the Writing of the National Language, includes a primary list of 2,500 characters and a secondary list of another 1,000 characters. For other than specialized and technical texts this is considered sufficient. Statistics show that the 1,000 most common characters account for about 90 per cent of all characters used in publications directed at a general readership. To cover the next 9 per cent, another 1,400 characters are necessary. Adding yet another 1,400 characters to a total of 3,800 raises the level to 99.9 per cent, and so on. In this way the progression continues. The relationship between frequency and rank on a frequency scale that is apparent here reflects another characteristic of natural language, known as Zipf's Law. It tells us that the relationship between frequency and rank is a constant across all languages (Zipf 1949). There are few high-frequency words and many low-frequency words, and the ratio of the former to the latter is steady. That is, the relationship between, for example, the five highest-frequency expressions and the five expressions ranking from 1,000 to 1,005 on a frequency scale is roughly the same for all languages. In the case of Chinese characters the rank/frequency constant moreover correlates with graphic complexity: the highest-frequency characters tend to be the lowest-complexity ones. Thus, in the list of 3,500 characters mentioned above, the one-stroke character — yī 'one' has a frequency of occurrence of 1.4585 ranking second on the frequency scale, while 鑷 niè 'forceps' consisting of 26 strokes occupies rank 3,472 and has a frequency of occurrence of 0.0001.

The 1,000 characters that account for 90 per cent of all contemporary texts are in the same order of magnitude as the signary of Sumerian cuneiform. This suggests that there is a pragmatic limit to the number of distinct signs that can be tolerated in a script. Yet, this is but 90 per cent and, while in the course of time the number of cuneiform signs diminished, that of Chinese characters grew. There is one reason why this was so. As we have seen above, the transfer of cuneiform signs to write homonyms or phonetically similar words led to the coming into existence of semantic determinatives. Homophony was likewise pervasive in Chinese, where the development took a similar course, with one important difference. While cuneiform determinatives were 'mute' but independent signs, their Chinese counterparts became integral components of characters. The Sumerians prefixed an extant determinative to an extant logogram to indicate a new usage, whereas the Chinese fused the two together to create a new character. As a result the total number of characters proliferated. This procedure has been by far the most productive strategy of forming new characters. It is still productive, as new characters need to be created, especially for technical terms and loanwords. There are various statistics and estimates referring to different corpora of characters (cf., e.g., DeFrancis 1984b: 84; Taylor and Taylor 1995: 53; Zhou 1992: 179). They all indicate that between 80 per cent and 90 per cent of all characters belong to this type, the fifth category of the *liù shū*. The vast majority of characters accordingly consist of a radical, the semantic determinative, and a phonetic.

The Chinese term for radical is 部首, *bùshǒu*. Radicals have been used early on as a lexicographic ordering principle, and they are still indispensable for this purpose today. The system of radicals developed over the centuries. Xǔ Shèn used 540 radicals in the *Shuō wén jiě zì* of 120 CE. The set of 214 radicals employed in contemporary dictionaries was used for the first time in a dictionary published in 1633, but became popular only with the dictionary compiled on orders of emperor Kāngxī (1662–1723), published in 1717. Radicals display the same statistical behaviour as characters, their frequency being inversely related to the number of

56   Signs of words

Table 3.5. *Chinese compound characters, formed of semantic determinatives and the phonetic indicator* gong

力	strength	工	功	effect	gong
穴	hole	工	空	empty	kong
絲	silk	工	紅	red	kong
水	water	工	江	river	jiang
木	tree	工	杠	staff	gang
攵	strike	工	攻	attack	gong

constituent strokes. For example, in excess of 250 characters contain the two-stroke radical no. 9 人 'human', while the 17-stroke radical no. 214 龠 'flute' is a component of no character except itself. Radicals of this sort are sometimes called 'dead radicals' because they are unproductive. This raises the question whether radicals serve any function other than that of a lexical ordering principle.

Linguistic structure

The meaning-indicating function of the radicals is variable. Some are more suggestive, and consistently so, than others, and some are plausible as semantic classifiers in some instances, but not in others. For instance, that 仇 *chó* 'enemy' includes the 'human' radical stands to reason, but in the case of 仍 *réng* 'still, yet' this is less obvious. As a matter of fact, the left-hand component of this character does not function as the 'human' radical, but as the phonetic *ren*. Yet, the character is listed in dictionaries under the 'human' radical. How then do radicals work? Because of the overwhelming numerical dominance of characters consisting of a radical and a phonetic, answering this question goes a long way towards explaining how the Chinese writing system works.

A number of radicals, such as those meaning 'human', 'thing', 'strength', 'to die', 'to be born', 'change', 'water', 'earth', 'fire', 'nothing', 'shape', 'place', are so general that taken together they might perhaps form an exhaustive system of ontological categories. But many other radicals, such as 'pig's head', 'shadow', 'poison', 'claw', 'dog', 'melon', 'millet', 'wheat', 'hemp', appear to represent categories of an altogether different order. Considering the great diversity of radicals it is impossible to see in them anything resembling a logically consistent and comprehensive system of semantic categories. Whether such a system is possible at all, or whether 214 would be the right order of magnitude of the necessary categories, or whether the earlier system of 540 radicals was more realistic is not known. Whatever the answer, for the most part radicals provide no more than a rather vague hint at the meaning of the character in question.

Except for the few dead radicals, however, radicals do not function alone but in conjunction with a phonetic. Both elements work together to mutually disambiguate each other, but what exactly do they contribute to determine an unequivocal interpretation of the character? Which of them carries more weight? Is it possible to measure their effect? The numbers would seem to indicate that phonetics are more important than radicals. Each character is interpreted as a meaningful syllable, usually a morpheme. Mandarin Chinese distinguishes roughly 1,300 tone syllables. Various dictionaries list between 888 and 1,040 phonetics. Given that 1,300 syllables need to be distinguished, this is proportionally much more than the 200-odd radicals available to distinguish a potentially infinite number of meanings. Phonetics, the conclusion seems to be inescapable, carry more weight in determining a character's interpretation than radicals. By and large this is true, but things are not quite so simple. For one thing, more than 10 per cent of characters do not contain a phonetic, and in many others it is not obvious which of the elements functions as the phonetic and which as the radical, because, like radicals, phonetics are also used as simplex characters with a meaning and a sound of their own. Further, only about one third of phonetics are accurate in the sense that the syllabic value of the phonetics and the characters containing them is the same. Finally, if about 1,000 shape-sound combinations must be remembered to secure unequivocal interpretation of the characters containing a phonetic, there is little advantage over remembering the 1,000 most frequent characters. This is apparently what proficient users of the Chinese writing system do because, on the whole, sound interpretation on the basis of phonetics is rather uncertain. This is not to say that the phonetics are ineffective, but that their effectiveness hinges on the other part of the system, the radicals, which by themselves are even less effective.

It is now widely recognized that the Chinese writing system is best described as a large syllabary with strong semantic elements that make up for the phonetic imprecision. In China and Japan Chinese characters are none the less commonly referred to as ideograms (*biǎoyì wénzì*), suggesting that the meaning component is stronger than the phonetic. While this is established usage, it does not reflect the most plausible analysis of the system. Unger (1990) has convincingly demonstrated that the very idea of ideography is not homegrown but a Western import. Empirical evidence supports the view, most vigorously advanced by DeFrancis (1984b, 1989), that both systematically and functionally the Chinese writing system relies more

58   *Signs of words*

Table 3.6. *Chinese words of location*

Monosyllabic		Disyllabic	
shàng	up	*shàngbiān*	above
xià	down	*xiàbiān*	below
lǐ	in	*lǐbiān*	inside
wài	out	*wàibiān*	outside
qián	front	*qiánbiān*	before
hòu	back	*hòubiān*	behind
páng	side	*pángbiān*	beside
zhōng	middle	*zhōngjiàn*	between

on sound than on meaning. It must be borne in mind, however, that the phonetic and the semantic interpretation of characters depend on each other. Whatever uncertainty remains on the part of the reader is neutralized by memorizing the whole character and by the fact that it is to be associated with a word already known. The writer, too, cannot but memorize the whole character. There is no way even a proficient writer could 'spell' an unknown character for a known word by combining a radical and a phonetic in a way similar to guessing the spelling of an English word never seen in writing. There are certain principles governing the position of radicals and phonetics within characters, but they are probabilistic regularities rather than strict rules. It is impossible, therefore, to master the Chinese script by learning a set of rules and the elements – radicals and phonetics – on which they operate. There is no way around learning to associate characters with words. To be more precise, 'word' is not really the appropriate term here. In most cases a character is not associated with a word but with a morpheme, but no distinction is made between the two in Chinese dictionaries, which follow long-established practice by listing characters rather than words.

Each character is associated with a syllable and a meaning, but the dictionary entries are not all of the same kind. Some are words, others are bound morphemes. This distinction overlaps with what in China is often referred to as disyllabic and monosyllabic words. For example, consider the list of 'words of location' in table 3.6.

Only the items in the disyllabic column are words in the technical sense explained at the beginning of this chapter in that they can be used alone and moved around in the sentence; the monosyllabic ones must be suffixed to nouns. The majority of modern Chinese words are disyllabic consisting of two characters. Chinese characters then cannot be said to express words, and the Chinese writing system is not described properly as logographic. This is partly because of the conceptual and perceptual dominance of characters and partly because words

中国这几年的变化的确很大。

| Gloss | zhōngguó
China | zhèjǐnián
these several years | de
GEN | biànhuà
change | díquè
really | hěn
very | dà
big |

Translation China underwent big changes during the past several years.

Figure 3.8 *Chinese example sentence. Characters do not show word boundaries which are indicated in the underlining and the Pinyin transcription.*

in Chinese do not behave as words in inflecting or agglutinative languages. In Chinese, an isolating language, words do not change their form and the word order in the sentence is fixed. At the same time, word classes are not as clearly differentiated. Taken together these typological features of Chinese imply that the distinction between compound words and syntactic phrases is not very pronounced. It is overshadowed by the graphic independence of the characters, the most conspicuous units of metalinguistic reflection induced by writing. The primacy of the character is reinforced by the invisibility of words in Chinese texts, which do not mark word boundaries. Each character occupies an equidimensional square, and character spacing is uniform regardless of whether two successive characters form a word, a phrase, or belong to different phrases. The most conspicuous linguistic unit corresponding to the character then is the monosyllabic morpheme.

Conclusion

A comparison of the two writing systems discussed in this chapter, the Sumerian and the Chinese, calls for a number of general considerations. First, to the question of whether there is any interesting relationship between linguistic type and type of writing system: the Sumerian language belongs to the agglutinative type, while Chinese is an isolating language, but both have plenty of monosyllabic homophonous morphemes. This has far-reaching consequences for the respective writing systems. Both of them are most commonly described as ideographic or logographic. But these terms must be properly defined to avoid confusion. In their mature form both systems assign considerable importance to the syllable as the unit of interpretation of signs. The term 'ideogram' is therefore undesirable. 'Logogram' is more appropriate, but inaccurate, because the term suggests that the word is the prominent unit of writing. This is, however, not the case in either Sumerian or Chinese, not in any event if the word is understood as a well-defined unit of linguistic analysis. In order to interpret Sumerian signs as words, a number of supplementary signs called phonetic complements and semantic determinatives are used as reading aids. They became necessary largely in order to differentiate homophones. Since these supplementary signs developed into a limited set, the total signary, too, was held within limits. The words of a language, by contrast, form an open set. From this fact alone it can be concluded that Sumerian is not a word-writing system in the strict sense that there is a word for every sign and vice versa. No logographic system in this sense ever existed anywhere.

The limitless nature of the lexicon is more clearly reflected in the Chinese system where homophone differentiation led to the incorporation of semantic radicals and phonetics into complex characters of which more than 50,000 developed over the centuries. Yet, like Sumerian signs, Chinese characters are not usually interpreted as words. Two to three thousand characters are sufficient for functional literacy, a number that is much smaller than the size of an individual speaker's lexicon, let alone the lexicon of the Chinese language at any given period of time. Syllables and morphemes are more relevant as linguistic units. Polyfunctionality of signs is inevitable. Words, it would appear, are simply too numerous. Or, to put it in evolutionary terms, once written signs were firmly associated with a linguistic interpretation, homophony was difficult and uneconomic to ignore. Evidence for this is found in another writing system that assigns the word a prominent function, Egyptian. Much like Sumerian cuneiform signs and Chinese characters, Egyptian hieroglyphs are multifunctional, serving as word signs, phonetic determinatives and semantic classifiers, as the case may be. Egyptian texts cannot be interpreted as successions of words on the basis of a simple bi-unique mapping relation between hieroglyphs and words. As is the case in Sumerian and Chinese, arrangements of written signs do not mirror lexical segmentation overtly. Rather the interpretation of words is a multilayered process involving reference to semantic, phonetic and lexical information, all of which is hinted at more or less vaguely. What is more, words are not easily defined in a uniform way across languages. They may also not be salient units of metalinguistic reflection in preliterate societies, which is to say that the notion of the word is influenced by interpreting written signs at least as much as these are based on a consistent definition of what a word is. The prominence of Chinese characters in China's lexicographical tradition certainly supports this assumption.

Questions for discussion

(1) How do we determine what a word is in a given language?
(2) In what sense can Sumerian and Chinese writing be said to be logographic?

(3)   Explain the devices used in Sumerian and Chinese to represent words. How do they differ, and what do they have in common?
(4)   How do we count words? How many words are there in a language, and how many signs are there in the Sumerian and Chinese writing systems, respectively? What can we learn by comparing these figures and calculating their ratios?

4

Signs of syllables

> Everybody is able to recognise a syllable, even if some difficulty is experienced in defining what a syllable is.   Anthony Burgess, *A Mouthful of Air*

Theoretical syllables

A number of writing systems are commonly described as syllabaries. Their basic operational graphic units are interpreted as speech syllables. Japanese kana is well known as one of the purest examples (see below), but there are many others, such as Akkadian cuneiform (von Soden and Rölling 1991), Elamite (Stève 1992), Hurrian (Wilhelm 1983), the Aegean scripts Linear B (Palaima 1989) and Cypriot (Baurain 1991), as well as the Vai (Scribner and Cole 1981) and several other West African scripts (Dalby 1970), and the Cree (Darnell and Vanek 1973) and Cherokee (Walker and Sarbough 1993) scripts of North America. A number of writing systems have developed a syllabographic component without shedding logography, a tendency exemplified by Hittite cuneiform (Laroch 1960), late forms of Egyptian (Schenkel 1994), as well as by Maya (Coe 1992). Some syllabic writing systems evolved gradually in antiquity (Sanmartín 1988), others were created deliberately in modern times (Burnaby 1985). Some undeciphered scripts such as the Iberian (Anderson 1988) and the Indus script (Parpola 1994) are thought to be syllabic or to contain strong syllabic elements. The letters of the Latin alphabet have names that, except for some peculiar cases such as English *double-u* and French *i grec*, usually have monosyllabic names used in sounding out the spelling of words. These same letters have occasionally been treated as syllables by scribes unfamiliar with the system, such as the Maya scribes who came into contact with the Latin alphabet through the Spaniards (Bricker 2000). All this testifies to the intuitive saliency of the syllable. But what is a syllable?

It is important to note at the outset that the speech syllable must not be confused with the graphic syllable. When we talk about speech syllables we refer to a body of sound regardless of whatever meaning may be associated with it. But this is already an abstraction. *She had a good laugh when he said 'let me tell you what I think'.* This sentence consists of monosyllables entirely. To conceive of them as meaningless is, perhaps, easier if we transcribe them phonetically: /ʃiː, hæd, ə, gʊd, lɑːf, wen, hiː, səd, let, mi, tel, juː, wɒt, aɪ, θɪŋk/. Or we can compile a list such as: /ʃiː/, /ʃiː-pɪʃ/, /ʃiː-nɪ/, /ʃiː-tɪŋ/ to show that the English syllable /ʃiː/ is not necessarily associated with a meaning. But can we conclude that this is so in other languages as well? The fact is that the syllable as a linguistic unit does not play the same role in all languages. Some languages join syllable after syllable to form long words, in others most of the words are only single syllables. This is a practical reason for the difficulty experienced in defining what a syllable is, as Burgess remarks in the passage quoted above. There are some theoretical reasons as well.

Intuitive notions of the syllable are vague. Attempts at precision move the discussion to a different level of analytical notions defined in a theoretically justified way. In phonology, the syllable is seen either as the minimum unit of sequential speech sounds or as a unit of the metrical system of a language. Certain theories consider the syllable as a basic phonological unit *sui generis*, while others derive its properties from those of the composite phonemes. Clearly, a syllable is a unit of articulation, and although a universally accepted articulatory definition is not available, phoneticians of different schools are agreed that syllables possess psychological reality for speakers. A syllable is a unit of speech that can be articulated in isolation and bear a single degree of stress, as in English, or a single tone, as in Chinese (see below). Different languages allow for different syllables. The specific structure of possible syllables is thus part of the phonological system of a language. In very general terms, syllables are units of speech consisting of an obligatory nucleus, usually a vowel (V), and optional initial and final margins, usually consonants (C). An alternative way of describing the structure of the syllable is to divide it into onset and rhyme, where the onset is the initial margin and the rhyme is further subdivided into peak and coda. A syllable with a vowel in coda position is called 'open', and a syllable with a consonant in coda position 'closed'.

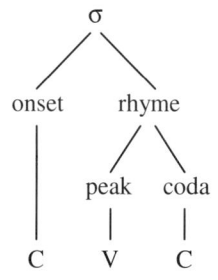

Figure 4.1 *The structure of a simple syllable*

Using these terms, the syllable structure of a language can be analysed as the set of possible C-V and V-C sequences and their combinations. The simplest syllable in any language is a single vowel. Certain consonants, especially nasals and liquids, can be syllabic too. That is, they can be in peak position. This depends on what is known as their relative sonority or audibility. The underlying idea is that margins and nuclei of syllables are arranged in a sequence of increasing and then decreasing sonority. The peak of the syllable is the nucleus, that part which has the highest sonority. Some speakers pronounce *squirrel* as one syllable, while *simple*, /sɪmpl/, and *rhythm*, /rɪðəm/, can be analysed as having two syllables rather than one. The liquid /l/ and the nasal /m/, respectively, have more sonority than the preceding consonant and therefore have syllabic status. Every syllable has one peak that is typically a vowel, but not every vowel is a syllable peak. Some languages of the Semitic family, Hebrew, for example, have what is known as 'reduced' vowels in interconsonantal position. The result is that a sequence such as /CVCV/ is regarded as a single syllable which, therefore, is sometimes alternatively transcribed as /C^{V}CV/. The types of syllable structure permitted is one of the more noticeable differences between languages. There is considerable cross-linguistic variation in syllabification as well as in the possible initial and final margins. Different languages may draw syllable divisions differently. A sequence such as CVCCV can be syllabified as CVC-CV or as CV-CCV. While some languages, like Arabic, have only C-onset syllables, others permit both C- and V-initial syllables, and likewise with final margins.

The syllable is also the domain of stress, another feature of cross-linguistic variation. In French, stress is not very important, it rarely affects meaning. In English it can be distinctive, as in *'increase* with stress on the first syllable, a noun, and *in 'crease*, a verb, stressed on the second syllable. But in other cases, such as *'for-mi-da-ble* vs. *for- 'mi-da-ble*, different stress distribution has no effect on meaning. In Russian, by contrast, stress is fixed. *Múka* with the accent on the first syllable means 'torture', but *muká*, stressed on the second syllable, is a different word which means 'flour'.

In some languages vowel length is distinctive, which means that there are minimal pairs of syllables that differ in phonological time only. Arabic, for instance, has three pairs of vowels that systematically contrast in length: /a, aː/, /i, iː/, /u, uː/. In English, vowels can be long and short, but length is not usually distinctive. For example, in *bit* the vowel is short and in *beat* it is long, but the vowel quality is also slightly different, [ɪ] and [iː], respectively. Most of the time, vowel length is predictable in English and therefore not distinctive. But Arabic systematically uses vowel length to differentiate meaning. There are pairs of words such as /laːm/ 'blamed' and /lam/ 'gathered', /fiːl/ 'elephant' and /fil/ 'to escape', /fuːl/ 'horse beans' and /ful/ 'Arabian jasmine', which are distinguished by vowel length alone. Syllables including a long vowel and those with a consonant in coda position of the types /CV:/, /CVC/ or more complex types such as /CCV:C/, /CCVCC/ and so on are called 'heavy syllables' as opposed to 'light' or 'open syllables', as mentioned above. In metrical terms heavy and light is a contrast of the relative duration of the syllable. For the description of languages that make use of this contrast systematically without combining it with other qualitative differences between sounds it is common to use a more specific term, which captures the difference, 'mora'. A mora is a unit of rhythmical time equivalent to a light syllable. The most common approach to matching syllables and moras is to count heavy syllables (long vowel and complex final margin) as two moras (Hyman 1985).

The syllable further functions as the unit to which a pitch level is assigned. Languages that use pitch level to distinguish words are known as 'tone languages', and distinctive pitch levels are called 'tones'. In tone languages it is relations between the pitch of different syllables rather than the absolute pitch that is important. Chinese, Burmese, Thai and other languages of the Sino-Tibetan family are tone languages. Chinese (Mandarin) has four tones, high, rising, falling and falling-rising. Thai distinguishes five tones and Burmese has four. Like length, tone is an essential feature in some languages but not in others. Where tone is important, the syllable, in addition to onset and rhyme, includes a tone that, however, must not be regarded as an optional element such as an additional consonant at the initial or final margin. In tone languages tone is a dimension of the phonological system that cannot be abstracted from an atonal body of the syllable, although this has often been done in providing phonological descriptions of tone languages. Tone is an inherent property of every stressed syllable. It is often the case that tone interacts with other phonological distinctions in such a way that certain tones are restricted to syllables of a certain segmental composition. In Thai, for example, heavy syllables can have only two of the five tones of the language.

To summarize, segmental composition, stress, duration and tone are properties of the syllable. The importance of these features varies across languages and, although

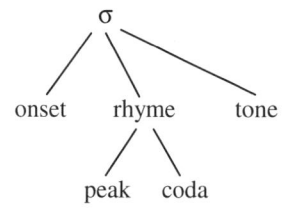

Figure 4.2 *The structure of a syllable in a tone language*

the syllable is crucial as a unit within which the distribution of phonological features can be stated, it is best defined as a unit for each language separately. This has important consequences for the analysis of syllabic writing systems.

Signaries and statistics

It is obvious that the complexity of the possible syllables of a language interacts with their number. A language such as Fijian that permits only open syllables is bound to have fewer syllables than one that permits syllables with complex initial and final margins of the type of English *strength*. Also it would appear that a language whose basic lexical stratum is monosyllabic needs more syllable types than one that has a basic stratum of polysyllabic lexemes. A writing system that targets the syllable as the key functional unit thus means different things for different languages. Let us consider as a complete syllabary a writing system in which a different symbol is used for each different speech syllable. Under this assumption Chinese, for example, would require over 1,300 symbols, although Chinese has a relatively simple syllable structure. The Chinese Script Reform Committee (*Hànyǔ Pīnyīn Lùnwén Xuǎn* 1988: 171) says that there are more than 1,200 syllables in Mandarin, while the syllable table of the *Xiàndài hànyǔ cídiǎn* dictionary of 1979 lists 1,332 syllables of which 34 are neutral-tone syllables. For most languages a complete syllabary would run into a much larger number of symbols. The Korean language with a rather complex syllable structure has more than 11,000 different syllables (Kim-Renaud 1997: 183). Vietnamese has more than 14,000 syllables, and Thai even as many as 23,000 (University of California, Los Angeles Phonological Segment Inventory Database). Yet more numerous are the syllables of languages such as German and English, which, if the languages of the world were ordered for syllable complexity, would range near the extreme of high complexity. Clearly, this is an order of magnitude that makes syllabaries unmanageable. In practice there are no, and never have been any, complete syllabaries in the above sense, which confirms the more general truth that no writing system encodes every distinction relevant in its language. Various strategies were developed for syllabic writing to get by with signaries much smaller than the number of speech syllables. An inevitable consequence of this is a certain degree of syntagmatic complexity in combining graphic symbols unambiguously to denote speech syllables.

Where syllabic writing evolved, the number of symbols was gradually reduced. For example, as we have seen in the previous chapter, close to 1,000 cuneiform signs were used in early periods of writing in Mesopotamia. Functional literacy at the time of Hammurabi (1728–1686 BCE) required at least 600 cuneiform signs plus hundreds of logograms. In the age of King Ashurbanipal (669–629 BCE) a list of 211 signs known as 'Syllabary A' was widely used as a basic standard. As applied to Babylonian, considered a dialect of Akkadian, the cuneiform syllabic signary decreased further to a set of about 110 signs. The decisive push towards syllabic writing came when Sumerian, the language for which cuneiform first evolved, was replaced by Akkadian as the principal written language. Parallel to this development, the proportion of logograms and syllabograms in cuneiform texts changed. While in Sumerian logograms account for between 60% and 42% of signs in running text and syllabograms constitute between 36% and 54%, the ratio is reversed in Akkadian with 85% to 95% syllabograms and only 3.5 per cent to 6.5 per cent logograms. (The rest in both cases is made up of determinatives.) When the cuneiform script was adapted to other languages, such as Elamite, a language spoken in western Iran, the shift towards sound writing continued. The Elamite signary consists of some 130 cuneiform signs, most of which are syllabograms. Hurrian, another language written in cuneiform script, had a syllabary of 77 signs, 43 (C)V and 34 VC. Of the 375 cuneiform signs of the Hittite signary (not to be confused with Hittite hieroglyphic) 86 were employed as syllabic signs.

A similar development took place when the Chinese script was transferred to other languages, Korean, Japanese and Vietnamese, in particular. The Koreans in a system called 'Hyangchal' first gave Chinese characters a Korean reading on the basis of the Chinese syllables associated with them. Since they continued to use the Chinese written language for most serious writing, they also developed a system of abbreviated characters for transcription. These Kwukyel characters were used for annotating Chinese texts. Yet another manner of using Chinese characters for Korean was the 'clerk reading' or 'Itwu' system (also 'Ido'), a mixed system containing logographic and syllabographic elements. Unlike Chinese, Korean is an agglutinating language with a rich grammatical morphology, which is cumbersome to write with Chinese characters. It was imperative, therefore, to use characters phonetically without regard to meaning.

The same problem arose when the Japanese first tried to write their language, although Japanese has a much simpler syllable structure than Korean. Early attempts to write Japanese fall into the category of Manyōgan, that is, kana of the '10,000 pages', so called after the Manyōshū poetry anthology of the eighth century. Manyōgana were Chinese characters unmodified in form but used primarily as phonetic symbols. The Japanese language of the time had 87 phonetic syllables, but over 970 Chinese characters were used to write them. Thus, for example, 32 different characters were utilized for the syllable /ka/ and as many as 40 characters were used for /si/. It is clear from the large number of Manyōgana that a standard had not yet been established. Moreover, Chinese characters were associated with Chinese syllables, which corresponded to Japanese syllables rather imperfectly

68 *Signs of syllables*

Table 4.1. *Some Manyōgana, Chinese characters used as phonetic symbols to write seventh-century Japanese*

Syllable	Chinese characters
/a/	安 阿 愛 吾 余 足 嗚 呼 鞅 我
/i/	伊 異 意 易 己 夷 怡 移 射 膽
/u/	宇 得 卯 有 菟 烏 汁 紆 雲 兎
/e/	愛 衣 得 可 依 榎 荏 江 吉 枝 兄
/o/	於 意 憶 愛 應 隠 乙
/ka/	加 架 蚊 日 家 可 賀 歌 嘉 鹿 汁 甘 香 介 閑 甲 伽 迦 箇 珂 訶 哥 河 柯 舸 呵 奇 軻
/si/	志 師 色 之 芝 士 始 時 詩 待 指 旨 思 信 伺 司 子 四 死 事 水 進 自 糸 私 石 斯 式 識 時 次 資 施 新 笑 趾 祀 枳 此 肆 矢

because the syllable structure of both languages is different. For one thing, Japanese is not a tone language, so Japanese scribes would tend to treat many Chinese syllables as homophonous which the Chinese perceived as distinct. The large number of Manyōgana further indicates that the characters had not been dissociated completely from meaning. The scribes would select one /ka/ rather than another because it seemed more fitting for the Japanese word in question. They would also use characters playfully and in idiosyncratic ways. It took a long time for the notion to take root that characters could be used for their syllabic values alone, and that the number of necessary characters could thus be drastically reduced. Notice also that some Manyōgana were given multiple syllabic interpretations. For example, 愛 the third character in the /a/ line of table 4.1, is also found in the /e/ line and the /o/ line. A one-to-one relation between characters and syllables was established only gradually. It went along with a process of graphic simplification, which erased the similarity of the phonetically used kana with their Chinese character models. When the graphic form of the characters changed, Manyōgana finally gave way to katakana and hiragana, the two Japanese syllabaries. With 48 characters each plus a few diacritics their signaries are many times less complex than the Chinese signary, which requires many more characters for even basic literacy, indicating a writing system of a different type.

Much has been made of the economic advantage of syllabic writing over word writing, which stems from the fact that the number of the speech syllables of a language is closed while that of words is open. Gelb (1963) in particular considered that economizing on the inventory of signs was the driving force in the development of writing. This is the cornerstone of his theory. To be sure, the structural unit of writing has an effect on the size of a writing system's signary. Yet, syllabaries range between a few dozen and several hundred signs. Cypriot has 55, Linear B has 59, Cree 45, Cherokee 85. With more than 200 signs the Vai syllabary is somewhat larger. In functional terms, economy of inventory is an advantage, but it is by no means the only factor that comes to bear in the development of writing. Plain conservatism, on the one hand, and changes brought about by adapting a writing system to an unrelated language are just as important, if not more so. Also, the size of the signary is just one of several factors that account for the relative simplicity of a writing system. Typically, syllabic writing reduces the burden on memory, as compared to word writing or morphosyllabic writing, but then the coding of words by means of a syllabary may involve complexities of its own.

Written syllables

How then do syllabaries encode speech syllables? As I have already remarked, syllabaries are incomplete, having fewer signs by a large measure than the languages they are used to write have speech syllables. The degree of incompleteness is different in different writing systems, their linguistic fit is subject to considerable variation. Some disregard minor distinctions such as the difference between aspirated and unaspirated final margin consonants, others are structured in such a way that major syllable types require convoluted circumscriptions. For the most part, these peculiarities reflect genealogical differences of the various syllabic writing systems. They all have in common that a good knowledge of the language is required for reading them.

Modern syllabaries

Syllabaries created in modern times, in a world where writing is widely understood as representing speech, targeted the syllable as the functional unit of the system to begin with. The syllable structure of the language was taken into

Table 4.2. *The Cherokee syllabary*

Ꭰ	*a*	Ꭱ	*e*	Ꭲ	*i*	Ꭳ	*o*	Ꭴ	*u*
Ꭶ	*ga*	Ꭸ	*ge*	Ꭹ	*gi*	Ꭺ	*go*	Ꭻ	*gu*
Ꭽ	*ha*	Ꭾ	*he*	Ꭿ	*hi*	Ꮀ	*ho*	Ꮁ	*hu*
Ꮃ	*la*	Ꮄ	*le*	Ꮅ	*li*	Ꮆ	*lo*	Ꮇ	*lu*
Ꮉ	*ma*	Ꮊ	*me*	Ꮋ	*mi*	Ꮌ	*mo*	Ꮍ	*mu*
Ꮎ	*na*	Ꮑ	*ne*	Ꮒ	*ni*	Ꮓ	*no*	Ꮔ	*nu*
Ꮖ	*gwa*	Ꮗ	*gwe*	Ꮘ	*gwi*	Ꮙ	*gwo*	Ꮚ	*gwu*
Ꮜ	*sa*	Ꮞ	*se*	Ꮟ	*si*	Ꮠ	*so*	Ꮡ	*su*
Ꮣ	*da*	Ꮥ	*de*	Ꮧ	*di*	Ꮩ	*do*	Ꮪ	*du*
Ꮬ	*dla*	Ꮮ	*dle*	Ꮯ	*dli*	Ꮰ	*dlo*	Ꮱ	*dlu*
Ꮳ	*dza*	Ꮴ	*dze*	Ꮵ	*dzi*	Ꮶ	*dzo*	Ꮷ	*dzu*
Ꮹ	*wa*	Ꮺ	*we*	Ꮻ	*wi*	Ꮼ	*wo*	Ꮽ	*wu*
Ꮿ	*ya*	Ᏸ	*ye*	Ᏹ	*yi*	Ᏺ	*yo*	Ᏻ	*yu*
Ꭵ	*ö*	Ꭼ	*gö*	Ꮂ	*hö*	Ꮈ	*lö*	Ꮕ	*nö*
Ꮛ	*gwö*	Ꮢ	*sö*	Ꮫ	*dö*	Ꮲ	*dlö*	Ꮸ	*dzö*
Ꮾ	*wö*	Ᏼ	*yö*	Ꭷ	*ka*	Ꮏ	*hna*	Ꮐ	*nah*
Ꮝ	*s*	Ꮤ	*ta*	Ꮦ	*te*	Ꮨ	*ti*	Ꮭ	*tla*

account when the systems were designed. The Cherokee (table 4.2) and the Cree (table 4.3) syllabaries, both of which were deliberately constructed by individuals in the nineteenth century, are good examples. Notice that these systems have graphemes for separate initial vowels, a design feature that gives them great flexibility. The Cherokee language has mostly open syllables, the only final margin C being /s/ for which a separate grapheme Ꮝ is provided. Glottal stop in coda position is ignored in writing. Initial margins can be complex for which the system provides CCV graphemes. The language has short and long syllables, and length is sometimes distinctive as in /àma/ 'water' vs. /áːma/ 'salt'. This distinction is ignored in writing, as is pitch, which is also distinctive in some words. Scancarelli (1992: 141) summarizes what she calls 'the shortcomings' of the syllabary: 'Any phonemic analysis would require certain distinctions to be made which are not

Table 4.3. *The Cree syllabary*

KEY TO THE CREE SYLLABIC SYSTEM.						
VOWELS.						
as in hate, á	as i in pin, e	as in no, o	as in pun, u	as in pan, a	Final Consonants.
▽	△	▷	◁	◁	
W wá ▽·	we △·	wo ▷	wu ◁·	wa ◁·	
P pá V	pe ∧	po >	pu <	pa ċ	'
T tá U	te ∩	to)	tu (	ta ċ	'
K ká ۹	ke ρ	ko ḋ	ku b	ka ḃ	`
Ch chá ๅ	che ſ	cho ⌐	chu ∪	cha ι̇	-
M má ⅂	me Γ·	mo ⌐	mu ∟	ma ᒼ	‹
N ná ɒ	ne σ	no ₀	nu ɑ	na ȧ	›
S sá ᔨ	se ⸝	so ⸝	su ካ	sa ካ̇	˄
Y yá ⸝	ye ⸝	yo ⸝	yu ⸝	ya ⸝	
Final w . . . °						
„ i . . . ·						
Aspirated final k ▪						
Extra signs— X = Christ, ℨ = r, ϟ = l, Ȧ = wi,						
" = h before a vowel.						
" = a soft guttural h when before a consonant.						

made in the syllabary. Distinctions would have to be made between ChV and CV syllables; between hCV and CV; between CVʔ, Cvh, and CV; between long and short vowels; and between vowels of different pitch and tone.' Since /s/ is the only consonant in coda position that can be written as such, other consonant clusters

72   *Signs of syllables*

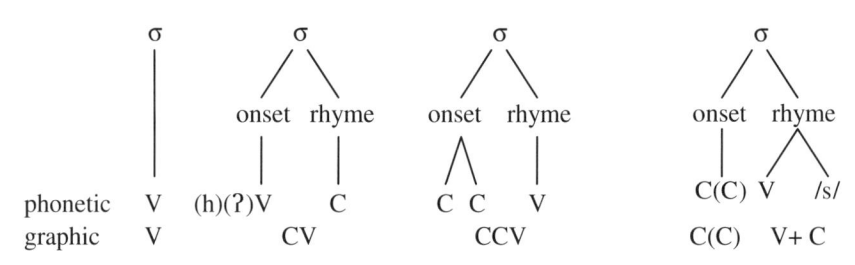

```
              σ              σ              σ                  σ
              |             / \            / \                / \
              |          onset rhyme    onset rhyme        onset rhyme
              |            |   |         /\   |             |   /\
phonetic   V        (h)(?)V    C        C C   V           C(C) V  /s/
graphic    V            CV              CCV               C(C)  V+C
```

Figure 4.3 *Cherokee syllables, phonetic and graphic*

that occur in the language must be written with CVCV sign sequences. In the event, a CV sign, which in its canonical usage is the notation of a consonant vowel sequence, must be interpreted as a single consonant. However, for speakers of the language these are not necessarily shortcomings, and it must be remembered that the requirements of a phonemic analysis are not the same as those of designing a practical writing system.

The Cree syllabary has signs for independent vowels and a set of CV syllables. In addition there are 'finals' to indicate closed syllables. Vowels are slightly underdetermined, since Cree has seven vowels, but only four vowel graphemes. Diacritics are used to indicate the three additional vowels. One of the diacritics, a large dot placed over the CV sign, marks length, which is generally distinctive in Algonkian languages of which Cree is one. This usage reflects conscious phonological analysis, since the diacritic refers not to a syllable or morpheme, but to a feature common to a number of different syllables. Another feature, too, reveals the planned design of the system. All V signs are triangles differing only in orientation, south for /e/, north for /i/, east for /o/, and west for /a/. Thus 'triangle' can be understood as indicating vocality. The directionality of the V signs is systematically repeated in the CV signs where the C part is indicated by the shape of the character and the V part by its orientation, as in /te/, /tu/, /to/, /ta/. Hence, the syllable is not really the smallest linguistic unit encoded in the Cree syllabary. It was chosen not because a segmental analysis of the language (see chapter 5) was not available, but because it was a convenient unit for the coding of Cree words that are very long. Combining the advantage of a small signary with that of giving words greater discernibility than an alphabetic notation, it is thought to be very suitable for the Cree language (Bennet and Berry 1991).

Other modern script creations have also chosen the syllable as the functional unit, for example, the Vai, the Mende and the Loma of West Africa. Invented in the 1820s, the Vai syllabary (table 4.4) consists of some 212 signs, the Mende, designed a century later, has a signary of 195 signs, and the Loma, which came into existence in the 1930s, has at least 185 signs (Dalby 1967). Since these scripts

Table 4.4. *The Vai syllabary*

[Table of Vai syllabary characters organized by consonant rows (left column labels: ʼ, b, ɓ, č, d, ɗ, f, g, g+ṽ, gb, gb+ṽ, h, h̃, ɟ, k, kp, kp+ṽ, l, m) and by consonant rows (right column labels: mb, mgb, n, nd, ń, ńj, ñ, ng, p, r, s, t, v, w, w̃, y, z, ṅ) across vowel columns a, ɛ, e, i, ɔ, o, u.]

were created in an environment where the Latin and Arabic alphabets were well known, it is quite obvious that keeping the signary small was not an important consideration. All three systems have independent Vs, Vai seven, Mende eight and Loma seven. The remainder are CV graphemes for open syllables with simple or complex initial margins of up to three consonants, (C)(C)CV, reflecting the predominance of CV syllable structure in these languages. The Vai syllabary uses points to distinguish varieties of consonant before the same vowel, likely an influence of the Arabic script. The phonetic fit of the Vai syllabary is relatively

74   Signs of syllables

poor (Scribner and Cole 1981), which is to say that readers rely heavily on context to interpret sequences of signs as words. Yet, the syllable has an appeal as an intuitive unit.

Ancient syllabaries

All syllabaries obviously reflect an awareness of the syllable as a linguistic unit. However, for the design of a syllabary it makes a difference whether syllables were intended as functional units or recognized as by-products of makeshift attempts to transfer an existing writing system to another language by applying the rebus principle. Not really a principle at all, rebus writing means to exploit accidental homophony of two unrelated words or parts of words of the same language or of two different languages. This is what happened when two of the oldest and most prolific writing systems, Sumerian and Chinese, were transferred to other languages. In both cases the adoption of the writing system for an unrelated language, Akkadian and Japanese, respectively, led to a change of type. In this sense it is misleading to say that scribes wrote syllables. Rather, extant logograms were reinterpreted as syllabograms. In both cases the transition was piecemeal and, perhaps, imperceptible to the scribes. 'The borderline between the logographic and syllabographic functions is in flux, especially in Sumerian writing' (Krebernik and Nissen 1994: 278). What the transition from logography to syllabography reflects, then, is the discovery rather than the deliberate representation of the linguistic unit of the syllable. The fact that the semantic aspect of the graphemes was not cancelled out with the beginning of their syllabic reinterpretation is evidenced by the fact that in writing Akkadian and Japanese, the Sumerian cuneiform signs and Chinese characters, respectively, were not just assigned syllabic values but also word values in these languages. The same kind of polyfunctionality can be observed in both cases, as illustrated in table 4.5.

When a writing system with a strong morphographic component is adopted for another language it is possible to assign new interpretations of words or morphemes of the recipient language to extant signs of the donor language. However, typological differences between the languages pose serious problems.

> In contradistinction to agglutinative Sumerian where syntactic changes are expressed by attaching grammatical elements to the word stem, Semitic Akkadian is an inflecting language where syntactic changes are effected by changes in the word stem. Such a language cannot be recorded in writing but by means of a phonetic script. Probably it was the need to write Semitic languages which led to the increase of using cuneiform signs for their phonetic values.
> (Nissen 1996: 13)

Table 4.5. *Parallel development of Sumerian cuneiform sign and Chinese character adapted to other languages. Elamite and Hittite, in the former case, and Korean and Vietnamese, in the latter, take the character as a logogram of the Sumerian and the Chinese loanwords, respectively. But in Akkadian and Japanese, the signs are given new interpretations of native words and are also used as phonetic signs.*

	Sumerian	Akkadian	Elamite	Hittite
⋈⊩	an dingir	šamû šamê ilu	an	nepiš

Meaning: god, heaven, sky; determinative for divine names; phonetic /an/

	Chinese	Korean	Japanese	Vietnamese
天	t'ien	cheon	ten, te* amatsu ame	thiên

*as Manyōgana and hence hiragana
Meaning: heaven, sky, nature, heavenly power, weather, god

The development of the Japanese syllabaries on the basis of Chinese characters can be described in very similar terms. The morphology of Japanese is much more complex than that of Chinese and cumbersome to represent by means of characters associated with lexical meanings. Sound writing was the obvious solution. Rebus writing was known prior to the transfer in both Sumerian and Chinese, and in both cases the syllable was the focal unit. Akkadian and Japanese syllabography is the result of systematically elaborating on this strategy. That the ensuing syllabaries are quite different must be explained in terms of the different syllable structures of the recipient languages. Since the syllable structure of Japanese is less involved than that of Akkadian a smaller and simpler syllabary could be developed for the former than for the latter.

The problem of syllable writing, as we have seen, is striking a balance between economy and clarity, between keeping the signary within limits and achieving a reasonable degree of unequivocal interpretation. More than one third of the cuneiform signs of 'Syllabary A' have multiple sound values, because the rebus principle

76 Signs of syllables

Table 4.6. *Basic grid of cuneiform 'Syllabary A'. With permission from P. T. Daniels and W. Bright*, The World's Writing Systems, *Oxford University Press, 1996, p. 57.*

	_a	_e	_i	_u	a_	e_	i_	u_
p b								
t d ṭ								
k g q								
s z ṣ								
š								
m n								
l r								
w y								
ḫ ʾ								
Ø								

a. The following CVC signs are also used: dim, dím, gír, ḫar, kal, kil, kin, kul, lag, lam, rig, suk, tan, tin. Table prepared by P. T. Daniels.

apparently operated on the basis of phonetic similarity rather than theoretically founded equivalence, the more so as it was applied across languages. The primary source of the syllabic values of cuneiform signs are Sumerian lexemes, for example /ga/ < Sumerian *ga* 'milk', /ig/ < Sumerian *ig* 'door'. However, in addition to /ig/ the syllabogram could also be interpreted as /ik/ or /iq/. Another syllabogram was to be interpreted as /eg, ek, eq/ and so on. In Sumerian writing, voiced, voiceless and emphatic stops in coda position were never distinguished, and the quality of the consonantal onset was likewise a matter of interpretation. Hence, there was one syllabogram each for /pa, ba/, /ta, da, ṭa/, /ka, ga, qa/ and so on. Syllabograms were generally associated with groups of similar syllables amongst which the intended one had to be selected according to context. This was economical, but added to the complexity of the system, a problem that was compounded in Akkadian. For Old Akkadian provided the cuneiform signs adopted from Sumerian with additional syllabic values. They were abstracted from Akkadian translations of Sumerian words, that is, Akkadian word interpretations assigned to Sumerian logograms. For instance, ⩟, Sumerian /kur/ 'land' was /maːtum/ in Akkadian, yielding the additional syllabic value /mat/. Another example is the cuneiform sign which is read /á/ 'arm' in a Sumerian context. In Akkadian it is used as a syllabogram for /id/ because 'arm' is *idu* in Akkadian.

Cuneiform

Cuneiform syllabograms are of the following types: V, CV, VC and CVC. In Late Assyrian writing, (C)VCV is also attested. In Old Akkadian certain syllabograms that later represent vowels are to be interpreted as CV signs. The consonantal onset of the syllables in question disappeared in later varieties of the language.

Three vowels are differentiated in writing, /a/, /i/ and /u/. Sumerian has CV signs distinguishing /i/ and /e/, but in Akkadian these vowels were not phonemically distinct and hence the Akkadian syllabary provides signs both for V and CV(C), whose vowel quality ranges between /i/ and /e/. For example, there is one sign for /šim/ and /šem/, another can be read /ri/ or /re/, according to context. However, in other instances different signs are available for /Ce/ and /Ci/, reflecting derivations from different Sumerian logograms. Inconsistencies of this sort show that the cuneiform syllabary is a historically grown system rather than having been designed on the basis of an analytic blueprint. The many so-called 'broken graphics' likewise make this clear. In the event, sequences of (-C)VC-VC signs must be interpreted as containing geminated consonants, as in *li-in-ik-ta* or *li-in-kat-ta* for /linkta/ 'he vowed'. At the same time, vowel notation is often pleonastic ('plene-writing'): the vowel of a syllabic sign of the CV type is repeated: CV_1-V_1. This practice made up for the indeterminate nature of the vowel

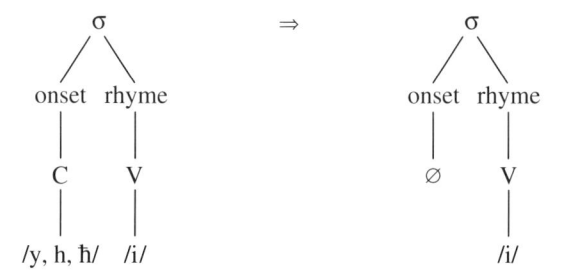

Figure 4.4 *Consonantal onset of Old Akkadian syllables is lost in Akkadian*

78 *Signs of syllables*

of CV signs. Where the vowel of a syllabic sign NI could be interpreted as either /i/ or /e/ an additional V sign makes the reading unambiguous. The same device is also used to mark vowel length, which is distinctive in Akkadian. Syllabic writing in Akkadian, then, involves a number of strategies to compensate for the limited number of syllable types encoded by the basic signs.

Redundant and incomplete coding of both vowels and consonants is quite common in cuneiform writing not only of Akkadian, but of other languages as well. In Elamite, for instance, CV and VC signs with their Old Akkadian values were taken over and a few CVC signs were added. There were only 113 signs in all, 25 of which were also used as logograms. The signaries of Hurrian and closely related Urartian were similarly small. In Hurrian writing five vowels, /a/, /e/, /i/, /o/, /u/, were encoded, as opposed to the Old Akkadian three. This suggests that these syllabaries were adapted to the expressive requirements of their languages. Logograms were used not because words were difficult to write syllabically, but out of convenience. Typically it was very frequent words that were so written. It is clear, then, that cuneiform syllabographic writing was well adapted and highly functional. That many texts strike us as rather convoluted and sometimes impenetrable has more to do with the fact that we have only vague ideas what spoken Akkadian, Assyrian, Babylonian, Hurrian or any of the other cuneiform languages were like than with the nature of the writing system, which suited the speakers of these languages just fine.

Kana

Turning now to the adaptation of Chinese characters to writing Japanese as the basis of generating the kana syllabaries, we can see a number of similar processes at work. The two syllabaries, hiragana, literally 'easy kana', and katakana, literally 'fragmentary kana', are identical in their phonetic values, but the symbols were graphically derived from different Chinese characters and used for different purposes. Chinese provided the phonetic values of the syllabograms which, however, were adjusted to Japanese needs. The syllable structure of Japanese allows for V, CV and ÇV syllables, where Ç is a palatalized consonant. The only consonant in coda position is /n/, but there are no CVC, that is, CV-n kana. This is because the nasal has syllabic value in Japanese. In the early period of kana when the system began to take shape, in the eighth to ninth centuries, /n/ was not encoded at all, but left to contextual interpretation (Seeley 1991: 97). Middle Chinese (MC) had many closed syllables, a feature alien to the phonological structure of the Old Japanese (OJ) language of the time. Two strategies were used when Chinese characters were given Japanese interpretations: one was to drop the final consonant, and the other was to add a vowel, as illustrated, respectively, in the upper and

Table 4.7. *Basic kana syllabaries: H, hiragana; K, katakana. Bracketed items are no longer used.*

		/a/	/i/	/u/	/e/	/o/
∅	H	あ	い	う	え	お
	K	ア	イ	ウ	エ	オ
/k-/	H	か	き	く	け	こ
	K	カ	キ	ク	ケ	コ
/s-/	H	さ	し	す	せ	そ
	K	サ	シ	ス	セ	ソ
/t-/	H	た	ち	つ	て	と
	K	タ	チ	ツ	テ	ト
/n-/	H	な	に	ぬ	ね	の
	K	ナ	ニ	ヌ	ネ	ノ
/h-/	H	は	ひ	ふ	へ	ほ
	K	ハ	ヒ	フ	ヘ	ホ
/m-/	H	ま	み	む	め	も
	K	マ	ミ	ム	メ	モ
/y-/	H	や		ゆ		よ
	K	ヤ		ユ		ヨ
/r-/	H	ら	り	る	れ	ろ
	K	ラ	リ	ル	レ	ロ
/w-/	H	わ	(ゐ)		(ゑ)	を
	K	ワ	(ヰ)		(ヱ)	ヲ
/n/	H	ん				
	K	ン				

Table 4.8. *Middle Chinese (MC) final consonants are dropped in Old Japanese (OJ)*

	MC	OJ
天	/t'ien/	/te/
安	/ân/	/a/
得	/tək/	/tø/
屋	/uk/	/o-ku/
宅	/dăk/	/ta-ku/
国	/kuək/	/ko-ku/

```
     Syllable analysis              Mora analysis
            σ                             σ
           / \                           / \
       onset rhyme                    mora mora
         |   / \                        |    |
         C  V  C                       CV    C
         |  |  |                        |    |
         h  o  n                       ho    n
                                        |    |
                                        ほ   ん
```

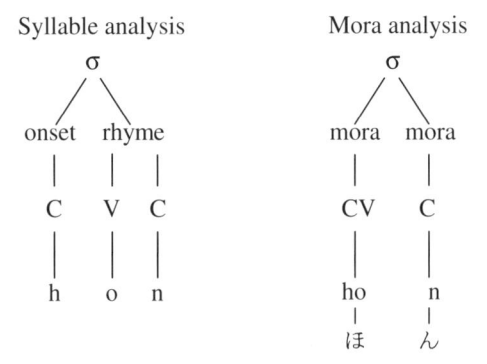

Figure 4.5 *Syllable analysis and mora analysis of Japanese* hon *'book' and the word's kana notation*

lower parts of table 4.8. What in Chinese is a heavy syllable is reduced to a light syllable in Japanese or turned into two syllables. In either case, the graphic sign preceded its phonetic interpretation. Japanese has a moraic structure, which means that phonological time is broken down into units of equal length, mora, rather than into short and long syllables. On the whole, this feature of Japanese phonology is reflected in the kana syllabaries, where each basic sign (table 4.7) is interpreted as one mora (Ratcliffe 2001). A long syllable is two mora and thus encoded with two graphemes.

Except for the syllabic nasal sign, all kana are either V or CV. This is very good in terms of economy. The basic hiragana and katakana listed in table 4.7 are just 48 signs each, including two that are no longer in use because, round about 1000, /wi/ and /i/ as well as /we/ and /e/ merged into single sounds. (The same is also true of /wo/ and /o/, yet the /wo/-kana were kept, although in modern standard orthography they are restricted in use to the direct object case marker /-o/.)

Table 4.9. *Hiragana, left, and katakana, right, for palatalized onset syllables*

	/a/	/u/	/o/
/ky-/	きゃ キャ	きゅ キュ	きょ キョ
/sy-/	しゃ シャ	しゅ シュ	しょ ショ
/ty-/	ちゃ チャ	ちゅ チュ	ちょ チョ
/ny-/	にゃ ニャ	にゅ ニュ	にょ ニョ
/hy-/	ひゃ ヒャ	ひゅ ヒュ	ひょ ヒョ
/my-/	みゃ ミャ	みゅ ミュ	みょ ミョ
/ry-/	りゃ リャ	りゅ リュ	りょ リョ

However, Japanese syllables are not quite that few and simple. For one thing, the basic kana do not differentiate voiced and voiceless stops and fricatives. Two diacritics are employed for this purpose. Two little strokes on the right shoulder of the kana of the /k-, s-, t-, h-/ groups indicate voicing, and a little circle in the same position on the kana of the /h-/ group turns the onset central fricative /h-/ into a voiceless bilabial, /p-/. Further, the onset consonants of the basic CV kana are short, but Japanese has tense or long consonants too. In terms of mora this means that a CVC_1C_1V sequence such as /kitte/ is counted as three mora. In kana this is encoded by prefixing the kana for /tu/ in smaller type to a CV kana whose onset consonant it copies: きって. Again, three kana, three mora. This principle is only compromised by the palatalized onset syllables of the /ky-/, /sy-/, /ty-/, /ny-/, /hy-/, /my-/ and /ry-/ groups. These are encoded by suffixing smaller type kana for /ya/, /yu/, /yo/ to the CV kana of the /i/ column (table 4.9). Thus, /myo/ is coded in kana as みょ, that is, mi-$_{yo}$. Although these are two kana, they count as one mora. While this may violate aesthetic and systematic principles, it does by no means undermine the system's efficiency or elegance.

Economy and accuracy

Kana comes close to an ideal syllabary in several respects. With a small signary that is easy to learn it achieves a high degree of accuracy. Contextual variation of phonetic interpretation of the kana signs is minimal. By and large, each kana is always pronounced the same. More than anything else this is thanks to the simple and regular structure of Japanese syllables which makes Japanese very suitable for syllabic writing. The system had reached its mature form in the tenth century. Yet, literary Chinese continued to play an enormously important role in the world of Japanese letters and, therefore, the Japanese did not shift to kana entirely, but used, and continue to use, logographic and syllabographic writing side-by-side and in a mixed style (see chapter 9). The kana system epitomizes the principle of economy in the development of writing more clearly than the cuneiform Syllabary A. This can be partially explained by the fact that the syllable structure of the recipient language, Japanese, is simpler than that of the donor language, Chinese, while it is the other way round in the cuneiform context, Akkadian having a more complicated syllable structure than Sumerian. Hence, the economic advantage of syllable writing over word writing or morphosyllabic writing is not the same for all languages but depends in large measure on the syllable structure of the language in question. This is evidenced, on one hand, by the inferior phonetic fit of some syllabaries, for example Cypriot and Linear B, and, on the other, by the inferior economy of other syllabaries, for example Yi.

The Aegean scripts Cypriot and Linear B have relatively small signaries of V and CV graphemes (tables 4.10, 4.11), but their phonetic fit is so poor that it is nearly impossible to reconstruct the phonology of the languages written. Both were used for early varieties of Greek, which apparently had many syllables with initial consonant clusters. In writing, these are not distinguishable from sequences of two or three CV syllable signs. Cypriot *ptolin* is written ǂ ├ ≤ ᛁᛋᛁ po-to-li-ne, CV_1-CV_1-CV_2-CV_3, and Linear B *pra* is written ǂ ιs pa-ra, CV_1-CV_1. There are syllabograms for open syllables only. It is assumed, however, that the language of both Cypriot and Linear B had consonantal codas, too. In Classical Greek, separated from these varieties by almost a thousand years, /s, n, l, r/ occur in coda position. There is much uncertainty as to what consonants occurred in clusters and in coda position in the syllables of the earlier forms of Greek. This is due, partly, to relatively scant documentation of these two scripts, but also to their inaccuracy. Although successfully deciphered, they do not allow for unequivocal interpretation at the phonetic level. As Bennett (1996: 126) remarks with regard to the phonetic interpretations of Linear B signs, 'it must be emphasized that . . . transcriptions are a modern convention and correspond exactly only to the shape, and not to any pronunciation or phonemic value of the sign'.

The Yi script – in the Western literature often referred to as Lolo or Wei – evolved in south-west China. It has an attested history of over five centuries but is believed to be much older. Its ancient varieties are morphosyllabic in structure following the model of Chinese writing. The total number of morphosyllabic

Table 4.10. *The Cypriot syllabary*

	a	e	i	o	u
	⚹	⚹	⚹	⚹	⋎
y	▽			⚹	
w	⋋⋌	I	⋋⋌	⌒	
r	Ω	⌒	⋎	⋎	)(
l	⋎	8	⋜	+	⋒
m	⋋⋌	⋋⋌	⋎	⊕	⋋⋌
n	⊤	⋋⋌	⋎	⋎	⋎
p	‡	⋎	⋎	ʃ	⋎
t	⊦	↓	↑	F	F
k	⇧	⋋⋌	⋎	⋀	⚹
s	V	⋎	⟨	⋎	)⋌
z	)⋌			⋎	
x	)(	(⊣			

Yi characters is estimated at as many as ten thousand. In modern times various attempts have been undertaken to devise a syllabic script on the basis of a selection of these characters (Bradley 2000). The new syllabary that was officially approved in 1980 drastically reduced the number of characters. The 819 characters each represent a tonal syllable (table 4.12). Like northern Chinese, Yi has four tones, three of which are treated like other phonological distinctions in the syllabary, while one, the mid level tone, is marked as a diacritic on syllabic signs of mid rising tone. In this manner, a highly accurate notation of Yi speech syllables is achieved. Most of the syllabograms are to be interpreted as a number of homophonous morphemes. This is clearly a major concession to economy

84   *Signs of syllables*

Table 4.11. *The Linear B syllabary*

	a	e	i	o	u
-	𐀀	𐀁	𐀂	𐀃	𐀄
d	𐀅	𐀆	𐀇	𐀈	𐀉
j	𐀊	𐀋		𐀍	
k	𐀏	𐀐	𐀑	𐀒	𐀓
m	𐀖	𐀘	𐀚	𐀗	𐀚
n	𐀜	𐀝	𐀛	𐀞	𐀢
p	𐀠	𐀡	𐀢	𐀡	𐀠
q	𐀣	𐀤	𐀦	𐀨	
r	𐀩	𐀫 ?	𐀪	𐀫	𐀬
s	𐀭	𐀮	𐀯	𐀰	𐀱
t	𐀲	𐀳	𐀴	𐀵	𐀶
w	𐀷	𐀸	𐀹	𐀺	
z	𐀼	𐀽		𐀿	

as compared to the old system, which graphically distinguished homophonous morphemes.

The Yi script is a syllabary. However, with more than 800 signs it is comparatively unwieldy. It fails to optimize the advantages of sound-based writing over meaning-based writing, as the relatively large number of syllables the designers of the modern script felt it was necessary to distinguish in writing does not allow the requirements of economy and accuracy to be balanced in a satisfactory way. The Yi syllabary, then, is a good example to show that the syllable is subject to a wide range of variation across languages and that, accordingly, it depends very much on the language in question whether or not the syllable can be fruitfully exploited as the key unit of a writing system.

Notice that the Chinese have grappled with the same problem. Among the various writing reform proposals that have been deliberated in the course of the

Table 4.12. *The standard Yi syllabary of 1980. Top line are onset consonants, vertical column on left side are nucleus vowels, and vertical column on right side are tones. Three tones are differentiated, indicated in the table as 't', 'p' and unmarked. Hence the arrangement of the syllable signs in groups of three.*

86 *Signs of syllables*

	Initial	Final	Pronunciation
來 =	落 +	哀	
	l(ak)	*ai*	*lai*
春 =	昌 +	脣	
	ch(ang)	(ch)*un*	*chun*

Figure 4.6 Fanqie, *the 'turn and cut' method of showing the syllabic value of a Chinese character*

twentieth century, there were some schemes that targeted the syllable as the basic unit (Chen 1996). In the mid-1930s, Zhai Jiaxiong advanced a scheme containing 454 characters which were meant to encode all Mandarin syllables without tonal differentiation. Another scheme proposed by Zhang Gonghui in 1947 comprised two syllabaries, one with more than 1,000 characters for all tone syllables, and another with some 400 characters disregarding tonal differentiation. There are always many reasons why writing reform schemes fail (see chapter 12), but in this case it is clear that the advantage of syllabic over morphosyllabic writing seemed too small to justify a deep-reaching reform. Interpreting Chinese characters as syllabic signs and thus limiting their number by assigning the same character to all homophonous morphemes leads to a syllabary which, much like the Yi syllabary, foregoes the advantage of semantic interpretability at the graphic level without reaping the benefits of a markedly smaller signary as compared to the morphosyllabic characters needed for everyday use.

The syllable has been known as a concept in China for many centuries (Wen 1995) and, as we have seen in the previous chapter, it does play an important role in the Chinese writing system. Chinese characters were understood as having syllabic interpretations which, however, were not always known. As early as the fourth century CE, Chinese scholars systematized a method of specifying the sound of a character called *fanqie* or 'turn and cut'. A select set of characters are used there strictly as phonograms. To show how a character is to be read, two other characters presumably known to the reader are written together, the first giving the initial, or beginning sound of the character to be assigned a syllabic interpretation, and the latter the final, the rest of the syllable and its tone.

The *fanqie* spelling method, which was brought to perfection as a reference tool in the Qieyun rhyming dictionary of 601, orders some 12,000 characters by syllabic finals or rhyme, that is, vowel, including diphthongs, plus final consonant, if any, and tone. In this manner, both the initial and final of every character were accurately identified. The tone is determined by the final. Thus, *mày* + *kā* yields

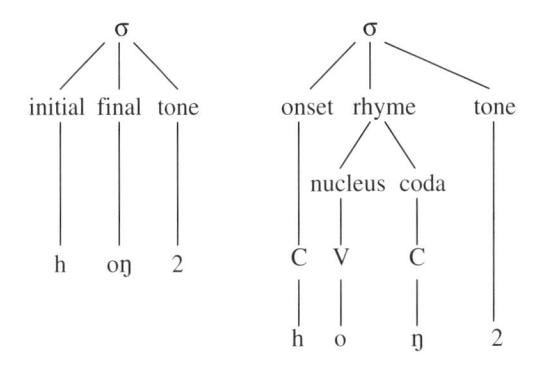

```
        σ                    σ
      / | \                / |  \
 initial final tone    onset rhyme  tone
    |   |    |          |    / \    |
    |   |    |          |  nucleus coda
    |   |    |          |   |    |   |
    h   oŋ   2          C   V    C   |
                        |   |    |   |
                        h   o    ŋ   2
```

Figure 4.7 Fanqie, *left, and phonetic, right, analysis of the syllable* hóng *'insect'*

mā 'mother' with level high (first) tone, whereas the *fanqie* for *mà* 'to scold' needs a final with the vowel /a/ in the falling (fourth) tone, for example *kà*.

The analytic division of the syllable into initial and final differs from modern phonology in that it does not further analyse the final as nucleus and a coda, but it is clear evidence, if any was needed, that the Chinese were aware not just of the syllable as a basic linguistic unit, but also of its analysability. It is particularly noteworthy that the concept of a consonant – the initial – was clearly understood, for this is essential for segmental writing to which we turn in the next chapter. Vowels are both syllables and segments, but the method of 'cutting' off the initial consonant from a syllable is unmistakable evidence of autosegmental analysis.

To conclude this chapter, we have seen that the syllable is the basic unit of a great variety of writing systems. Its functional suitability depends on the syllable structure of the language written. Most syllabaries are defective or incomplete if we take the encoding of all distinct speech syllables of the language in question as a measure of completeness. This, however, is a theoretical ideal rarely approximated in practice. The Aegean systems of a few dozen signs only and the modern standard Yi system consisting of in excess of 800 signs exemplify the two problems faced by all syllabaries: inadequate linguistic fit and an extensive signary. Few languages have a syllable structure that is simple enough to allow for the development of a system that is both economical and easy to interpret. Of the historically grown systems Japanese kana is the prime example.

Questions for discussion

(1)   What does it mean for a syllabary to be incomplete or defective?
(2)   Why would English be difficult to write with a syllabic script?

(3) Explain the difference between a syllable and a mora.
(4) How do you account for the fact that syllabic writing systems vary on a large scale in the size of their signaries?
(5) How does a rhyme in Chinese rhyming dictionaries differ from a rhyme in modern phonology?

5
Signs of segments

> The powers of letters, when they were applied to a new language, must have been vague and unsettled, and therefore different hands would exhibit the same sound by different combinations.   Samuel Johnson

> Aur prezent english langweij iz inefisient, autdated, deflated, irregular, feilur-cawzing, distorted, regressiv, retardant, and often repulsiv!
> Internasional Union For Kanadan

> Each natural language has a finite number of phonemes (or letters in its alphabet) and each sentence is representable as a finite sequence of these phonemes (or letters).   Noam Chomsky, *Syntactic Structures*

> Question: What is an agnostic dyslexic insomniac?
> Answer: Someone who lies awake all night worrying about the existence of dog.

This is an alphabetic pun. People who do speak English but do not write it much never laugh when they hear it. It plays with the interchangeability of letters that, with an alphabetically trained ear, you can 'hear' – or is it 'see'?[1] It is English spelling that makes us perceive one word as the reverse of another, that is, as the same sequence of segments turned backwards. Segments, more specifically phonemic segments, are, it is widely believed, what alphabetic letters encode. However, alphabetic writing has been cited as evidence both for the psychological reality of segments (Cohn 2001: 198) and for the view that segments are a mere projection (Morais *et al.* 1979). The argument cuts either way. How would it be possible to encode speech as a sequence of discrete graphical elements (letters) unless there were corresponding units in the mental representation of language?! But where are they, and if they are in our mind, how did they get there? Illiterate adults find it difficult to divide the stream of speech into segments (and cannot laugh about *dog*), but even a little reading instruction enables them to do so.[2] This

---

[1] Notice that the technical limitation of the term 'letter' to writing is a recent development. Abercrombie (1949) quotes John Bulwer's (1648) remark that 'Letters are the true elements of Speech made of motions of the Mouth' and other statements where 'letter' refers to speech or to both speech and writing.
[2] For an argument about the effects of English spelling on phonemic representation, see Skousen 1982.

raises questions about the nature of the relationship that holds between speech and alphabetic writing.

Theoretical segments

One way of looking at segments is as the speech sounds the letters of the Greek and Latin alphabets are interpreted as. This seems a bit roundabout, perhaps, but there are reasons for such a view, as will become clear. Segments happen in time, but letters are arrayed in space. That a temporal duration corresponds to a spatial extension is not self-evident. Phonologists define segments as ensembles of distinctive features referring to manner and place of articulation. These features are the cornerstone of phonological theory. Their combinations yield segments called 'phones' when they are not viewed as elements of a particular language. Say *p*, to take a simple case. We are talking here, of course, not about the name of the letter, but about the phone [p], a consonant produced as a bilabial voiceless stop, which we can pronounce regardless of the language to which it belongs. However, this is much like pronouncing the letter *p* in isolation, and it may be just that. The production of phonetic features in connected speech extends over a period of time, starting before a segment begins and coming to an end only after it has been terminated (Günther 1988: 15). Where, then, is the segment? According to Prince (1992: 384), 'one common intuition about talking is that we proceed by emitting a sequence of discrete articulations, *rather like the letters of an alphabet*' (emphasis added). It is quite common to equate segments with the letters of the alphabet in this manner, as witnessed, for instance, in the quote by Noam Chomsky at the beginning of this chapter. However, over the past several decades, phonologists have moved away from the segment, since they were not able to discern it in the speech signal. Inspection of phonetic reality (connected speech) has not revealed segments corresponding to discrete phonemes (corresponding in turn to discrete graphemes), because articulators – that is, the physical organs of speech production – work continuously, exhibiting, at any point, the influence of the preceding and following sound. There is hence broad agreement that 'it is impossible, in general, to disarticulate phonological representation into a string of non-overlapping units' (Prince 1992: 386). This is a real problem, for how shall we interpret letters as overlapping units? The problem disappears if, for descriptive purposes, we accept a model of language where there is a phonemic level, at which discrete segments are lined up one after another, as in writing.

All attempts to prove that speech actually *works* on the basis of principles determining the sequential organization of discrete segments have failed. At the same time, Chomsky's above-quoted statement that, on an abstract level, speech is *representable* in terms of finite sequences of segments is indisputable. As a matter of fact, descriptions of this sort have been highly successful. But a good description of an object need not be isomorphic with it. Who would claim that a beautiful woman consists of black and white dots just because a picture of her does? In like manner we must not confuse a segmental *description* of speech with the speech itself. In a sense, alphabetic orthographies can be understood as descriptions of their respective languages, but in any event the relationship between sequences of alphabetic letters and speech is never a one-to-one mapping relation. It is complex in both directions, and, as any description, hinges on a certain point of view highlighting some aspects at the expense of others.

Alphabetically written words can be read and can be pronounced, even words like *chlororophenpyridamine*. The pronounceability of alphabetic words rests on a process known as 'phonological recoding', that is, the transformation of mental representations of sequences of letters into mental representations of sequences of sounds. A great deal of reading research deals with the question of whether and to what extent phonological recoding is necessary for reading alphabetic texts, a problem to which we will return in chapter 9. For present purposes suffice it to note the obvious fact that alphabetic texts can be given a phonetic interpretation, they can be read aloud. While this is true of all writing, more or less, it is widely assumed that in alphabetic writing this rests on the fact that each letter represents a sound. The question then is, what sound?

Phonemes

As pointed out above, the prime candidate, the phonetic segment or phone, has proven to be elusive. Phonologists have recourse to a more abstract unit, the phoneme defined as a phone which fulfils a meaning-differentiating function in a given language. Although there are problems with the phoneme, too, many phonologists continue to use this concept, telling us, for example, that on average languages have 22.8 consonant phonemes and 8.7 vowel phonemes. Maddieson (1984) reports these figures on the basis of studying 317 languages. While he found that they differed on a large scale in their sound inventories, distinguishing between a poor 6 and a luxurious 95 consonants and between an equally disparate 3 and 46 vowels, this is clearly an order of magnitude altogether different from that of words, morphemes and syllables, however counted. In this regard, Cicero's (106–43 BCE) Latin was a plain-vanilla language. With 28 phonemes (tables 5.1, 5.2) it is pretty close to the average. What this means is that in the sound pattern of first-century Latin we find 28 important contrasts that are systematically used to differentiate meaning. A contrast is not the same as a unit, although this distinction is often ignored. Consider, for example, the following definition.

Table 5.1. *Latin vowels and diphthongs*

	front	central	back
high	i iː		u uː
mid	e eː		o uː
low		a aː	
diphthongs			ae au

Table 5.2. *Latin consonants*

	labial	dental alveolar	palatal	velar	uvular	glottal
stop	p b	t d		k g	q	
fricative	f	s				h
nasal	m	n				
liquid		l r				
glide			j	w		

Segmental phoneme: a consonant and vowel sound of a language that functions as a recognizable, discrete unit in it. To have phonemic value, a difference in sound must function as a distinguishing element marking a difference in meaning or identity.   (Ives, Bursuk and Ives 1979: 253)

The difference between a unit and a contrast is often glossed over like this because our inability to pin down the segment can thus be concealed. It is, however, possible to give every contrast a name, say a letter, which is then used to mark it. This kind of relationship between phonological distinctions and letters has often been interpreted as meaning that 'the purpose of alphabetic orthographies is to represent and convey phonologic structures in a graphic form' (Frost 1992: 255). Who, if anybody, stipulated this purpose is unknown. If orthographies have a purpose it is to encode and retrieve linguistic meaning in a graphic form. To represent and convey phonologic structure is at best a means to that end, which is of no interest to anyone except linguists. Instead of assuming a purpose at all it seems more prudent to consider an alphabetic orthography as a possible interpretation or description of the phonological structure of a language, and not usually an ideal one for that matter, if by ideal we mean being parsimonious and as simple as possible.

Written segments

The Latin alphabet had 23 letters (A B C D E F G H I K L M N O P Q R S T V X Y Z), its modern roman form has 26, as <I, J> and <U, V> were not distinguished in classical times and <W> was added much later as a ligature of *UU* or *VV*. What kinds of segment, if any, do they encode? When talking about the letters of the roman alphabet as such, it does not make sense to say that they correspond to phonemes, because phonemes are units of individual languages. We can of course study the characteristics of Latin spelling and try to discover the correspondences between graphemes and phonemes. To list phoneme-grapheme correspondences and reveal their underlying regularities is the main task in analysing alphabetic orthographies. In the case of Latin, thanks to its relatively simple phonology, this is not too difficult, but notice that our evidence for the phoneme inventory of Latin comes from the written record. We find, for instance, that V graphemes are used indistinguishably for short and long vowels which, as we know from metrical analyses, were phonemically distinct, as in *malus* 'bad' vs. *mālus* 'mast'. We also find that geminate C graphemes are frequent but do not seem to regularly mark phonemic contrasts. And we find a great deal of variation in spelling, pointing both to phonetic changes and to inconsistencies. One scribe writes *poena* 'punishment', another *pena*. Similar examples are legion. They could be indicative of a diachronic process of monophthongization or of dialectal variation, or both. Common though these spelling variations are, Latin is often cited as the prototype of phonemic writing, which one influential scholar defines thus: 'In a purely phonemic system of writing, there is a one-to-one correspondence between phonemes and their written representation' (DeFrancis 1989: 185).

This is a straightforward definition, but it does not apply to any particular orthography. It is, as some would say, just an ideal, much like a complete syllabary as defined in the previous chapter is an ideal, an abstract principle that is at best approximated by actual writing systems. As Jaffré and Fayol (1997: 41f.) observe,

PHONEMES   GRAPHEMES

[1] ←--→ <1>
[2] ←--→ <2>
[3] ←--→ <3>
[4] ←--→ <4>
⋮   ⋮
n ←--→ n

Figure 5.1 *The ideal model of phonemic writing*

'none of the European alphabetic orthographies is the fruit of deliberate linguistic calculation. They are all natural children of tinkering and groping in the dark which, nonetheless, have reached a quasi-functional balance.' By 'groping in the dark', I take it they refer to the uncertainty that Samuel Johnson in the quote at the beginning of this chapter diagnosed as accompanying the application of the Latin alphabet to other languages. In Johnson's day, a letter was a thing with three attributes, a name (*nomen*), a graphical form (*figura*) and a power (*potestas*), that is, its pronunciation. Form and name were relatively unproblematic,[3] but the power was 'vague and unsettled'.

Uncertainty and polyvalence

This uncertainty has three aspects. One is that, even assuming that each letter of the Latin alphabet was interpreted as a phoneme, these interpretations were clear only as contrasts, that is within the system of Latin phonology as reflected in spelling. Secondly, some uncertainty is bound to arise whenever the letters whose phonetic correspondences are defined with respect to the relevant contrasts of one language are applied to another where at least some of the contrasts are different. There is no complete congruence. Finally, there is the uncertainty of which contrasts are relevant in the hitherto unwritten language and how they should be marked. This is far from trivial, for, while Latin may have served as a model, the Latin alphabet at no point in its long history was a neutral instrument. It was always biassed, that is, adjusted to and informed by a particular language. With the wisdom of hindsight it is interpreted as exemplifying phonemic writing, although it embodied the principle of sound writing in a much more general and imprecise sense. Phonemic writing in the ideal sense of DeFrancis' above definition presupposes a phonemic analysis resulting in an inventory of the phonemes of the language in question which are then assigned letters. This, it can be said with confidence, was never done when the Latin alphabet was applied to other languages, except in modern times when linguists were charged with or set themselves the task of 'reducing languages to writing' and designing orthographies. Rather, the transfer usually happened in a more or less spontaneous, makeshift way, if only because the twenty-three letters of the Latin alphabet usually were not enough to mark the relevant contrasts. The result of this is the multiplicity of sounds associated with each letter if compared across alphabetic orthographies. Consider, for example, the letter *x* (see figure 5.2).

---

[3] Notice, however, that on the graphic level, too, much variation evolved prompting the development in 800 of the Caroline minuscule by Alcuin of York as a unified script for the Latin world. (Mallon 1982)

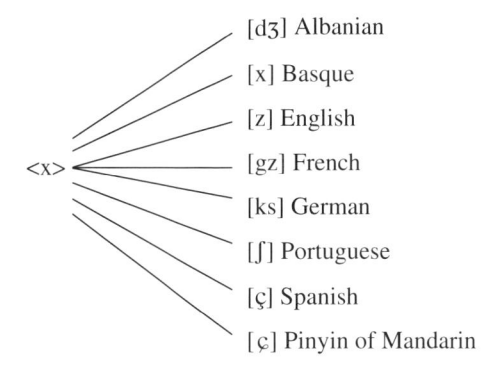

```
<x> ─┬──── [dʒ] Albanian
     ├──── [x] Basque
     ├──── [z] English
     ├──── [gz] French
     ├──── [ks] German
     ├──── [ʃ] Portuguese
     ├──── [ç] Spanish
     └──── [ɕ] Pinyin of Mandarin
```

Figure 5.2 *The letter* x *and some of its phonetic interpretations*

The phonetic interpretations of the letter *x* are so varied that it is difficult to find a common core. And this is only a simplified picture, because the grapheme <x> is often given several different phonetic interpretations. In English it is [z] only in word-initial position and otherwise [ks] as in *excellent* or [gz] as in *exist*. In French, [gz] is only initial as in *Xavier*. In intervocalic position as in *deuxième* it is pronounced [z], and in final position it is written but not pronounced, as in *deux* [dø]. [ks] is yet another pronunciation as in *préfixe*. Spanish <x> can also be pronounced [x] in certain contexts, and so on, in other languages. If we add to this all possible orthographic renditions of the sounds we have identified as possible interpretations of <x> we arrive at a very complex set of relations. Now, it might be argued that *x* is a special letter which has some strange properties. After all it is the only Greek-derived letter which in Latin is both redundant and encodes two phonemes. It occurs always in final position in words like *lex* 'law' and *rex* 'king' where it is interpreted as the consonant cluster [ks] which could be written <ks> just as well. However, there are many other 'special letters', and if we look at the twenty-three letters one by one we will not find a single one that has but one phonetic interpretation. Even within one language's orthographic system most letters are multivalent, not to speak of orthographies of different languages. As the result of the vernacularization of the Latin alphabet and its use over the centuries, all of the letters have a multiplicity of phonetic interpretations, which vary depending on the language the letters are applied to.

What is more, the same is also true for the other direction. It is rare indeed that we can answer the question 'How do I write this sound?' by naming a single letter. Consider the English vowel *schwa*[4] /ə/, the pronunciation of the third letter of *analytic*. It is not difficult to find out that, in English, any vowel letter is sometimes pronounced [ə] (see figure 5.3). Again, the relevance of this example could be

---

[4] The name *schwa* derives from Hebrew *šewa*, a diacritic indicating a neutral vowel.

96 *Signs of segments*

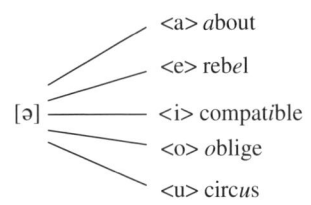

```
            <a> about
            <e> rebel
[ə]         <i> compatible
            <o> oblige
            <u> circus
```

Figure 5.3 *Graphic representation of [ə] in English*

called into doubt, because as a neutral, central vowel [ə] exhibits great variability as far as place of articulation and degree of rounding are concerned and, therefore, is encoded by several different vowel letters in most alphabetically written languages. But the other vowel letters, if not quite as promiscuous, still exhibit a considerable degree of variation, too.

There are several reasons for the polyvalence of the letters of the Latin alphabet within and across languages and the multiplicity of graphic representations of sounds by means of the Latin alphabet. They can be grouped under three headings: historical, systematic and haphazard.

Historical change

Over time, the gap between spelling and pronunciation is bound to widen in alphabetic orthographies, as spoken forms change and written forms are retained. Many of the so-called 'silent' letters in French can be explained in this way. Catach (1978: 65) states that 12.83 per cent of letters are mute letters in French, that is, letters that have no phonetic interpretation whatever. Many of them once had phonetic counterparts that, by regular processes of sound change, have been effaced. Returning to figure 5.2, it is inadequate, therefore, simply to list the various phonetic interpretations of French <x>. Inspecting the distribution of mute letters, we will notice (1) that not only <x> but other C graphemes, too, fail to be pronounced in word-final position; (2) that the same C graphemes once were pronounced in Old French or, prior to that, in Latin; and (3) that they still are pronounced in intervocalic position, both within words and at word boundaries, as in *deux études* [døzetyd]. Unravelling the underlying rules of sound change will go some way towards explaining the intricate relations between graphemes and phonemes in French, but not all the way. For many supposedly historical spellings are artifacts such as modern *poids* 'weight', which was erroneously modelled on Latin *pondus*, although the Old French word was spelled *pois* and pronounced /pois/. The pseudo-etymological spelling *poids* has been around for several hundred years, and its present pronunciation /pwa/ is hard to explain on the basis of general rules.

Another historical factor that undermined simplicity and cross-linguistic uniformity in sound-letter correspondences of the Latin alphabet has to do with the gradual reversal of the relationship between speech and writing. 'How shall I write this word?' used to be the initial question where the application of the Latin alphabet to an unwritten language was at issue. As time went by, it was superseded by the question 'How shall I pronounce this word?' The great *ad litteras* reform initiative carried out in Charlemagne's name in the Latin-speaking world in the ninth century is the prime example testifying to this change of attitude. To halt the 'corruption' of the language, Latin was to be pronounced as it was spelt. Spelling pronunciation was thus born both as a concept and as a linguistic reality. Consider, for instance, Latin-derived words such as *habit*, *heretic*, *hotel* and *hospital* in English where the initial <h> is pronounced, although it had already ceased to be pronounced in Middle French whence these words were borrowed. Some frequently used words like *hour* are still pronounced without the /h/, despite the spelling. But the others are evidence that writing had become an agent of linguistic change, transcending its role as a means of expression. The image became the model.

Some linguists consider that this is an inevitable consequence of writing, as, for example, the title of Kenneth Pike's 1947 book suggests: *Phonemics: A Technique for Reducing Languages to Writing*. Phonemes are here seen in direct correlation with alphabetic writing, which, from Pike's point of view, is a reduction, an abstraction, rather than a neutral and faithful representation. A letter is a stabilizer, something like a catalyst, which introduces shape where in phonic reality is flux. It is worth noting that this is a problem not just of description, but of standardization and the power of a fixed norm. Writing by means of letters that supposedly represent sounds fosters an awareness of the necessity to settle on a variety embodying the canonical form of the language in question.

Systematic multifunctionality

Systematic reasons for the complex relations between sounds and the letters of the Latin alphabet are many. One is that groups of similar phones are divided up into phonemes differently in different languages. For instance, [b], [p], [p^h] are such a group. In English, voiced [b] as in *bill* differs from voiceless [p] as in *pill*. The first letter of *pill* is pronounced [p^h] in *pill*, with aspiration, whereas the same letter is a non-aspirated [p] in *spill*. But unlike *bill/pill*, this distinction is not phonemic. [p] and [p^h] are positional variants or allophones in English and, therefore, not distinguished in spelling. In Mandarin, by contrast, aspiration marks a phonemic contrast which is why *Beijing* is spelt with a <b> standing for a de-voiced [b] in Pinyin, whereas <p> is for [p^h]. Hence the range of phonetic interpretations of letters varies across languages.

Phonetic contrasts may be phonemic in some instances and non-phonemic in others. In German, /g/ and /k/ are two phonemes usually distinguished in spelling as in *gerben* 'to tan' vs. *kerben* 'to notch'. Yet, <g> has two phonetic interpretations, [g] and [k] (not counting [x], a common pronunciation of *ich mag* 'I like to', which is not the point at issue here). This duplicity as that of other C letters is quite systematic. <g> is pronounced [k] only in final position, as German has no final voiced consonants. Another reason for ignoring the phonetic distinction [g], [k] in writing is preserving the graphic word in its various derivational forms, as in *Tag* [taːk], *Tage* [taːgə] 'day, days'. A similar strategy explains the <ti> – [ʃə] correspondence in English, as in *connection, perfection, election*, which are recognizable morphological derivations of *connect, perfect, elect*. But notice that the graphic uniformity of word paradigms is observed in some languages but not in others. In Dutch, the same phonological fact as of German, that voiced consonants do not occur in final position, is the rationale for *not* preserving the graphic word form. Examples such as *ik reis* 'I travel', *wij reizen* 'we travel' are again quite systematic, but the underlying principle is different. In the event Dutch spelling is more phonetic than German.

I have now mentioned in passing a major reason for the apparent polyvalence of the letters of the Latin alphabet. Their usage is determined not just by the phonetic interpretations of individual letters but by higher-level units, morphemes and words. In spite of the persistent notion that letters are associated with sounds or sets of sounds, it is impossible to construct an algorithm for the spelling of the words of a language like English on the basis of a list of all, or even the most commonly used, graphemic representations of the phonemes of English. An algorithm for the opposite direction, providing the graphemes of English with a phonetic interpretation is equally hard to construct. Such an algorithm is needed, for example, for a reading machine that produces a synthesized voice output. For illustration, consider just some of the many English graphemes that can be, but are not always, interpreted as the phoneme /uː/ (table 5.3).

Some of the spellings in table 5.3 are more regular than others; some may be classified as exceptional, historical or foreign spellings. But they serve to illustrate one point: it is not segments that are encoded but words. Notice also that the list comprises no proper names, such as *McLuhan*, which invariably add to the complexity, or words where [uː] occurs as part of a palatalized syllable, as in *new* [njuː], *continue* [kəntɪnjuː] *nuisance* [njuːsns] and *euphemism* [juːfɪmizəm].

There is, of course, structure below the word level. As table 5.3 demonstrates, many graphemes consist of several letters, which moreover are subject to numerous context restrictions. But arriving at the correct spelling of English words by matching phonemes one-by-one with graphemes would require an algorithm so complex that relying on long word lists instead is more economical. Alternative

Table 5.3. *Some ways of spelling /uː/ in English*

<u>	truly
<o>	do
<oe>	shoe
<oo>	soon
<ue>	true
<ui>	lawsuit
<ou>	routine
<wo>	two
<ew>	screwed
<ewe>	jewel
<oeu>	manoeuvre
<ous>	rendezvous
<ough>	throughout
<oups>	coups

graphemes for the same phoneme (or combination of phonemes) would have to be ordered for probability in such a way that, for example, the algorithm produces *Fred* as a first or unmarked option and *Phred* as a highly marked option, but in the case of *phrase* <ph> must be the first and only option for [f].

Similarly, building up the correct phonetic interpretation of English words from the relevant graphemic units – individual letters, digraphs, trigraphs etc. – is sometimes impossible and often difficult. Again, word lists and morphological rules are hard to avoid. It is quite obvious, then, that for a language like English the ideal model of phonemic writing sketched in figure 5.1 is meaningless. Even a more complex model such as figure 5.4 does not apply, because in many instances it is not individual graphemes, including digraphs and trigraphs, that are the relevant units, but morphemes and lexemes.

Spellings like *to*, *too*, *two*, *see*, *sea*, and *phrase*, *frays*, multiplied by hundreds of other examples, make for complex grapheme–phoneme correspondences, but the interpretation of written texts does not depend on these correspondences alone. Exploiting other systemic levels of language is equally common and practical. The plural of both *dog* and *cat* is uniformly indicated by <s>, although it is [dɔgz] but [kæts]. In the event <s> can be understood as indicating the plural morpheme rather than a sound. Accordingly, such spellings are sometimes referred to as morphograms. Another very obvious case in point is word separation. It introduces structural organization in alphabetic writing that has nothing to do with the stream of speech, let alone grapheme–phoneme correspondences.

100   *Signs of segments*

PHONEMES   GRAPHEMES

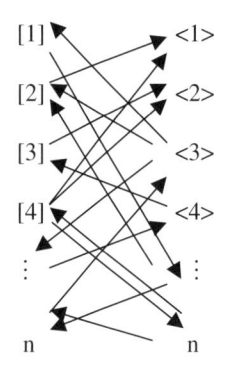

Figure 5.4 *Complex phoneme–grapheme correspondences*

Haphazard choices

Finally, there are miscellaneous processes and events that introduce irregularities and disharmonies between orthography and pronunciation. In several European languages, the letter *h* has been employed for purposes not directly related to the spoken form of words. Spanish <h> is an example. Before <u> and <v> were distinguished, <h> was used in front of initial /we/ to exclude the phonetic interpretation [v]. Hence *huevo* [weβo] 'egg' < Lat. *ovum*. In other orthographies <h> fulfils quite different functions. In French it is usually interpreted as a glottal onset barring the liaison of a final C with a following initial V. Hence *les enfants* [lɛz̃ãfã] but *les halles* [lɛʔal]. In German, in addition to encoding the consonant [h], <h> is used to mark vowel length, as in *mahnen* [mɑːnən] and to mark a syllable boundary before an unstressed V, as in *drohen* [dRo.ən]. As a part of digraphs *h* occurs in many orthographies, such as English *th*, *sh*, *gh*, *ph*, *ch*, among others. Double C graphemes variously indicate consonant length (Italian *addio* [ad-ˈdiːo]), vowel quality (German *Motte* [mɔtə]), a sound not otherwise encoded as Spanish <ll> for the palatal lateral [ʎ], or are used in logographic function (English *butt* vs. *but*).

Digraphs and trigraphs tend to have more variable phonetic interpretations across languages than simple consonant letters. The *th-* spelling of English for /θ/ as in *think*, /ð/ as in *brother* and /t/ as in *Thailand* has no counterpart in most European languages. <ous> for /u/ is regular in French, but unknown in other languages, except in French loanwords. <oe> for /u/ is unique to Dutch, as is <sch> for German /ʃ/, <nh> for Portuguese [ɲ], and <ld> for Norwegian /lː/. Idiosyncrasies of this sort reflect the fact that digraphs and trigraphs represent a major strategy of redressing the paucity of the signary of the Latin alphabet. They were usually tailored or developed spontaneously to suit the needs of individual languages.

Other haphazard factors that contribute to arbitrary grapheme–phoneme correspondences include loanwords kept in their original spelling, inconsistent spelling reforms, and technical innovations. The pseudo-archaic English *ye* is an example of how a grapheme came into existence on purely technical grounds. It was introduced by William Caxton (*d.* 1491), who brought the printing technology to England from the continent. Not having a thorn <þ> – a letter still used for /θ/ in Icelandic – in his letter case, he used <y> instead.

Linguistic interpretation

The three causes of polyvalence and uncertainty just discussed, historical change, systematic multifunctionality, and haphazard choices, together bring about orthographies that tend to operate on more than one level. While graphemes map onto speech sounds, phonetic interpretations are supplemented, to a greater or lesser extent, by graphotactically encoded morphological and lexical information. To some extent, spelling conventions reflect phonological structure, but this is usually the phonological structure of words or morphemes rather than connected speech. Graphic words are formed according to the graphotactic regularities of the orthography in question, which can be related to phonetic words formed according to the phonotactic regularities of the phonology in question. This relationship usually relies on several structural levels of the linguistic system, rather than on phonemic segmentation alone. Alphabetic orthographies, no matter how simple the phoneme–grapheme correspondences, are not systems of transcription. They constitute systems in their own right which ought to be investigated as such, rather than as insufficient representations of phonological phrase and sentence structure.

The question remains as to how grapheme–phoneme correspondences can be calculated and what they mean for alphabetic orthographies. Many dictionaries include a pronunciation key that could serve as a rough and ready estimate. *The American Heritage Dictionary*, for instance, posits 43 phonemes and 232 graphemes for American English, a ratio of 1 : 5.39. But, as Nyikos (1988) has demonstrated, it is quite unclear on what kind of data figures of this sort are based. His own comprehensive survey of a number of dictionaries yielded a ratio almost five times as complex: 40 phonemes and 1,120 graphemes occurring in common English words, a ratio of 1 : 24. Calculations of this sort are a matter of contention, because they are informed by different theoretical assumptions. What can be said, however, is that the higher the ratio the further removed the spelling system is from phonemic writing. The phoneme–grapheme ratio is one of the more obvious points distinguishing the various orthographies that make use of the Latin alphabet. Those with a very high ratio are sometimes called 'deep orthographies', while those with a ratio closer to the ideal of 1 : 1 are called 'shallow or surface orthographies', where 'depth' means being further removed from the phonetic interpretation of strings of graphemes. Surface orthographies such as Finnish, Spanish and Turkish are characterized by relatively regular grapheme–phoneme correlations, whereas in deep orthographies such as English and French elementary grapheme–phoneme correlations are frequently superseded by fixed graphic syllables, morphemes and lexemes. 'Deep' and 'surface' mark extreme points on a scale along which many other intermediary orthographies are located.

Augmenting the Latin alphabet

Surface orthographies are often considered simpler and thus superior to deep orthographies because they seem to conform more closely to the ideal the Latin alphabet is thought to embody. This is one reason why many attempts have been made to expand the Latin alphabet, which was felt to be inadequate for many of the languages that use it (Wells 2000). Digraphs and trigraphs, we noticed above, are important devices for doing this as they do not drastically alter the outer appearance of written texts. It is the only such device used in English, but many other languages employ two further devices to enlarge their signaries: diacritics and additional letters. The latter is generally undesirable because it undermines the purported universality of the Latin alphabet, except for orthographies designed by linguists in modern times, which make use of, for example, the 'Africa alphabet' (figure 5.5) developed in 1930 by the International Institute of African Languages and Cultures in London. Many languages have a velar nasal phoneme /ɲ/ but <ɲ> is rarely used as a grapheme. Yet there are letters such as Danish <Æ, æ>, Dutch <IJ, ij>, German <ß> (lower case only) and <Ŋ, ŋ> used in certain West African languages, which are specific.

More commonly, diacritics are used to supplement the basic set of Latin letters (table 5.4). Notice, however, that the difference between diacritics and additional

---

Aa Bb Ɓɓ Cc Dd Ɖɖ Ee Ɛɛ əəFf *Ff* Gg
ɣɣ Hh Xx Ii Jj Kk Ll Mm Nn Ŋŋ Oo Ɔɔ
Pp Rr Ss Ʃʃ Tt Uu Vv Ww Yy Zz Ʒʒ '

Figure 5.5 *The Africa alphabet*

Table 5.4. *Commonly used diacritics to enlarge the scope of the Latin alphabet*

Symbol	name	Example	Function
<´>	Acute accent	Polish Ź	palatalization
<`>	Grave accent	Italian *città*	stress accent on last syllable
<^>	Circumflex	French *bête*	on Vs which formerly preceded an [s]
<ˇ>	Háček (reversed circumflex)	Czech *č*	palatalization
<~>	Tilde	Portuguese *ã*	nasalization
<¨>	Umlaut	German *ü* [y]	V quality modification
	Diaeresis	English *coördinate*	separate pronunciation of two Vs
<¯>	Macron	Latin *hērēditās*	vowel length
<,>	Cedilla	French *ç*	pronunciation of <c> as [s] before <i>
</>	Slanted bar	Polish *ł*	velarization

letters is rather fuzzy and unimportant for graphemic and graphotactic analysis. Both *ä*, an *a* plus the diacritic ¨, and the additional letter *æ*, derived from the ligature *a+e*, count as separate graphemes of the orthographies where they are used.

Digraphs and trigraphs, diacritics, and new letters make up for the shortcomings of the Latin alphabet, but their number is limited. The alphabet of most languages does not exceed thirty basic letters, although the number of graphemes, which includes all upper case and lower case letters, all diacritically modified letters, and all letter combinations that function as graphotactic units, is much higher. Even shallow orthographies rarely approximate the ideal of a bi-unique grapheme–phoneme mapping relation. The International Phonetic Alphabet (IPA) (figure 5.6) is still committed to this ideal. Since its inception in 1886, it has been continuously expanded and now includes a total of 111 basic symbols plus 31 diacritics and 33 symbols for suprasegmental features. This is a far cry from the original 23-letter Latin alphabet, a clear indication that, although derived from the Latin alphabet, the IPA is functionally very different from alphabetic orthographies. These have, however, inherited some of the same characteristics, especially an inadequacy in dealing with suprasegmental features.

Suprasegmentals

In one respect all alphabetic orthographies are underdetermined with regard to the spoken sounds of utterances. Sound features such as stress and pitch are essential parts of utterances, but the Latin alphabet provides no means of encoding

CONSONANTS (PULMONIC)

	Bilabial	Labiodental	Dental	Alveolar	Postalveolar	Retroflex	Palatal	Velar	Uvular	Pharyngeal	Glottal
Plosive	p b			t d		ʈ ɖ	c ɟ	k g	q ɢ		ʔ
Nasal	m	ɱ		n		ɳ	ɲ	ŋ	ɴ		
Trill	ʙ			r					ʀ		
Tap or Flap				ɾ		ɽ					
Fricative	ɸ β	f v	θ ð	s z	ʃ ʒ	ʂ ʐ	ç ʝ	x ɣ	χ ʁ	ħ ʕ	h ɦ
Lateral fricative				ɬ ɮ							
Approximant		ʋ		ɹ		ɻ	j	ɰ			
Lateral approximant				l		ɭ	ʎ	ʟ			

Where symbols appear in pairs, the one to the right represents a voiced consonant. Shaded areas denote articulations judged impossible.

CONSONANTS (NON-PULMONIC)

Clicks	Voiced implosives	Ejectives		
ʘ Bilabial	ɓ Bilabial	ʼ as in:		
ǀ Dental	ɗ Dental/alveolar	pʼ	Bilabial	
ǃ (Post)alveolar	ʄ Palatal	tʼ	Dental/alveolar	
ǂ Palatoalveolar	ɠ Velar	kʼ	Velar	
ǁ Alveolar lateral	ʛ Uvular	sʼ	Alveolar fricative	

SUPRASEGMENTALS

ˈ	Primary stress	ˌfoʊnəˈtɪʃən
ˌ	Secondary stress	
ː	Long	eː
ˑ	Half-long	eˑ
˘	Extra-short	ĕ
.	Syllable break	ɹi.ækt
|	Minor (foot) group	
‖	Major (intonation) group	
‿	Linking (absence of a break)	

TONES & WORD ACCENTS

LEVEL			CONTOUR		
e̋ or ˥	Extra high		ě or ˦˥	Rising	
é or ˦	High		ê or ˥˦	Falling	
ē or ˧	Mid		e᷄ or ˦˥	High rising	
è or ˨	Low		e᷅ or ˨˩	Low rising	
ȅ or ˩	Extra low		e᷈ or ˧˦˧	Rising-falling	
↓ Downstep			↗ Global rise		etc.
↑ Upstep			↘ Global fall		

Figure 5.6 *The International Phonetic Alphabet (revised to 1993)*

VOWELS

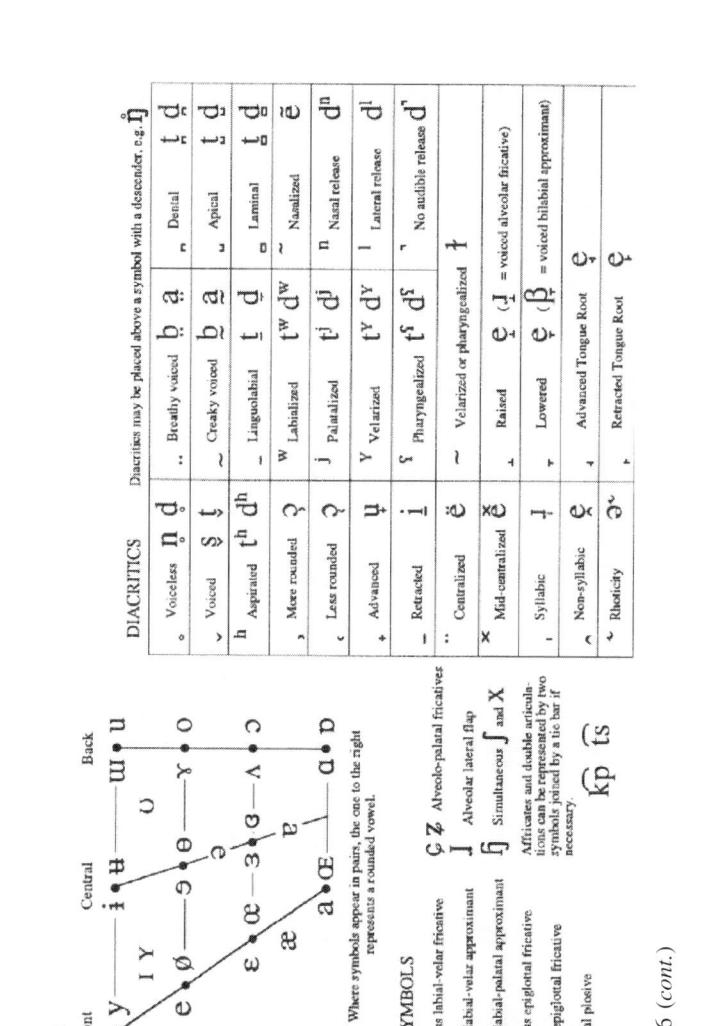

	Front	Central	Back
Close	i • y	ɨ • ʉ	ɯ • u
Close-mid	e • ø	ɘ • ɵ	ɤ • o
Open-mid	ɛ • œ	ɜ • ɞ	ʌ • ɔ
	æ	ɐ	
Open	a • ɶ		ɑ • ɒ

Where symbols appear in pairs, the one to the right represents a rounded vowel.

OTHER SYMBOLS

ʍ Voiceless labial-velar fricative ɕ ʑ Alveolo-palatal fricatives
w Voiced labial-velar approximant ɺ Alveolar lateral flap
ɥ Voiced labial-palatal approximant ʃ x Simultaneous ʃ and x
ʜ Voiceless epiglottal fricative
ʢ Voiced epiglottal fricative Affricates and double articulations can be represented by two symbols joined by a tie bar if necessary.
ʡ Epiglottal plosive

k͡p t͡s

DIACRITICS

Diacritics may be placed above a symbol with a descender, e.g. ŋ̊

̥ Voiceless	n̥ d̥	̤ Breathy voiced	b̤ a̤	̪ Dental	t̪ d̪
̬ Voiced	s̬ t̬	̰ Creaky voiced	b̰ a̰	̺ Apical	t̺ d̺
ʰ Aspirated	tʰ dʰ	̼ Linguolabial	t̼ d̼	̻ Laminal	t̻ d̻
̹ More rounded	ɔ̹	ʷ Labialized	tʷ dʷ	̃ Nasalized	ẽ
̜ Less rounded	ɔ̜	ʲ Palatalized	tʲ dʲ	ⁿ Nasal release	dⁿ
̟ Advanced	u̟	ˠ Velarized	tˠ dˠ	ˡ Lateral release	dˡ
̠ Retracted	i̠	ˤ Pharyngealized	tˤ dˤ	̚ No audible release	d̚
̈ Centralized	ë	̴ Velarized or pharyngealized	ɫ		
̽ Mid-centralized	ɛ̽	̝ Raised	e̝ (ɹ̝ = voiced alveolar fricative)		
̩ Syllabic	n̩	̞ Lowered	e̞ (β̞ = voiced bilabial approximant)		
̯ Non-syllabic	e̯	̘ Advanced Tongue Root	e̘		
˞ Rhoticity	ɚ	̙ Retracted Tongue Root	e̙		

Figure 5.6 (*cont.*)

them. These features are called 'suprasegmentals' because they do not occur before or after, but together with other vowels and sonorants. They relate not to segments but to syllables and sometimes larger units. Consider as an example Danish *stød* (literally 'thrust'), a kind of glottal stop occurring within affected vowels. *Stød* marks a phonological distinction, as in *mor* 'mother' vs. *mord* 'murder', homophone words only distinguished by the presence of *stød* in the latter (Haberland 1994: 322). The graphemic distinction is <r> vs. <rd>. The segmental notation of the alphabet forces us to encode these features as segments or features of segments. Traditional phonology treats suprasegmentals as distinct from segments. The latter can be isolated, the former cannot. But, as we have seen earlier, the segment is a theoretical construct that is not easily matched with an observable unit in the sound stream. In a sense, therefore, suprasegmental features only accentuate the fundamental difficulty of the principle of segmentation on which the alphabet is based.

This is a particular problem with the many tone languages of the world. Various conventions have been developed to deal with it. Romanization schemes for Mandarin Chinese have played a prominent role in this connection. An early article by Yuan Ren Chao (1930), a prominent Chinese linguist, is still widely quoted. It represented contour tones with number combinations based on a pitch scale of 1 (lowest) to 5 (highest) and is thus able to capture the process quality of tones. However, interspersed number symbols radically change the visual impression of alphabetic writing. Therefore, Chao's system is not used in any orthography. Another system, *Gwoyeu Romantzyh*, has no accent marks, but provides a different internal spelling to all vowels in all four tones and thus forms a different graphic image for each tonal syllable in Mandarin. In this system, several alphabetic letters are regularly used without any segmental correlate. For instance, the <r> in *jarng* 'to assist' is to be interpreted as rising tone rather than an alveolar consonant. Similar solutions have been chosen for other tone languages. Some recently devised orthographies for Sino-Tibetan languages use orthographic strategies to encode tonal distinctions. For example, Lahu, which distinguishes seven tones, uses roman letters suffixed to the tone-bearing V as follows: no symbol for mid-level neutral, <l> mid-fall, <d> high-fall, <q> mid-rise, <r> low-fall, <t> high-to-mid-high, <f> low-level. However, the fact that roman letters are employed by such systems in two radically different functions has generally worked against their acceptance. The official romanization of Chinese, Pinyin, uses accent marks on the tone-bearing Vs: <⁻> flat, <′> rising, <ˇ> falling-rising, <`> falling. With just four distinctions Mandarin has a moderately simple tone system. Diacritical tone marks for other languages require more complex solutions. For instance, Vietnamese spelling uses diacritics for both vowel quality and tone. The basic V letters of Vietnamese are <Aa, Ââ, Ăă, Ee, Êê, Ii, Oo, O'o', Uu, U'u'>.

These combine with six contrastive tone diacritics: no mark, an acute accent, a grave accent, a hook, a tilde and a dot-under. The result is that there are several graphemes consisting of a letter base and double accents, for example, <Ấ ấ, Ẫ ã̃, Ẩ ẩ, É̂ ế, Ễ ẽ̂, Ệ ệ>.

Two lessons can be learned from Vietnamese spelling. First, the Latin alphabet is characterized by a general shortage of V letters, which becomes more obvious as alphabetic orthographies are designed for languages that are typologically unrelated to Latin. The second point to note is that through the poverty of V letters the Latin alphabet, and by extension the IPA, still betray its origin in the universe of Semitic writing, to which we will turn in the next chapter. To the extent that universality can be claimed for alphabetic notation, it is a universality grounded in a particular tradition that, for example, analytically distinguished segmental from suprasegmental features.

Conclusion

The Latin alphabet is the most widely used script of all time. Its simplicity and elegance as the writing system of the Latin language suggests universal applicability on the basis of the common principle of segmentation. More than any other script it is associated with the idea of the sound segment. However, it has never been the neutral tool it is sometimes thought to be but which its modern offspring, the IPA, still strives to be. All alphabetic writing systems do not function in the same manner. In this chapter we have seen that, although the letters of the Latin alphabet are impressionistically interpreted as sound segments and are often considered the units of phonemic writing, encoding phonemes is just one of several functions that letters fulfil as graphemes of particular orthographic systems. The phonetic interpretation of Latin letters is variable both within and, in greater measure, across languages. They typically operate on different levels ranging between phonetic features and phonemes and, being combined to form complex graphemes, serve the encoding of syllables, morphemes and lexemes. The distinctions recognized by alphabetic orthographies vary across languages, as do their grapheme inventories. Phoneme–grapheme correspondences, which form a central part of alphabetic orthographies, are variously supplemented by higher-level graphic regularities, many of which have no correlates in speech. In various complex ways alphabetic writing allows for a phonetic interpretation and is thus related to speech, but at the same time fosters a segmentalist projection of it. The isolated letter bears a conceptual semblance to the phoneme and pushes the insight that distinctive features rather than whole sounds are the basic building blocks of speech into the background. 'Linguistic notations, like the International Phonetic

Alphabet and the Americanist phonetic alphabet, are obviously influenced by the modular principle of the standard typographic alphabet' (Bigelow 1992: 197). Supporting a conception of language as consisting of segmental, unitary and distinct sounds, the Latin alphabet thus is a Janus-faced medium of linguistic expression, functioning as both model and image.

Questions for discussion

(1) What is a letter?
(2) How does the number of the letters of the alphabet of a language relate to the number of the graphemes of its orthography?
(3) What is the difference between shallow orthographies and deep orthographies?
(4) Why has the Latin alphabet been supplemented by additional letters and diacritical marks?
(5) What distinctions in alphabetic writing can you think of that have no correlate in speech?

6
Consonants and vowels

> Take care of the sense, and the sounds will take care of themselves.
> Lewis Carroll

> The practical utility of having separate signs for vowels will vary according to the phonological structure of the language concerned.
> Roy Harris, *The Origin of Writing*

It is a recognized fact, and has been for millennia, that there are two complementary classes of speech sounds, consonants and vowels. Segmentalism, we noted in the previous chapter, is a view of language that treats both classes exactly alike, inspired to do so, perhaps, by interpreting the Graeco-Latin alphabet as an iconic map of speech sounds where letter order represents the sequence of articulated sounds. As a matter of principle, letters for vowels and consonants are assigned equal space in writing systems derived from the Greek alphabet, and as a class V letters are indistinguishable in form from C letters. Indeed, the equalization of both is usually quoted as the crucial accomplishment of Greek writing. Yet, there are some conspicuous differences between vowels and consonants. Let us briefly consider some of them.

Differences between consonants and vowels

Early definitions of vocalic phonemes as units that have the faculty of forming a word by themselves have proven too restrictive, but independence as a syllable, though only a rough-and-ready criterion, is more tenable. As discussed in chapter 4, vowels have syllabic status, consonants usually do not. Certain consonants such as /n/, /l/ and /w/ are syllabic in some languages and, on the other hand, there are also non-syllabic vowels, but generally speaking syllabicity is more closely associated with vowels than with consonants. Vowels rather than consonants bear stress accent, pitch and tone.

Another difference between the two classes of speech sounds is seen in their relative volatility. On the stage of sound change vowels play the leading roles,

110   *Consonants and vowels*

while consonants are usually assigned walk-on parts. In the following examples of the Great Vowel Shift from Old English (OE) to Modern English (ME) in the fifteenth century, the vowels changed, but the consonants were preserved.

    OE āþ   bāt   bān   hām   rād   stān   hāl
    ME oath boat bone home road stone whole

Vowels are also more prone to get changed in paradigmatic derivations such as *foot, feet, tooth, teeth, mouse, mice, breathe, breath, sit, sat*. Consonants form the skeleton of these words, vowels provide the flesh. Regular vowel alternation of genetically related words is furthermore observed across languages, as in F *trois* /trwa/, I *tre* /tre/, Gr *drei* /drai/, E *three* /θriː/; L *fenestra*, F *fenêtre*, Gr *Fenster*. To be sure, consonants too change over time, but vowels are of their nature more unstable, especially long vowels, which often end up being diphthongs, as in *house* < OE *hūs*.

Consonants and vowels differ in production and sound quality. Vowels are pure sing-song that opera singers can use when practising their voice, a e i u æ o. Vowels are more likely than consonants to be uttered in isolation and to form words and interjections. In vowels the air stream released from the lungs is uninhibited, differences between them resulting from modifying the shape and length of the resonant cavities that the sound passes through. By contrast, consonants are hisses, hums, buzzes and puffs of air forced through the relatively constricted, or completely closed, vocal tract. They are produced by moving the tongue, the most important of the speech organs, around the mouth, obstructing the flow of air in various ways or bringing it to a stop by closing the lips. Though consonants can be produced in isolation, *ssssssss, krrr*, they are typically articulated in combination with a vowel, *pooh, ugh*.

Yet another difference between consonants and vowels concerns their distributions and functions in different languages. Most languages have a clear division of labour between vowels and consonants: syllables begin with consonants and end with vowels; clusters are rare. These are general tendencies, but there are marked differences on other levels of the language system. Some languages rely more heavily on consonants than others. The Semitic languages, including modern Arabic and Hebrew, are well-known as a linguistic family that is poor in vowels and rich in consonants. The classical vocalic system is limited to three pairs of vowels, short and long /a, i, u/. The diphthongs /aw/ and /ay/ later developed into /o/ and /e/, respectively. The elaborate consonantal system is made up mostly of sets of three parallel consonants, voiced, voiceless and emphatic. Consonants are all-important in Semitic languages because of the lexical functions they fulfil. **Consonantal roots** embody basic semantic information and are combined with vocalic prefixes, infixes and suffixes, which indicate grammatical information, as in

Table 6.1. *The Semitic root* qbr *'to bury', imperative forms*

	Hebrew	Syriac	Ugaritic	Arabic	Ethiopic
sing. 2 m.	qəbur	qəbor	qbr	'uqbur	qəbər
2 f.	qibir	qəbor	qbr	'uqburi	qəb(ə)rī
plur. 2 m.	qibru	qəbor	qbr	'uqburu	qəb(ə)rū
2 f.	qəborna	qəbor	qbr	'uqburna	qəb(ə)rā

Classical Arabic *šrb* 'drink': *šurb-* 'drinking', *šaːrib* 'drinker', *šariba* 'he drank', *mašuruːb-* 'a drink'. The formation principle of a fixed triconsonantal root and variable vowels is a distinctive characteristic of these languages, many of which share a common lexical stock of such roots, as illustrated in table 6.1.

Finally, there are differences in regard to how vowels and consonants are encoded in phonographic writing. Consonants, which usually constitute the margins of syllables, are always present, but vowels are dealt with in diverse ways. These differences are so conspicuous that phonographic writing systems have been classified according to how they handle vowels. Four major modes of vowel indication can be distinguished: no vowel indication, auxiliary vowel indication, inherent vowel indication, and independent vowel indication. All Greek-derived alphabets belong to the last type providing the same kind of graphic signs for Cs and Vs. However, V letters are typically more polyvalent than C letters. The five basic V letters of the Latin alphabet, A, E, I, O, U, are enough for all of the Vs of very few languages only. For instance, the number of Vs and composite Vs in German is 18, in French 20, in English 23, and in Danish as many as 27. The latter three have augmented the five basic V letters by diacritics and extra letters, but graphic distinctions are still outnumbered by phonemic distinctions. The relative shortage of V letters, characteristic of the alphabets of many other European languages as well, testifies to the descent of the Graeco-Latin alphabet from its Semitic precursor where vowel indication was even more sparing. It is the Semitic mode of vowel indication that we discuss next, that is, no vowel indication and auxiliary vowel indication. The fourth mode, vowel incorporation, is characteristic of most writing systems of the Indian subcontinent, which will be discussed in detail in chapter 7.

Semitic writing systems

The Semitic language family is subdivided generally into three branches, East Semitic (sometimes called North Semitic), West Semitic and South Semitic. The writing system of the East Semitic languages, Akkadian, Assyrian and

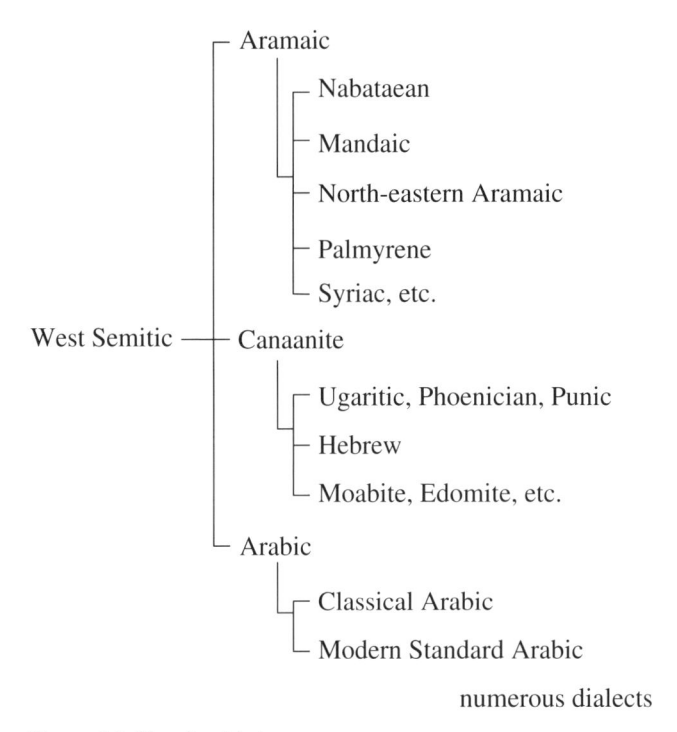

```
                    ┌─ Aramaic
                    │      ┌─ Nabataean
                    │      ├─ Mandaic
                    │      ├─ North-eastern Aramaic
                    │      ├─ Palmyrene
                    │      └─ Syriac, etc.
  West Semitic ─────┼─ Canaanite
                    │      ┌─ Ugaritic, Phoenician, Punic
                    │      ├─ Hebrew
                    │      └─ Moabite, Edomite, etc.
                    └─ Arabic
                           ┌─ Classical Arabic
                           └─ Modern Standard Arabic
                                        numerous dialects
```

Figure 6.1 *West Semitic languages*

Babylonian, is cuneiform, which does not concern us here. The writing system developed for South Semitic languages, especially Amharic, is of the V incorporating type and will, therefore, also not be considered here. Semitic writing systems in the narrow sense of this chapter are writing systems developed for and associated with the West Semitic languages shown in figure 6.1.

From around 700 to 200 BCE, Aramaic was the dominant language of the ancient Near East where, in the form of Imperial Aramaic, it served the Assyrian, Babylonian and Persian empires, including the western provinces in Arabia and Egypt, as the administrative language. This status was afforded it mainly thanks to the simplicity of its writing system, as compared to the morphosyllabic cuneiform system of Akkadian. Around the beginning of the Common Era Aramaic had replaced Hebrew as a vernacular language of the Israelites. Other offshoots of Canaanite were Ugaritic, spoken in a city state on the Syrian coast, and Phoenician in the area of modern Lebanon whence it spread to many places on the Mediterranean coast, notably Carthage in modern Tunisia where it is called Punic. Attested over a period of fourteen hundred years from the twelfth century BCE to the end of the second century CE, Phoenician is of particular importance for the history of writing (see chapter 10) because it was in the form of the Phoenician alphabet that the Greeks came into contact with Semitic writing. Arabic rose to prominence with the spread of Islam. Originating from the Arabian peninsula, it captured much of North Africa and the Middle East whence it spread further east.

Typological classification

For the West Semitic languages numerous writing systems evolved, which are generally known as consonantal alphabets, although Daniels (1990) prefers the term 'abjad' which is based on the beginning of the order of letters in Arabic (corresponding to A, B, J, D), the most widely used Semitic script in modern times, instead of Greek letter names from which, of course, the established 'alphabet' is derived.[1] But 'alphabet' is an idiomatic expression, a name and a term not restricted in meaning to its etymological origin. The Semitic consonantal alphabets are all of the same type, focussing, as the name suggests, on consonants rather than vowels, which are indicated optionally and, therefore, not included in the sequence of basic symbols. From this apparent fact, which is clearly evidenced by the earliest known forms of the West Semitic signary, it has sometimes been concluded that vowels were unimportant to ancient Semitic scribes, and, even more unfortunately, that the Semitic alphabets were defective. Both these tenets are wrong. As became clear in the previous chapter, all phonographic writing systems, however refined and concerned with language-specific phonetic detail, omit great numbers of phonetic distinctions. Practical writing systems need not lend themselves to providing faithful transcriptions. The point is to enable the reader to provide written documents with an interpretation. Thanks to the special role played by consonants in Semitic word formation, consonants are crucial to this end, although vowels are by no means unimportant. Semitic alphabets can only be called 'defective' when Greek or Latin is considered the yardstick of supposedly 'full' alphabetic writing.

Expressions such as 'defective' or 'incomplete alphabet' are not merely a matter of unfortunate terminology. They raise the issue of how Semitic writing systems should be classified. Robins (1978: 116), for instance, in a textbook of general linguistics states:

> The ancient Semitic writing system used by the Phoenicians and the Hebrews was of the syllabary type; modern Hebrew writing is a development of this, and so is the Arabic script in the Middle East today.

This classification echoes a proposal by I. J. Gelb (1963) who argued that each sign of ancient Semitic writing encoded a syllable, although, in contradistinction

---
[1] For a discussion of this terminology, see Bright 1999 and Watt 1998.

114   *Consonants and vowels*

to other syllabaries, Semitic 'syllabaries' do not specify the vowels. Each sign is thus assumed to encode a C plus any V. The rationale for this peculiar assumption, which claims syllabic status for the signs while leaving the specific nature of the encoded syllables undetermined, is that, according to Gelb, it is inconceivable that the ancient Semitic scribes could have conceptually grasped the abstract unit of an isolated consonant. As O'Connor (1996: 88) points out, this makes no linguistic or historical sense and only satisfies Gelb's evolutionist theory of the history of writing, which postulates a syllabary as a necessary stage prior to the development of a 'true' alphabet. Harris (1986: 36), quoted at the beginning of this chapter, emphasizes the point that having separate signs for vowels is not equally important for all languages. As we noted above, consonants play a distinctive role in Semitic languages which makes their load-bearing function in writing plausible. The Semitic writing systems that were evidently viable for Semitic languages should not be judged against their later adaptations to other, typologically distinct languages, notably the Greek alphabet. Following O'Connor (1996) I, therefore consider Semitic writing systems as encoding the consonants of the West Semitic languages. A great variety of Semitic scripts evolved, which do not in all instances coincide with the Semitic languages. Figure 6.2 summarizes the most important Semitic scripts and their derivational relationships.

Notice that the above family tree includes Semitic scripts for Semitic languages only. Many other languages of various families use Semitic-derived writing systems, too. Indo-European languages with their Greek-derived alphabets of the Latin

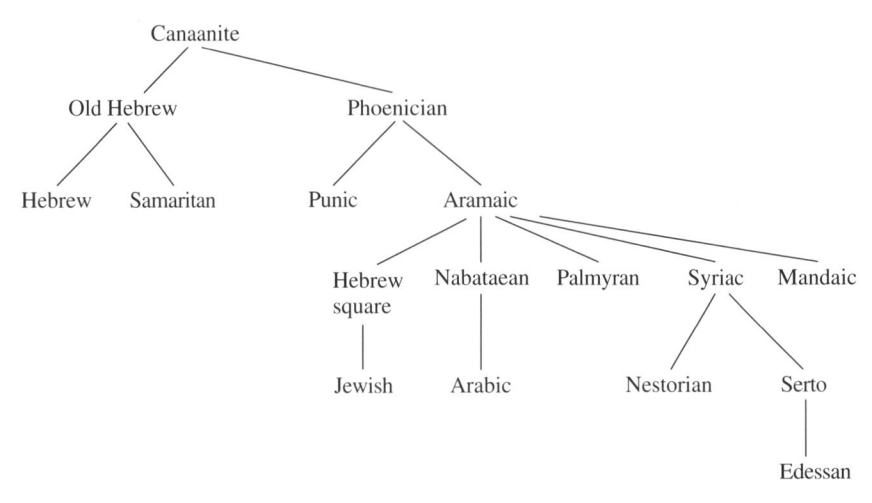

```
                        Canaanite
                       /        \
              Old Hebrew         Phoenician
              /      \           /        \
         Hebrew   Samaritan   Punic      Aramaic
                                        /  |   \   \    \
                                  Hebrew Nabataean Palmyran Syriac Mandaic
                                  square    |        |      /  \
                                    |       |        |  Nestorian Serto
                                  Jewish  Arabic              |
                                                           Edessan
```

Figure 6.2 *Lineage of ancient Semitic scripts*

Table 6.2. *The Aramaic alphabet*

ʾ	𐡀	l	𐡋
b	𐡁	m	𐡌
g	𐡂	n	𐡍
d	𐡃	s	𐡎
h	𐡄	ʿ	𐡏
w	𐡅	p	𐡐
z	𐡆	ṣ	𐡑
ḥ	𐡇	q	𐡒
ṭ	𐡈	r	𐡓
y	𐡉	š	𐡔
k	𐡊	t	𐡕

variety, in the West, and the Cyrillic variety, in the East, are most widespread, but Iranian languages such as Parthian, Middle Persian, Sogdian and Avestan, as well as languages of the Altaic family including Uigur, Mongolian and Manchu, in their literary history also acquired scripts derived from the ancient Aramaic script. Thus from the Aramaic alphabet (table 6.2) descended, directly or indirectly, most of the modern world's writing systems, the Chinese and Indic spheres of writing being the main exceptions, although the latter, too, may be related to Semitic writing. Since the relationship between Semitic and Indic writing systems is uncertain, and since the Indic systems are structurally quite different they will be discussed separately.

Graphic development

Once the Semitic alphabet had come into existence in the late Bronze Age somewhere in Palestine or at the Phoenician coast, it developed various forms under the hands of local scribes in many parts of the ancient Near East. They are attested, throughout their long history, mostly in stone inscriptions but also on papyrus and parchment, as in the famous Dead Sea scrolls of the first century BCE. Syriac, Mandaic, Palmyran and Nabataean are all graphic varieties of the later Aramaic script, as is the Jewish or Hebrew 'Square' script – not to be confused with the Paleo-Hebrew script which became extinct in antiquity when the Hebrews adopted a cursive variety of the Aramaic alphabet from which eventually the 'Square' Hebrew/Jewish script evolved. This script is still used for modern Hebrew. Another offshoot of Aramaic, the Nabataean script, which developed in the first century CE on the Sinai peninsula and in north Arabia, is the immediate forebear of the Arabic script. Although it is quite different from the Arabic script that evolved in the fourth and fifth centuries CE, it foreshadows certain graphic features, such as the existence of separate final forms for some letters. Like Hebrew Square, the Arabic script continues to be used today. It is the main script of Arabic and, in modified forms, for a host of other languages in Asia and Africa. The Nabataean script was rounded and cursive, while the Hebrew Square script had a more angular appearance. Graphically the Hebrew and Arabic scripts are quite dissimilar therefore, but originating from a common source they share many structural features which we will examine in what follows. Although some other Aramaic-derived scripts are still in use, notably the Syriac scripts used in liturgical contexts by Christian communities in Syria, Lebanon and Iraq, Hebrew Square and Arabic are the major modern descendants of the Aramaic alphabet.

Hebrew writing

Like the Phoenician alphabet (Paleo-Hebrew), which was first used to record the Hebrew language, the Hebrew alphabet consists of twenty-two basic consonant letters. Since Hebrew makes some phonetic distinctions not encoded in the Phoenician alphabet, some letters were modified to express these distinctions. There are thus seven pairs of closely related letters, distinguished by a dot, called *dagesh*, placed inside the basic letter. These letters are *bet* בּ, *gimmel* גּ, *dalet* דּ, *kaf* כּ, *peh* פּ, and *tav* תּ. How exactly the pronunciation of the consonants thus encoded differed from those encoded without the dot is not known, but the difference is systematic and mostly predictable. It is traditionally interpreted in such a way that the letters with *dagesh* are pronounced as the stops /b g d k p t/, while their unpointed counterparts are pronounced as fricatives /v ɣ x f θ/. Similarly, two pronunciations of the s-sound were distinguished by putting a dot on the right שׂ or left שׁ shoulder of the letter *shin*, transliterated <ś> for שׂ and <š> for שׁ. But the

Table 6.3. *Scripts for Hebrew. Adapted from Avrin 1991: 126f.*

	Paleo-Hebrew *8th century BCE*	Jewish script *Temple Scroll*	Ashkenazi *14th-15th century*
alef	𐤀	א	א
bet	𐤁	ב	ב
gimmel	𐤂	ג	ג
dalet	𐤃	ד	ד
he	𐤄	ה	ה
vav	𐤅	ו	ו
zayin	𐤆	ז	ז
ḥet	𐤇	ח	ח
tet	𐤈	ט	ט
yod	𐤉	י	י
kaf	𐤊	כ	כ
final kaf		ך	ך
lamed	𐤋	ל	ל
mem	𐤌	מ	מ
final mem		ם	ם
nun	𐤍	נ	נ
final nun		ן	ן
samech	𐤎	ס	ס
ayin	𐤏	ע	ע
peh	𐤐	פ	פ
final peh (feh)		ף	ף
ẓade	𐤑	צ	צ
final ẓade		ץ	ץ
qof	𐤒	ק	ק
resh	𐤓	ר	ר
shin	𐤔	ש	ש
tav	𐤕	ת	ת

phonetic interpretation conventionally assigned to them, /s/ and /ʃ/, respectively, is conjectural as is the exact pronunciation of *samech* ס, another s-letter. Five letters, *kaf*, *mem*, *nun*, *peh* and *zade* have separate final forms. Taken together these signs form the Hebrew consonantal alphabet.

Hebrew is written from right to left on horizontal lines running from top to bottom. The alphabet in table 6.4 encodes the consonantal distinctions of the language. Some of them have been neutralized in the modern language. There are two letters for laryngeal consonants, א and ע, which must have encoded different consonants in antiquity, but in modern Hebrew they have collapsed into one. א is sometimes not pronounced at all. This *alef quiescens* or 'silent alef' occurs in etymological spellings where it is part of a consonantal root that is fully pronounced in other related words. Purely consonantal writing is unproblematic when the written language is reasonably close to the vernacular language, as used to be the case when Hebrew was first written. Already in this period, however, three consonant letters, ה, ו and י, were assigned interpretations as vocalic signs. This practice is first attested in the Gezer Calendar dating from the tenth century BCE. At first, the consonant letters were only used for long vowels in word-final position. Eventually, the following convention of vowel interpretations in addition to the consonantal values of these letters stabilized.

ה was interpreted as *ā* or any long vowel in final position, e.g. מה = *mā*.
ו was interpreted as *ō* and *ū* both in interconsonantal and final position, e.g. לו = *lō* or *lū*.
י was interpreted as *ī* and *ē* both in interconsonantal and final position, e.g. לי = *lī* or *lē*.

In vocalic function these three letters are called *matres lectionis* or 'mothers of reading' (Zevit 1980). Using *matres lectionis* constitutes *plene* or 'full' writing, while their omission is called 'defective writing'. Notice that Hebrew vowels are conventionally distinguished as short and long, although it is uncertain whether the *matres lectionis* really reflected duration or, perhaps, stress or both. The word sign מלך *mlk*, spelt without *matres lectionis*, could be interpreted as *mélik*, 'king', *malkāh* 'queen', *mōlēk* 'ruling', *mālak* 'he rules', *mālǝkû* 'they ruled'. In *plene* spelling, some measure of disambiguation is accomplished:

mālǝkû מלכו they ruled
malkî מלכי my king
malkāh מלכה queen

Matres lectionis were never used totally consistently, and even with this system in place complete vowel interpretation was possible only for words in context. Generally, this was not a problem, but the development of *matres lectionis* is a

Table 6.4. *The Hebrew alphabet*

Name	Letter	Final form	Transliteration	Sound-value
alef	א		ʼ	/ʔ/
bet	בּ		b	/b/
	ב		ḇ	/v/
gimmel	גּ		g	/g/
	ג		ḡ	/g/
dalet	דּ		d	/d/
	ד		ḏ	/ð/
he	ה		h	/h/
vav	ו		w	/w/
zayin	ז		z	/z/
het	ח		ḥ	/H/
tet	ט		ṭ	/t/
yod	י		y	/j/
kaf	כּ	ךּ	k	/k/
	כ	ך	ḵ	/x/
lamed	ל		l	/l/
mem	מ	ם	m	/m/
nun	נ	ן	n	/n/
samech	ס		s	/s/
ayin	ע		ʻ	/ʕ/
peh	פּ	ףּ	p	/p/
	פ	ף	p̄	/f/
zade	צ	ץ	ṣ	/ts/
qof	ק		q	/q/
resh	ר		r	/r/
shin	שׂ		ś	/s/
	שׁ		š	/ʃ/
tav	תּ		t	/t/
	ת		ṯ	/θ/

120 *Consonants and vowels*

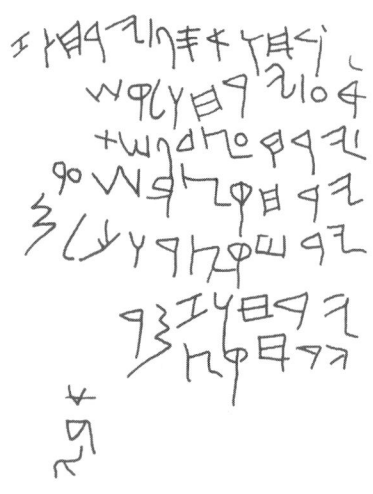

Figure 6.3 *The Hebrew Gezer Calendar, tenth century* BCE, *in Phoenician script*

clear indication that encoding vowels was sometimes found desirable, because around the end of the sixth century BCE Hebrew had been abandoned as a vernacular language by the Jewish community in favour of Aramaic. As the historical gap between written language and vernacular speech widened, the need to indicate vowels was felt more urgently. Since Hebrew continued to function as the Jews' liturgical language, a more elaborate system of indicating vowels in writing came into existence. Over a long period of time Jewish scholars (the Massoretes) developed a system of diacritics, points and lines added to C letters to indicate Vs. The best known and most widely used system is 'Tiberian pointing', so called after the city of Tiberias in north Israel, a centre of Jewish study and liturgy. There are two other systems of pointing, the Babylonian and the Palestinian, but as the system used for printing the Bible Tiberian pointing is considered the most important of the Massoretic traditions. Its standardized form on which the Massoretes settled in the ninth century CE is summarized in table 6.5.

The vocalization diacritics are points and lines mostly placed under the C letter after which the V is to be pronounced. For instance, <ָ> is interpreted as the long V *ā*, the combination <לָ> is thus read *lā*. There is one diacritic where the order is reversed. The glide [a] marked by <ַ> below a final guttural C is pronounced before it, as in שְׁמֹעַ *šəmō*[a]ʿ 'to hear'. Pointing is used in conjunction with *matres lectionis* to form an intricate system of V indication. Since ה, ו and י are doubly employed as C letters and *matres*, bi-functional usage sometimes occurs. Co-occurrence of the consonant י *y* with vocalic י *y*, that is, *mater lectionis*, is common, as in נָכְרִיָה *nokrîyāh* 'strangers', alternatively transliterated *nokriyyāh*.

Table 6.5. *Tiberian pointing in relation to C letter* ב b *and* ח ḥ

Name	simple	+ mater l. י y	+ mater l. ו w	+ mater l. ה h
patah	בַ ba	-	-	-
qames	בָ bā/bo	בָי bâ	-	בָה bā
hireq	בִ bi/ī	בִי bî	-	-
sere	בֵ bē	בֵי bê	-	בֵה bēh
segol	בֶ be	בֶי bê	-	בֶה beh
holem	בֹ bō	-	בוֹ bô	בֹה bō
qibbus	בֻ bu	-	בוּ bû	-
shwa	בְ bə			
hateph-patan	חֲ hă			
hateph-seghol	חֱ hĕ			
hateph-qames-hatuph	חֳ hŏ			

A special role is played by < ְ >, the schwa (šəwā, in correct transliteration) sign of 'reduced vowels'. It is read as /ə/ whenever the preceding syllable contains a long vowel, and has no phonetic interpretation otherwise. In the event, 'vowel indication' is a purely graphic exercise. This is not true of the Tiberian pointing system as such, which provides accurate information about vocalization and syllabification. To this end another mark is inserted into the consonantal text. The *meteg* is a short vertical line placed under a C letter to the left of a V diacritic, if any. Of its several functions the most important are

– to mark a long V where a schwa would be expected;
– to indicate the pronunciation ā for < ָ > which can be interpreted as short unstressed *o* or long ā;
– to indicate that a C is not to be geminated where this would be expected.

In sum, Biblical Hebrew has the vowels and the graphic means for their encoding shown in table 6.6.

Considering the elaborate system of diacritical vowel indication, it is of some interest that in the above account I had to point out on several occasions that we do not know for sure how the sounds encoded by the Hebrew alphabet and its various auxiliary signs were pronounced in Biblical Hebrew. The brackets in table 6.6 should not obscure this point. The symbols enclosed therein represent no more than assumed contrasts. This says a lot about sound writing in general. The Jewish scribes had a keen interest faithfully to preserve the phonetic form of religious texts. The notation they developed did that, in some measure, but it is still like a musical score, allowing wide room for interpretation. Reading and, in the case

Table 6.6. *Hebrew vowels and their graphic indication*

ī <˙.> [i]	i <.> [ɪ]		ū <˙ı> [u]
ē<˙..> [e]	e<˙̣> [ɛ]	ə <̣> [ə]	u <̣> [uː]
ā <˙, > [ɑ]/[ɔ]		a <_> [a]	ō<ı̇> [o]
			o <,> [ɔ]

of many Massoretic texts, chanting phonographic texts amounts to a patterned approximation rather than a precise reproduction.

One further point needs to be mentioned. The Jewish scribes continued to use their consonantal alphabet, with and without vowel pointing, long after it had been transferred to the Greeks who further developed the *matres lectionis* transforming the auxiliary and diacritical mode of vowel indication into an integral part of the linear system. The Greek alphabet was, of course, well known to the Jewish scholars who, however, held on to their literary tradition. This testifies both to the conservative nature of writing and to the fact that the consonantal alphabet in the guise of the Hebrew Square script was found suitable for Hebrew (as well as many other Jewish languages). Modern Hebrew, a spoken language again, makes do without V pointing because readers need not be informed about the appropriate vowels, let alone their exact pronunciation. Reading as they do for sense they can let the sounds take care of themselves.

Arabic writing

The Arabic alphabet is the youngest branch of the family of Semitic consonantal alphabets. It has twenty-eight letters encoding consonants and long vowels. In addition there are a number of diacritic lines and points for short vowels, which, however, are usually not written. Unlike Hebrew, Arabic has remained a vernacular language since the beginning of its literary history. The need to indicate vowels was, therefore, felt less urgently, although a wide rift developed between the classical language of the Qur'an and the vernaculars on the Arabian peninsula and between Baghdad, in the East, and Agadir, in the West. A paradigm case of what is known as the sociolinguistic situation of diglossia (Kaye 2001), the difference between classical and vernacular Arabic is a powerful testimony to the influence of writing on language, Classical Arabic being a language that lives through writing.

As we noted above, the Arabic script stems from the Nabataean script, an immediate descendant of the Aramaic alphabet (Gruendler 1993). Graphic development of the Arabic alphabet led to the formation of several very similar letters which in turn had an influence on their conventional ordering. As distinct from the ancient Semitic alphabets, the Arabic alphabet is ordered after graphic similarity of letters in the following sequence, using conventional transliteration: ' b t ṭ ǧ ḥ ḫ d ḏ r z s š ṣ ḍ ṭ z ʽ g f q k l m n w h j. Another feature of the Arabic script is that letters have four different shapes for isolated, initial, medial and final position in a **writing group**. A writing group does not always coincide with a word, because the six non-connecting letters, 'alif, dāl, ḏal, rā', zāy and wāw can occur in non-final position. Otherwise letters are always connected in writing, including print.

Consonants can be geminated and are then pronounced as long consonants. In writing this is expressed by the diacritic *šadda* <$\overset{\omega}{\_}$>

Šadda

ّ

رّ ـمّ/murr^{un}/ 'bitter', مّ ـمّ/muhimm^{un}/ 'important'

placed above the C letter in question. The three C letters *'alif*, *wāw* and *yā'* are given a secondary interpretation as the long vowels /aː, iː, uː/ in which function, however, they are never used in word-initial position. *'alif* is combined with *wāw* and *yā'* to encode the diphthongs /aw/ and /ay/, respectively. In initial position the glottal stop /'/ is always encoded with *'alif*, but in word-internal position *wāw* and *yā'* are often used instead.

Another diacritic, *hamza* is then placed above *wāw* or *yā'* to indicate that the pronunciation is to be glottal stop.

Hamza

ء

أ إ ؤ ئ
رأس/ra's^{un}/ 'head'; سؤال/su'āl^{un}/ 'question'; بئر/bi'r^{un}/ 'a well'
'alif, *wāw* and *yā* as 'seats' of *hamza*

Hamza is also used in conjunction with *'alif* whenever it is pronounced as /'/, especially word-initially, because not every word-initial *'alif* is pronounced as glottal stop. While *ā* is usually written with *'alif*, there are some words where a superscript *'alif* or 'dagger *'alif*' is used instead. The short vowels /a, i, u/ are encoded as diacritics, placed above or below the letter after which they are pronounced.

Table 6.7. *The Arabic alphabet*

Name	Transliteration	Transcription	Isolated	Initial	Medial	Final
'alif	a	[ʔ]	ا			ا
bā'	b	[b]	ب	ب	ب	ب
tā'	t	[t]	ت	ت	ت	ت
θā'	t, th	[θ]	ث	ث	ث	ث
ǧīm	ǧ	[dʒ]	ج	ج	ج	ج
ḥā'	ḥ	[ħ]	ح	ح	ح	ح
xā'	ḥ, kh	[x]	خ	خ	خ	خ
dāl	d, dh	[d]	د			د
dal	d, dh	[ð]	ذ			ذ
rā'	r	[r]	ر			ر
zāy	z	[z]	ز			ز
sīn	s, sh	[s]	س	س	س	س
šin	š	[ʃ]	ش	ش	ش	ش
ṣād	ṣ	[ṣ]	ص	ص	ص	ص
dād	ḍ	[d]	ض	ض	ض	ض
ṭā'	ṭ	[ṭ]	ط	ط	ط	ط
ẓā'	ẓ	[ð]	ظ	ظ	ظ	ظ
'ayn	'	[ʕ]	ع	ع	ع	ع
ġayn	gh	[ɣ]	غ	غ	غ	غ
fā'	f	[f]	ف	ف	ف	ف
qāf	q, k	[q]	ق	ق	ق	ق
kāf	k	[k]	ك	ك	ك	ك
lām	l	[l]	ل	ل	ل	ل
mīm	m	[m]	م	م	م	م
nūn	n	[n]	ن	ن	ن	ن
hā'	h	[h]	ه	ه	ه	ه
wāw	w	[w]	و			و
yā'	y	[j]	ي	ي	ي	ي

ي و ا
ā ī ū

In normal Arabic texts, long vowels are written, short ones are not. Since, thanks to the relatively simple syllable structure of Arabic, short V phonemes are rather predictable this causes few problems of interpretation. Virtually without exception syllables begin with a C followed by a V or a Vː. A consonantal coda can follow a short V. Where short Vs are written, as in the Qur'an and some other religious texts, they are encoded by diacritical marks, as illustrated for the letter fā'.

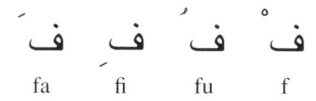

ف　ف　ف　ف
fa　fi　fu　f

An additional diacritic, a superscript circle called *sukūn*, indicates that a C is not followed by a V. A special convention governs the encoding of the endings of the indefinite noun /-un/, /-in/, /-an/. They are only pronounced in connected speech. The form ملك m-l-k 'king' thus has two phonetic interpretations, [malik] and [malikun]. Endings omitted in connected speech are transcribed as raised letters, /malik^{un}/. A special sign is used for the feminine ending /-at^{un}/, the letter hā' with two dots ة. It encodes the consonant [t] as the grammatical morpheme, feminine ending, as in ملكة /malikat^{un}/ 'queen'. The sequence 'ā is often written as *'alif 'madda*, a tilde placed on top of the *'alif*.

Madda
/'ā/　آ
آلآن /'āl'ān^a/ 'now'
القرآن /'alquar'ān^u/ 'the Qu'rān'

As a result of these and some other orthographic rules, an Arabic text is 'not a direct representation of its phonemic equivalent' (Fischer 1992: 93). Arabic writing thus illustrates even more clearly than other phonographic systems that writing is autonomous, but at the same time allows for, and calls for, phonetic interpretation.

The Arabic alphabet is not really a consonantal alphabet, for long Vs are regularly written. However, Arabic orthography relies on consonants much more than on vowels. V indication is possible where needed, but vowels, short and long, are not always pronounced where indicated, because Standard Arabic is highly logographic. Discrepancies between the graphemic forms of inflectional endings and their phonetic realizations are common, and many lexemes are graphically encoded as such rather than being built up letter-by-letter on the basis of regular grapheme–phoneme correspondences. Standard Arabic is rarely used in common speech, and since the Arabic speech community is spread out over a wide area dialect variation is considerable. Being relatively far removed from speech, the Arabic writing system is quite congenial to this state of affairs, allowing as it does a broad range of different phonetic interpretations. Like other writing systems using an alphabetic notation, its relation to speech is not an iconic mapping relation. It is thanks to, rather than in spite of, its skeletal nature and phonemic underdetermination that it can be read by speakers of vastly different dialects. The sense is taken care of by the consonantal framework, and as this is being interpreted by the reader the vocalic sounds take care of themselves.

Notice that in Arabic writing as in other Semitic languages vowels are not omitted by default because the writing system provides no means for encoding them. As we have seen, it does so in various ways. But Semitic writing systems treat consonant signs as fundamental and vowel signs as diacritics or dispense with the latter altogether. Some Semitic languages, such as Hebrew and Arabic, are usually written without V diacritics, while others, such as Syriac, are more commonly written in a pointed variety. In any event, exact V indication is possible. The concept of interpreting basic letters as vowels – *matres lectionis* – was firmly established long before the Arabic writing system took on its present form. At the time, moreover, the encoding of Vs in the basic signary had been common practice for many centuries in another offshoot of the ancient Semitic alphabet, the Greek alphabet, to which we turn next. Evidently, therefore, what is commonly and misleadingly called 'defective' writing was never felt to be defective by the Arab scribes. It is also worth noting in this connection that the practice of diacritical V indication was maintained in other languages to which the Arabic alphabet was applied, such as Persian and Urdu, for which some additional C letters were introduced. Assigning consonants a privileged position in writing, then, must not be seen as a compromise solution or incomplete realization of phonography but as a viable principle on a par with other systems that exploit certain aspects of the sound pattern of language to encode words.

Greek writing

The Greeks traditionally call their alphabet *phoinikeia grammata* (φοινιχήια γραμματα), 'Phoenician letters', because they learned the art of writing from the advanced civilization of the Phoenician coast (see chapter 10). With its introduction into Greece the Semitic consonantal alphabet was for the first time applied to a non-Semitic language, a consequential event that resulted in significant changes to the system. One of the reasons why consonants play such a dominant role in Semitic writing is that Semitic syllables and hence words begin with a C. Semitic letters, it is generally agreed (Driver 1976), came into existence on the basis of the principle of acrophony ('initial sound'), that is, using a sign for the first sound of the word it stands for (instead of for the entire word). Semitic letter names are meaningful words. The triconsonantal root *'lf*, for example, means 'bull', *'elef*, in Hebrew whence *alef*, the first letter of the Semitic alphabet. *Bēth* whence <b> means 'house', *gīmel* <g> 'camel', *dalet* <d> 'door', *kaf* <k> 'palm', *mem* <m> 'water' and so on. Since there are only C-initial words, only C letters are generated by this principle. This is a plausible explanation for the absence of V letters in the basic Semitic signary and the development of auxiliary V indication for writing Semitic languages. *Matres lectionis* and V diacritics never occur in initial position, because it is not necessary. But what if V-initial words and words with no recognizable consonantal root need to be written?

This was the case when the Semitic alphabet was applied to Greek. Consider words such as (1) ἀνοησία [anɔisia] 'nonsense', (2) ἄνοια ['ania] 'feebleminded', (3) εὔνους [evnus] 'favourable', (4) οὐλή [uli] 'scar', (5) ὄνομα [ɔnɔma] 'name', (6) ὑγίεια [i'jia] 'health'. Take away the vowels, and almost nothing is left: (1) ns, (2) n, (3) ns, (4) l, (5) nm, (6) j. Clearly, a consonantal alphabet applied to such a language would yield seriously defective texts. Notice that the order of the Phoenician alphabet and the names of the letters were largely preserved in Greek, but the acrophonic principle could not readily be transferred because the letter names were meaningless in Greek. Moreover, the glottal stop /'/ encoded by the letter *alef*, and the emphatic laryngeal /'/ encoded by the letter *ayin*, are not phonemic in Greek and therefore not easily perceived by speakers of Greek. The Greeks were likely, therefore, to pronounce the initial sound of the name of the first letter of the Phoenician alphabet not as a glottal stop but as /a/. *Alpha* thus came to be interpreted as a V, whereas *alef* is a C letter. Other Phoenician letters were similarly reinterpreted as follows: *hē* as *e psilon*[2] /e/, *ayin* as *o mikron* /o/, *wāw* as *digamma* /u/, and *yōd* as *iōta* /i/. Later on, short *e* and *o* sounds were graphically distinguished from their long counterparts by two additional letters, *ēta* derived from Phoenician *et* for /ɛː/, and *ō mega*, whose graphic origin is unclear, for /ɔː/. An original Greek creation of the letter on the basis of the sign for the 'little o', *o mikron*, seems possible. The Greeks also invented the three letters Φ, Χ, Ψ for the consonants /ph/, /kh/, and /ps/ which were not encoded in the Phoenician alphabet. Together with Ω and Υ they were added at the end of the list.

What in Semitic writing was a functional extension of C letters, the use of *matres lectionis* for final Vs, had thus been turned into the regular integration of V letters into the linear graphical encoding of language. Greek has nothing like the C roots of Semitic languages which, for words in context, allow the reader to supply the grammatical information mostly borne by Vs. A more explicit mode of encoding than that afforded by the twenty-two letters of the Semitic consonantal alphabet was needed for this language in which lexical information is borne by Vs almost as much as by Cs. The principle of interpreting letters as vowels was known from the *matres lectionis* mode of V indication. In an adaptation process that took centuries[3] the Greeks discarded the consonantal interpretation of the

---

[2] A 'high' or 'spirited' e. *Psili* is later the term for *spiritys lenis*, an aspiration mark.
[3] Many local alphabets were developed before the 'Ionian standard alphabet' gained general currency. For details see Jensen 1970 and Sass 1991.

128 *Consonants and vowels*

Table 6.8. *Greek vocalic reinterpretation of Phoenician consonant letters*

Greek			Phoenician		
alpha	A	/a/	'alef	𐤀	/ʔ/
e psilon	E	/e/	he	𐤄	/h/
o micron	O	/o/	'ayin	𐤏	/ʕ/
iōta	⌇	/i/	yōd	𐤉	/j/
ēta	H	/ɛː/	ḥēt	𐤇	/H/
o mega	Ω	/ɔː/			
digamma	F	/u/	wāw	Y	/w/

above-mentioned Phoenician letters and claimed full segmental status for vowels. To them the Phoenician letters as applied to their language were signs of sounds rather than meaning.

Indirect evidence of this can be seen in the manner and direction of writing. In archaic documents Greek is written from right to left, like Phoenician, the letter forms having a left-facing orientation. For some time both horizontal directions of writing were possible, the direction being reversed with every line in what is known as *bustrophedon* or 'ox turning' style. This way of writing frequently manifests itself in *scriptura continua* or writing without word separation. Ifyoudonotbreakupthesequenceoflettersitishardtorecognizewordsorothermeaningfulunitswhichtendtojumpoutofthepageinconsonantalwritingofsemiticlanguages. From this point of view, encoding the vowels of Greek words was crucial for reading. More than anything else it was the many V-initial Greek words that favoured the development of V letters on a par with C letters.

However, as we noted at the beginning of this chapter, vowels are in many regards more volatile than consonants. The encoding of vowels, accordingly, exhibits more variation than that of consonants. It is doubtful whether Greek spelling conventions ever approximated the ideal of a one-to-one relation between letters and sounds. In classical Greek the one-symbol-one-sound principle is violated for the Vs <α>, <ι> and <υ>, which encode both short and long vowels, and for the digraphs <ει> and <ου> which are no longer interpreted as diphthongs. In modern Greek Vs remain the Achilles heel of phonetic writing. The five Vs of modern Greek are variously encoded as follows: /a/ : <α>; /e/ : <ε, αι>; /i/ : <ι, ει, η, οι, υ, υι>; /o/ : <ο, ω>; /u/ : <ου>. In <υα> and <ευ> *u psilon*, <υ>, relapsed to consonantal status being interpreted as [f] before voiceless stops and as [v] elsewhere. The classical Greek alphabet eventually consisted of the following twenty-four letters in this order: Α, Β, Γ, Δ, Ε, Ζ, Η, Θ, Ι, Κ, Λ, Μ, Ν,

Ξ, Ο, Π, Ρ, Σ, Τ, Υ, Φ, Χ, Ψ Ω (in roman transliteration A, B, G, D, E, Z, Ē, Th, I, K, L, M, N, Ks, O, P, R, S, T, U, Ph, Kh, Ps, Ō).

```
ΒΑΣΙΛΕΟΣΕΛΘΟΝΤΟΣΕΣΕΛΕΦΑΝΤΙΝΑΝΨΑΜΑΤΙΧΟ
ΝΑΥΤΑΕΓΡΑΨΑΝΤΟΙΣΥΝΨΑΜΜΑΤΙΧΟΙΤΟΙΘΕΟΚΛΟΣ
ΕΠΛΕΟΝΗΛΘΟΝΔΕΚΕΡΚΙΟΣΚΑΤΥΠΕΡΘΕΥΙΣΟΠΟΤΑΜΟΣ
ΑΝΙΗΑΛΟΓΓΟΣΟΣΔΗΧΕΠΟΤΑΣΙΜΤΟΑΙΓΥΠΤΙΟΣΔΕΑΜΑΣΙΣ
ΕΓΡΑΦΕΔΑΜΕΑΡΧΟΝΑΜΟΙΒΙΧΟΚΑΙΠΕΛΕQΟΣΟΥΔΑΜΟ
```

Βασιλέος ἐλθόυτος ἐς Ἐλεφαντίναν Ψαματίχō ταῦτα ἔγραψαν τοι σὺν Ψαμματίχōι τōι Θεοκλος ἔπλεον ἦλθον δὲ Κέρκιος κατύπερθε υἶς ὁ ποταμὸς ἀνίη ἀλογγόσōς δ' ἦχε Ποτασιμτο Αἰγυπτίōς δὲ "Αμασις ἔγραφε δ'ἀμὲ "Αρχōν Ἀμοιβίχō καὶ Πέλεqος ὁ 'Υδάμō

When King Psammetich came to Elephantine, the people of Psammetich, son of Theokles, wrote this. They sailed and came to above Kerkis, as far as the river permitted. The foreigners guided Potasimto, and the Egyptians Amasis. Archon, son of Amoibichos, and Peleqos, son of Eudamos, wrote this.

Figure 6.4 *Ionian Greek inscription of the early sixth century* BCE *without word boundaries (Jensen 1969: 449)*

Conclusion

The Greeks reinterpreted the Phoenician alphabet to suit their language in such a way that segmental status was accorded both consonants *and* vowels. In view of the many V-initial words and the general importance of vowels at the level of lexical information, this was an important development. Greek V letters helped to solidify the notion that vowels like consonants were fixed units of speech. Yet, a marked difference in the encoding of consonants and vowels remained. Relative to the phoneme inventory of Greek there are proportionately fewer V letters than C letters, and as a direct consequence the range of phonetic interpretations of V letters tends to be wider than that of C letters. This feature of the Greek alphabet has been communicated to virtually all alphabets derived from it. That it echoes the origin of the Greek alphabet in the Semitic consonant script is obvious; whether it is also indicative of genuine phonetic differences between consonants and vowels, which are encoded so differently in the ancient Semitic alphabet, remains to be determined.

Questions for discussion

(1) Why is it easier to read 'nglsh cn ls b wrttn wtht vwls' than 'Ei a ao e ie io oe'?
(2) What are *matres lectionis*?
(3) Why were *matres lectionis* never written in word-initial position?
(4) How do Semitic and Indo-European languages differ with regard to the functional distribution of consonants and vowels?
(5) What is *scriptura continua*? Discuss its linguistic significance.

7
Vowel incorporation

> It is clear that the Kharoṣṭī and Brāhmī scripts as we know them were elaborated by ancient pandits who had a high degree of sophistication in phonetics.
> William Bright

Most writing systems are interpreted as referring in some way to the phonetic composition of speech forms. In the process the natural continuous flow of sound is artificially broken up into discrete units of various size. The syllable is an intuitively salient unit exploited to this end by several ancient and modern writing systems such as Assyrian cuneiform, Cypriot and Japanese kana, as we saw in chapter 4. It also plays a critical role in the Indian writing systems, which are the subject of this chapter. Syllables are typically composed of consonants and vowels, which, in the Western tradition, as a reflection of the Greek alphabet are both uniformly considered sound segments, while in Semitic writing consonants and vowels are conceptualized and symbolized differently. The use of *matres lectionis* in archaic Semitic documents, discussed in chapter 6, is clear evidence that the Semitic scribes had a notion of a vowel as a unit of language. For reasons having to do with the conservative nature of writing systems in general and with the semantic significance of consonants in Semitic languages, they chose not to, or were not able to, treat both classes of sounds in the same manner.

This holds true for the many Indian writing systems, too. While acknowledging the significance of the syllable, they also, in their own characteristic way, distinguish between Cs and Vs. Jensen (1969: 351f.) and Gelb (1963: 191) have, for different reasons, classified Indic scripts as alphabets. Jensen is not too concerned with terminology and uses the term 'alphabet' in a very broad sense. Gelb, on the other hand, being committed to an evolutionist theory of the history of writing, cannot be satisfied to call a system that came into existence long after an alphabet with full vowel indication had been developed anything but an alphabet, because any other classification would suggest a relapse to pre-alphabetic writing, and that is not supposed to happen in a linear evolution. However, since this type of writing system displays both the syllable

132 *Vowel incorporation*

and its internal structure, scholars less committed to an evolutionist view have variously called it *neosyllabary* (Février 1948), *semisyllabary* (Ullman 1989 following Diringer 1968), *syllabic alphabet* (Coulmas 1989) and *alphasyllabary* (Bright 1999).

Sources of descent

Writing has a long tradition in South Asia. Although intellectual development in India has always favoured oral over written means of communication, an astounding variety of scripts evolved on the subcontinent. The oldest palaeographic monuments are in the undeciphered Indus script (Parpola 1994) dating from the mid-third millennium BCE. So far, all attempts to establish a connection with the two Indian scripts of the earliest historical period, known in Sanskrit as Kharoṣṭhī and Brāhmī, have been frustrated (Bright 1990: 118f.). In the absence of major archaeological discoveries, it is unlikely that we will ever know whether writing fell into disuse together with the Indus script in India, or whether there is a thread however tenuous and twisted that connects to Kharoṣṭhī and Brāhmī (Salomon 1995).

Separated from the Indus script by some two thousand years, Kharoṣṭhī and Brāhmī are first attested in the Buddhist inscriptions of the Mauryan Emperor Aśoka in the third century BCE. Theories about their origin are on somewhat firmer ground than the genealogy of the Indus script. On the basis of the graphic similarity of some signs, they have been linked by Diringer (1968: 262) and Jensen (1969: 355) following Bühler (1896) to the Aramaic script, which at the time of Aśoka extended to the western frontiers of the Mauryan empire. Like Semitic scripts, Kharoṣṭhī was always written from right to left. It was limited to the north-western parts of India and died out in the second century CE without any descendants. Brāhmī, by contrast, was far more consequential for the development of writing in India. In this case, too, a Semitic origin or significant Semitic influence on its creation seems likely. The first documents in Brāhmī, too, were written from right to left, but the direction of the script was later reversed. Throughout most of its history Brāhmī, like all of its descendants, was written from left to right. Deshpande (1993: 168) has adduced converging letter shapes and their phonetic interpretations in support of the Semitic origin hypothesis, which, however, is not universally accepted because several Brāhmī signs cannot be derived from the Aramaic or Phoenician alphabets, or any other Semitic script. A connection with the Greek alphabet has also been hypothesized (Brāhmī ⊙ resembles the Greek Θ in form and phonetic interpretation), while some scholars, especially in South Asia, prefer to see in it an original creation.

Table 7.1. *Correspondences between Phoenician and Brāhmī signs*

Phoenician		Brāhmī	
ʾ	⪥	⪥	a
b	⟋	◇	b
g	⟍	∧	g
d	△	⪥	d
h	⪥	⨆	h
w	Y	⪥	v
z	I	⊏	ŋ
ḥ	H	⊔	gh
ṭ	⊕	⊙	th
y	Z	↓	y
k	⪥	+	k
l	⪥	⪥	l
m	M	⪥	m
n	⪥	⊥	n
s	⪥	⪥	ṣ
ʿ	○	⌒	e
p	⪥	⪥	p
ṣ	⪥	⪥	c
q	φ	⪥	ch
r	◁	⪥	r
š	⪥	∧	ś
t	+	⪥	t

Many unresolved questions concerning the development of Brāhmī remain, but there is no doubt about its general importance as the source of all modern Indian scripts, which in spite of many marked differences follow the same structural design.

134 *Vowel incorporation*

Table 7.2. *Brāhmī primary vowels*

	Short		Long	
low central	ꓭ	a	ꓬ	ā
high front	∴	i	∷	ī
high back	L	u	Ŀ	ū

Table 7.3. *Brāhmī secondary vowels*

	Long		Diphthongs	
front	▷	e	⟩	ai
back	ι	o	⩜	au

Structural design

Two major design features of Brāhmī are: (1) independent or initial vowel signs and (2) diacritic vowel indication in postconsonantal position. Vowels are grouped into two classes, primary and secondary, as shown in tables 7.2 and 7.3. Secondary vowels are encoded as graphic modifications of their more basic counterparts. Originally the signs for *e* and *o* were interpreted as the diphthongs *ai* and *au* but came to be pronounced as [eː] and [oː].

The two sets of signs given in tables 7.2 and 7.3 reflect the fact that the languages written, that is, various Prakrits or Indo-Aryan 'dialects', had V-initial words and syllables consisting of a V only. However, the majority of syllables were C-initial with many consonant clusters and a final V. It is this syllable type, that is, CV, CCV, that the characteristic unit of Brāhmī developed, the graphic syllable called *akṣara* in Sanskrit. An *akṣara* consists of one or more consonants followed by a vowel, which in the event is not encoded by the independent V sign but by a diacritic sign called *mātrā* adjoined to the consonant sign, which is considered basic. Typically, the consonantal base is clearly recognizable in all derived graphic syllables, as illustrated for *k* and *l* in table 7.4. The most frequently used vowel, usually a reduced vowel [ə] or [ʌ], but traditionally transliterated as *a*, represents the unmarked case, that is, consonant signs are interpreted as incorporating it together with the consonant unless otherwise indicated. This 'inherent' vowel is

Table 7.4. *Brāhmī* mātrās, *diacritic vowel signs on consonant letters* k *and* l

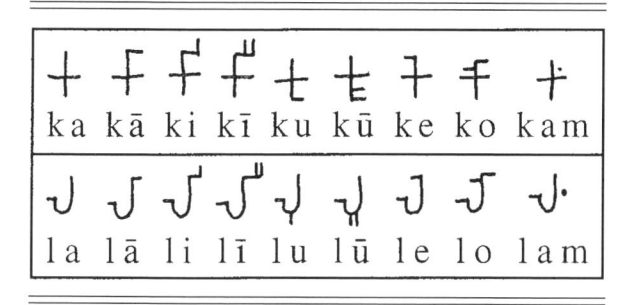

+	ꓕ	ꓞ	ꓞ	╇	╘	┼	┿	┿
ka	kā	ki	kī	ku	kū	ke	ko	kam

↲	↲	↲	↲	↲	↲	↲	↲	↲·
la	lā	li	lī	lu	lū	le	lo	lam

Table 7.5. *Brāhmī* akṣaras, *consonants with inherent* a

k	+	kh	ȝ	g	∧	gh	ധ		
c	d	ch	ɸ	j	⊏	jh	⊢	ñ	⊤
ṭ	⊂	ṭh	O	ḍ	ſ	ḍh	ȯ	ṇ	Ɪ
t	⋏	th	⊙	d	⊅	dh	◯	n	⊥
p	∪	ph	⊌	b	◇			m	ⵖ
y	⋓	r	⟩	l	↲	ḷ	⊢	v	△
s	⊥	ṣ	⊢	ś	∧	h	⊔		

superseded by the other vowel diacritics, which are grouped around the base. A dot placed on the right shoulder of the basic *akṣara* indicates nasal interpretation. A matrix like this where the common graphic element of all listed items can be interpreted as a consonant is clear evidence that the notion of a consonant as such was available to whoever designed the system, unless you want to argue that the inherent neutral vowel is part of all the other vowels.

While simple syllables of the CV type are encoded by obligatory diacritics attached to the consonantal base, more complex syllables require secondary devices.

136   *Vowel incorporation*

In syllables of the type CCV, that is when a consonant occurs before another consonant, conjunct consonant signs are used. Consonant clusters are common in the Prakrits, as in the modern Indian languages that descended from them, and accordingly there are numerous conjunct consonant signs or ligatures derived from the basic consonant signs. For example, the last sign of the sequence ष ा र भि त्प *a-ra-bhi-tpa* is composed of त *ta* and प *pā* to encode *tpā*.

Devanagari

The system of conjunct consonant signs or ligatures fully developed only in the scripts derived from Brāhmī. They are illustrated in table 7.9 for Devanagari, the major script of Sanskrit and other Indo-Aryan languages such as Hindi, Marathi, Sindhi and Nepali. In conjunct consonants one consonant sign takes a reduced form, in many cases omitting the characteristic perpendicular stroke on the right-hand side. As a result speech syllables are not always congruent with graphic syllables: The *akṣara* sequence अल्प 'small', which must be transliterated *a + lpa*, would be pronounced [alˈpa] rather than [aˈlpa]. Almost 200 Devanagari conjunct consonants make for rather involved rules of phonetic interpretation.[1] The incongruence of graphic and phonetic syllables which becomes apparent here reminds us once again of the autonomy of the graphic system which does not in all of its systematic features reflect properties of speech, but must be given a phonetic interpretation on the basis of more or less complex rules.

Another diacritic, called *virāma* (lit. 'stop'), underscores the independence of graphic from phonetic structures. A stroke slanting from left to right below an *akṣara*, it changes its interpretation to the effect that the inherent vowel is muted, for example नामन् *nāman* 'name'. A device corresponding to *virāma* in speech is hard even to imagine: first pronounce a sound [-nʌ] and then pronounce another [ø] to repeal it, yielding [-n]. It makes little sense to interpret *akṣara* cum *virāma* in such a way, that is, to interpret a spatial sequence of graphic signs – first *akṣara*, then *virāma* – as a temporal sequence of sounds. Rather, an *akṣara* with a *virāma* attached must be seen as one unit, not a sequence of units. *Virāma* is used only in word-final position when the word itself is used in pause or followed by a punctuation mark. In other instances involving the internal structure of *akṣaras* the sequential organization at the graphic level also fails to reflect that at the phonetic level. Although *akṣaras* are interpreted as CV syllables, the V part sometimes precedes the C part. Obligatory diacritic vowel indication also shows the graphic syllable as a unit that is two-dimensional rather than linear. The diacritic for *ā* is

---

[1] In his *History of Printing and Publishing in India* Kesavan (1997:127) speaks of Devanagari 'needing as many as 500 to 800 symbols for its conjunct characters'.

Table 7.6. *Devanagari plosives*

	Voiceless unaspirated	Voiceless aspirated	Voiced unaspirated	Voiced aspirated	Nasals
Velar	क k	ख kh	ग g	घ gh	ङ ṅ
Palatal	च c	छ ch	ज j	झ jh	ञ ñ
Retroflex	ट ṭ	ठ ṭh	ड ḍ	ढ ḍh	ण ṇ
Dental	त t	थ th	द d	ध dh	न n
Labial	प p	फ ph	ब b	भ bh	म m

Table 7.7. *Devanagari sonorants and fricatives*

	Palatal	Retroflex	Dental	Labial
Sonorants	य y	र r	ल l	व v
Fricatives	श ś	ष ṣ	स s	ह h

Table 7.8. *Devanagari vowel signs for Hindi*

Primary vowels

अ आ इ ई उ ऊ ऋ
a ā i ī u ū ṛ

Secondary vowels

ए ऐ ओ औ आं अ:
e ai o au am ah

on the right side of the associated C, that for *e* on top, that for *u* beneath the C, that for *i* on the left, and that for *ī* on the right. That is, in linear terms, medial and final *i* is written before the C after which it is pronounced. Thus, [miːl] 'mile' is spelt *m-ī-l*, but [mɪl] 'meet' (imp.) is spelt *i-m-l*. This is indicative of the operational salience at the graphic level of the syllable, which is seen as a whole rather than a succession of isolated Cs and Vs.

Anusvāra (lit. 'after-sound') is yet another diacritic that disrupts the correspondence of spatial extension and temporal duration by exploiting the

Table 7.9. *Devanagari conjunct consonants*

क्ष	=	क	+	ष
kṣa		ka		ṣa
त्र	=	त	+	र
tra		ta		ra
ज्ञ	=	ज	+	ञ
jña		ja		ña
श्र	=	श	+	र
śra		śa		ra

two-dimensionality of the script. While nasals in prevocalic position are written with their own *akṣaras*, as indicated in the last column of table 7.6, the unmodified nasal following a vowel is written with *anusvāra*, a dot placed above the *akṣara* after which it is pronounced, much like what we hear at the end of French *bon*. In this connection it is well to remember what we discussed in chapter 5 concerning the production of phonetic features such as nasalization. It extends over a period of time, starting before a segment begins and coming to an end only after it has been terminated. As a diacritic attached to the *akṣara* as a whole, the *anusvāra* would seem to do justice to this aspect of phonetic reality at least as well as an alphabetic notation, which is commonly interpreted as a segmental representation of speech sounds. The *visarga*, a colon placed after the *akṣara*, likewise must be interpreted as operating over the entire *akṣara*. Indicating hard breathing it is pronounced as a final *h* plus homorganic echo of the preceding vowel. Finally, notice that ligatures, many of which are composed of two modified signs in vertical rather than horizontal arrangement, disrupt the sequential parallelism of sound and sign. The fact that this parallelism is considered essential at the level of syllables only is further highlighted by the existence of the ligatures for certain syllables in both vertical and horizontal combination of the constituent parts.

To sum up the main points of this section, Devanagari uses as its main functional unit the *akṣara*. The unmarked *akṣara* is interpreted as a syllable consisting of a C and an inherent weak V. Other non-final Vs are written with diacritics on the C base, which supersede the inherent V. Additional diacritics are employed to indicate that an *akṣara* is not interpreted as an open syllable. Initial Vs, bothlong and short, have their own freestanding signs, which are also considered *akṣaras*. The syllable, then, is the privileged unit of writing in Devanagari, but there is no one-to-one mapping relation between graphic syllable and phonetic syllable. The *akṣara* is the functional unit of all scripts derived from Brāhmī, but there are a number of characteristic differences, which will be illustrated below with three other examples, the Tamil, Tibetan and Thai scripts. To a greater or lesser extent they bear witness to the high level of sophistication in phonetics for which William Bright, quoted at the outset of this chapter, praises the ancient Indian pandits and which is so manifest in Devanagari.

Linguistic analysis

All writing systems are based on, and hence more or less explicitly incorporate, a linguistic analysis. In the case of Indian writing systems this is especially obvious. Phonetic analysis was cultivated in India as early as the sixth century BCE. It arose in the oral context of studying sacred texts and the need to preserve their phonetic form. The two parameters for describing speech sounds on which modern phonetics is based, place and manner of articulation, were recognized and systematically applied by the ancient Indian linguists to the analysis of speech. Vowels are grouped into two categories, simple and compound. Simple Vs are described as glottal [a], palatal [i] and labial [u], corresponding to modern descriptions of these Vs as open back, close front and close back. Long Vs and diphthongs are considered compound Vs. Consonants are grouped into classes according to places of articulation, which are specified from the back of the vocal tract upward: glottal, velar, palatal, retroflex,[2] dental and labial.

By explaining differences of sound by reference to the organs of speech, the ancient Indian scholars anticipated the results of modern phonetics by almost two and a half thousand years. Their acute insight into the articulatory mechanisms is clearly reflected in the traditional arrangement of Indian letters, which represents what in modern terms are known as natural classes of sounds. Voicing and aspiration are recognized as vital distinctions in the manner of articulation, as is the distinction between plosive and nasal. Sonorants and fricatives are distinguished from stops, which in turn are grouped according to their place of articulation from the back to the front of the vocal tract: velar, palatal, retroflex (alveolar), dental and labial. Tables 7.5 and 7.6 follow this pattern, representing the traditional arrangement of letters in Indian scripts.

---

[2] As a descriptive category 'retroflex' refers to both place and manner of articulation. It means that the consonant is made by the tongue tip against the alveolar ridge.

Another conspicuous feature of Devanagari is the continuous horizontal top line, which in many cases extends across word boundaries. It is broken by *anusvāra* and *visarga* and word-initial consonants, but continues in all other cases. Sanskrit does not mark wordboundaries. Sentences are marked by a perpendicular stroke. The sequences of syllables held together in Sanskrit writing by an unbroken top line corresponds to a continuum of sounds in speech to which apply the euphonic rules of sandhi, that is, the phonological modification of grammatical forms that have been juxtaposed, for example: *na asti iha* 'not is here' becomes *nāstīha*; *devīiva* 'like the goddess' becomes *devīva*. Both in internal sandhi, within words, and external sandhi, across words, elision and fusion of vowels occur regularly. Sanskrit orthography is sensitive to these phonological processes in that it does not encode words in their isolated forms but as parts of a pause group. Hence, ligatures are used not only within words, but also across word boundaries where a final and initial C coalesce. In modern languages using Devanagari words are divided by spaces much like European languages written in Roman or Cyrillic.

Tamil writing

Tamil, a member of the Dravidian family of languages, is the most important literary language of southern India. First written in Brāhmī-derived Grantha, it developed a script of its own, called *tamiz euttu* in Tamil. Although it shares a common origin with Devanagari it differs from it significantly both in appearance and structure. From angular Devanagari and other northern scripts it differs through its more rounded letter forms, which are attributed to the typical writing surface of early documents, palm leaves which tend to break more easily when incised by a pointed stylus with straight and angular strokes. More important, however, are two structural features distinguishing Tamil from other Indian scripts: the small number of basic signs and the absence of ligatures.

As Georg Bühler, whose groundbreaking *Indian Palaeography* was first published in 1896, observed 'the great simplicity of the [Tamil] alphabet...is explained by the phonetics of the Tamil language' (Bühler 1980: 93). Like the other Indian scripts the Tamil writing system is a syllabic alphabet. Its basic consonant signs (table 7.10) include the inherent vowel *a*. Other postconsonantal Vs are written with obligatory diacritics (table 7.11), while twelve independent signs are provided for initial Vs (table 7.12).

A comparison of the Tamil signary with other Brāhmī-derived scripts reveals its special position in the sphere of Indian writing. Brāhmī itself has thirty-six basic signs, and of the northern group of its descendants Bengali, Sindhi, Kashmiri, Oriya and Devanagari have thirty-nine, while Gurmukhi (for Punjabi) has forty-two. Of

Table 7.10. *Tamil consonant signs*

	Transliteration	Sound
க்	k	[k, g, ɣ, x]
ங்	ng	[ŋ]
ச்	c	[tʃ, dʒ, ʃ, s]
ஞ்	ñ	[ɲ]
ட்	ṭ	[t, d, ɽ]
ண்	ṇ	[ɳ]
த்	t	[t, d, ð]
ந்	n	[n]
ப்	p	[p, b, β]
ம்	m	[m]
ய்	y	[j]
ர்	r	[ɾ]
ல்	l	[l]
வ்	v	[ʋ]
ழ்	ẓ	[ɻ]
ள்	ḷ	[ɭ]
ற்	ṟ	[r, d]
ன்	n̲	[n]

Table 7.11. *Tamil vowel diacritics*

த	ta	தா	tā	தெ	te	தே	tē	தை	tai
தி	ti	தீ	tī	தொ	to	தோ	tō	தௌ	tau
து	tu	தூ	tū						

Table 7.12. *Tamil independent vowel signs*

Primary vowels			Secondary vowels		
	Transliteration	Sound		Transliteration	Sound
அ	a	[ʌ]	எ	e	[e]
ஆ	ā	[aː]	ஏ	ē	[eː]
இ	i	[i]	ஐ	ai	[ʌy]
ஈ	ī	[iː]	ஒ	o	[ɔ]
உ	u	[u]	ஓ	ō	[oː]
ஊ	ū	[uː]	ஔ	au	[ʌʋ]

the southern group Telugu has thirty-nine signs and Kannada and Malayalam each have forty. Tamil makes do with thirty basic signs, including six derived letters, and in earlier versions had only twenty-one. Voiceless and voiced stops are not distinguished, voicedness being largely predictable. There is no series of aspirated Cs. The virtual absence of ligatures for conjunct Cs makes Tamil writing on the whole more linear than writing in Devanagari and other Indian scripts. This is achieved by the vowel muting sign *puḷḷi*, a dot placed above the consonant sign. It corresponds to the Devanagari *virāma*, but is governed by different rules. While the *virāma* typically occurs in final position only, the *puḷḷi* is more freely used in medial position, too, which makes it easier to write consonant clusters.

In spite of its greater linearity in comparison with other Indian scripts, Tamil, too, uses the *akṣara* as its basic unit. Individual signs are interpreted as syllables, not as sequences of Cs and Vs. In some instances the linear order of phones is the

Table 7.13. *Tamil Grantha letters for Sanskrit sounds*

	Transliteration	Sound	
ஜ	j	[dʒ]	
ஷ	ṣ	[ṣ]	
ஸ	s	[s]	
ஹ	h	[h]	'Aaytam', for fricatives following a stop
க்ஷ	kṣ	[kṣ]	

reverse of the order of the C part and V part within the *akṣara*. To illustrate, notice that the six vowel diacritics on the right-hand side in table 7.11 for -*e*, -*ē*, -*ai*, -*o*, -*ō*, and -*au* precede or surround the *t*-.

Tibetan writing

The Tibetan writing system dating from the seventh century CE is a syllabic alphabet of the Indian type. Although its origin is not well attested, it is widely assumed that it is patterned on the Gupta script, an offshoot of Brāhmī. It is written horizontally, from left to right. *Yi ge*, the Tibetan term for *akṣara*, denotes the basic functional unit of Tibetan writing. The thirty basic consonant signs (table 7.14) are each interpreted as a C plus inherent V *a*, in the usual way. But in contradistinction to the Indian syllabic alphabets, Tibetan has only one independent V letter, for *a*. Like consonant letters it serves as the base to which vowel diacritics for *i*, *u*, *e* and *o* are attached. The V diacritics for *i*, *e* and *o* are superscripts, that for *u* is a subscript (table 7.14).

The C letter for *ha*, *achung*, is also used as a subscript to compensate for the scarcity of V letters. The letter to which it is attached is to be pronounced with a long vowel. Modern Tibetan has twelve distinct vowels and two tones, but in writing only the five short vowels just mentioned are distinguished, long vowels being of foreign origin, mostly Sanskrit. Tone is not marked.

The polyvalency of V signs and many etymological spellings make for difficult reading. Ligatures are formed by combining basic C letters according to fixed rules.

Table 7.14. *The Tibetan syllabic alphabet*

	Voiceless	Occlusives	Voiced	Nasals
Velar	k	kh	g	ng
Palatal	c	ch	j	ny
Dental	t	th	d	n
Labial	p	ph	b	m
Affricate	ts	tsh	ž	
Semivowels and other continuants	w y sh	zh r s	z l h	'
Independent vowel	a	i u e o		

Table 7.15. *Vowels of modern Tibetan*

	Front	Central	Back
High	i ė ü	ʌ	o' u
Low	e ɛ ö	a	ɔ o

For example, *y* combines as a subscript with seven other C letters to form conjunct consonant signs for the palatalized syllables *kya, khya, gya, pya, phya, bya* and *mya*. Similarly, subscript *l* combines with six C letters, which are then interpreted as the syllables *kla, gla, bla, zla, rla* and *sla*. Other ligatures are formed by attaching reduced C signs to basic C signs as superscripts or on either side. As in Indian scripts, the graphic syllable is a two-dimensional form to be interpreted as a whole, rather than a linear string of Cs and Vs. The composite elements can be identified, but in many cases the internal structure of a ligature no longer corresponds to the phonetic interpretation. Especially prescript *b* and postscript *d* are in most cases morphological or etymological spellings without any phonetic interpretation. For instance, the word pronounced [sɛ] 'killed' is spelt *bsad*.

There is no V muting diacritic in Tibetan writing. A superscript dot, called *tsheg*, placed on the right shoulder of a letter indicates syllable closure. Two consecutive

C letters not separated by a *tsheg* are interpreted as a cluster. Put differently, in isolation basic letters are interpreted as syllables, but in the context of other letters, unless otherwise marked, as Cs. This amounts to the structural possibility of encoding C clusters without ligatures, which might be regarded as a step towards the linear encoding of phonemes. However, as in Tamil writing, the graphic syllable is conceptually and systematically the crucial unit of the system.

Thai writing

The next example of Brāhmī-derived alphasyllabic writing to be examined in this chapter is the Thai writing system. Its chief significance for this discussion is the fact that it encodes a dimension of the sound pattern of language that is ignored by most other writing systems, tone. As in all Brāhmī-derived scripts, the functional unit of Thai writing is the graphic syllable consisting of a consonant base with various diacritics grouped around it. There are forty-two basic C letters (table 7.16). No signs are available for syllable-initial Vs. Instead the glottal-stop sign อ is used as a base to which V diacritics are attached as superscripts or subscripts, or on either side. Long vowels and diphthongs are written as circumscripts (table 7.17). Four superscript tone marks form a second layer of diacritics (table 7.18). They are placed on the right shoulder of the C letter, above the V diacritic, if any. Two additional diacritics are used, a superscript circle on the right marks nasalization, and a superscript hook is sometimes used to indicate etymological spelling. Etymological spellings, not all of them marked by this diacritic, are frequent, especially with Indic loanwords, which entered the Thai language together with the Buddhist scriptures that brought writing to South-east Asia. For instance, the series of retroflex consonant signs is used mainly in Indic loanwords which, however, have been assimilated phonologically. Thus, the orthographic distinction between retroflex and dental (alveolar) Cs has no phonetic interpretation. Once again, an aspect of the autonomy of the graphic system manifests itself here.

Thai is said to have five contrastive tones, canonically described as falling, high, mid, rising and low. Tone is unknown in Semitic and Indo-European languages, that is, the languages for which segmental alphabets developed. In alphabetic notations, including the IPA, tones are therefore distinguished from segmental features as 'suprasegmentals'. The general idea underlying this terminology is that speech can be analysed as a succession of discrete segments that are modulated by continuous features such as pitch contours or tone melodies. Clearly, these features do not apply to segments, but to syllables or even larger units. However, the distinction between segments and suprasegmentals is an abstraction. Thai orthography is a paradigm example to illustrate how problematic it is.

146   *Vowel incorporation*

Table 7.16. *The Thai syllabic alphabet*

	Occlusives		Nasals
	Voiced	Voiceless	
Velar	ก k^1	ข kh^2	
		ฃ kh^3	
		ฆ kh^3	ง ng^3
Palatal	จ c^1	ฉ ch^2	
		ช ch^3	
		ซ s^3	
		ฌ ch^3	ญ $ň^3$
Retroflex	ฎ d^1	ฏ t^1	ฐ th^2	
		ฑ th^3	
		ฒ th^3	ณ n^3
Dental	ด d^1	ต t^1	ถ th^2	
		ท th^3	
		ธ th^3	น n^3
Labial	บ b^1	ป p^1	ผ ph^2	
		ฝ f^2	
		พ ph^3	
		ฟ f^3	
		ภ ph^3	ม m^3
Resonants	ย y^3	ร r^3	ล l^3	ว w^3
Others	ศ s^2	ษ s^2	ส s^2	ห h^2
	ฬ l^3	อ $'^1$	ฮ h^3	

Table 7.17. *Thai vowel diacritics*

Simple vowel diacritics				Compound vowel diacritics			
short		long					
◌ั	a	◌า	ā	เ◌าะ	o	เ◌ือะ	ua
◌ิ	i	◌ี	ī	โ◌ะ	ō	เ◌ือ	uā
◌ุ	u	◌ู	ū	เ◌ะ	e	ไ◌	ai
				เ◌ียะ	ia	เ◌ีย	iā
◌ึ	u'	◌ื	ū'	เ◌	ē	ใ◌	ăi
				เ◌า	au	◌ํา	am

Table 7.18. *Thai tone diacritics*

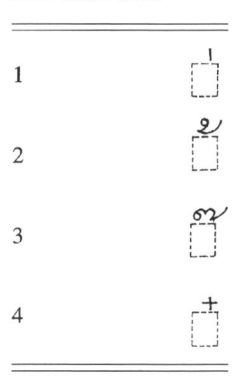

1	◌่
2	◌้
3	◌๊
4	◌๋

Consider what a leading expert on Thai linguistics has to say about the inventory of thirty-three segmental phonemes of the language: 'This is based on a spelling-pronunciation interpretation of the traditional orthography' (Diller 1992: 150). In other words, spelling, however indirectly through spelling pronunciation, is the ultimate base of phonological knowledge. Diller further explains that 'a single Thai consonant sound may be represented in writing by multiple *letters, which sometimes determine readings of tones*' (Diller 1992: 151f., emphasis added). Thai letters are grouped into three classes called *klāg* 'mid', *sung* 'high' and *tam* 'low', referring to different tones. They are distinguished by superscript numbers 1, 2, 3, respectively, in table 7.16. Tone is thus encoded in two ways: by the basic C letters, which are interpreted as incorporating a weak inherent V, and by the presence or absence of a tone diacritic. The latter must be understood not as adding tone to an otherwise atonal syllable, but as modifying the tone of the syllable in question. For instance, a tone class 3 consonant letter without tone marker is interpreted as a mid tone syllable, which tone marker 1 turns into a syllable with falling tone. Tone marker 2 attached to the same basic letter yields a high tone syllable.

Diller's just quoted statement that letters sometimes determine readings of tones suggests an atonal syllable as the primary unit of writing. There are, perhaps, certain historical reasons for such a view, because in Indic languages tone is not distinctive, and the Indic syllabic alphabets, accordingly, do not encode tone. Tone marks, it seems to follow, had to be added to the system to make it suitable for Thai. However, such a description either presupposes that a syllable can be stripped of its tone or that tone bore a lesser functional load in the thirteenth century when Thai was first written. But it is counter-intuitive that the medieval Thai scribes ever interpreted the imported *akṣaras* as applied to their own language (which has many monosyllabic words) as atonal syllables. The presence in the Thai writing system of tone-class letters and tone diacritics can be understood, with at least as much plausibility, as indicating that the graphic syllable of Thai has always been interpreted as a tone syllable. This is certainly the case today, although the phonetic interpretation of Thai writing is very involved because of many etymological spellings.

In sum, two lessons can be drawn from the Thai syllabic alphabet that have wider implications. First, there is an analogy with respect to tone to what was said in chapter 5 about the reality of phonetic features as continuous events that extend across abstract segment boundaries. Tones are continuous events connected with one another. The syllable is the relevant unit, but adjacent syllables influence each other yielding variable contours. Neither tone-class letters nor tone diacritics add an isolated feature of tone, but mark contour changes. Second, structurally Thai writing is highly analytic, each graphic syllable comprising elements that can be interpreted as referring to consonantal, vocalic and tonal features. At the same time, the two-dimensional rather than linear arrangement of these components indicates that this analyticity does not reflect temporal sequentiality. This is a basic principle of all Brāhmī-derived scripts.

Brāhmī-derived scripts

Already in 1877 K.F. Holle, a Dutch scholar, upon request of the Batavia Society of Arts and Sciences published a table of 198 scripts of Indian origin,

Table 7.19. *First page of K. F. Holle's 'Tabel van oud en nieuw-Indische alphabetten'*

150 *Vowel incorporation*

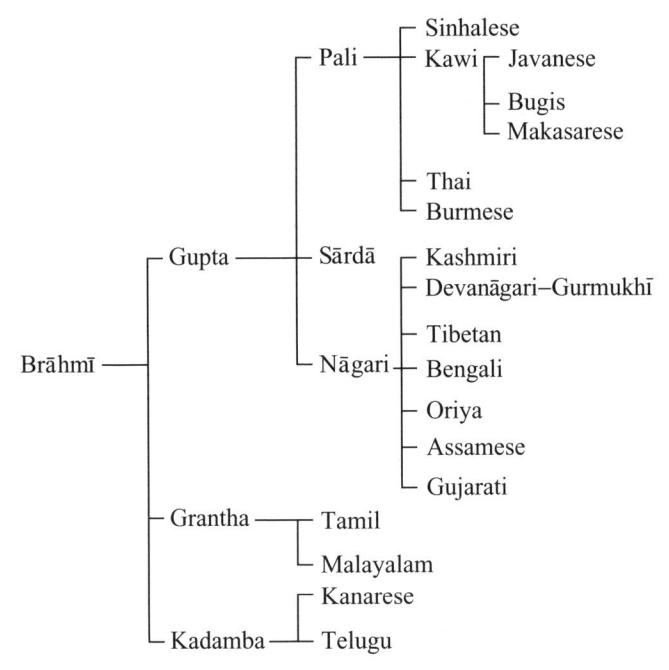

```
                                    ┌─ Sinhalese
                          ┌─ Pali ──┼─ Kawi ┌─ Javanese
                          │         │       ├─ Bugis
                          │         │       └─ Makasarese
                          │         ├─ Thai
                          │         └─ Burmese
              ┌─ Gupta ───┼─ Sārdā ─┬─ Kashmiri
              │           │         ├─ Devanāgari–Gurmukhī
              │           │         ├─ Tibetan
  Brāhmī ─────┤           └─ Nāgari ┼─ Bengali
              │                     ├─ Oriya
              │                     ├─ Assamese
              │                     └─ Gujarati
              ├─ Grantha ──┬─ Tamil
              │            └─ Malayalam
              │            ┌─ Kanarese
              └─ Kadamba ──┴─ Telugu
```

Figure 7.1 *Scripts descended from Brāhmī*

focussing on manuscripts collected in the Dutch Indies. Gaur (1985: 108) refers to about 200 scripts descended from Brāhmī. The total list of all Brāhmī-derived scripts ever used on the Indian subcontinent, in South-east Asia and in Central Asia is even more comprehensive and keeps growing, as manuscripts redacted in hitherto undocumented scripts surface in archives and inscriptions are discovered in remote places. Indian scripts have been applied to languages of four different families: Indo-Aryan, Dravidian, Sino-Tibetan and Austronesian. Figure 7.1 lists the most important of them.

Questions for discussion

(1) How do speech syllables and graphic syllables relate to each other in Indian scripts?
(2) Vowel graphemes and consonant graphemes are dealt with differently in Indian scripts. What is the linguistic motivation?
(3) What distinguishes the Thai script from other Brāhmī-derived systems?

8
Analysis and interpretation

> The linguistic level at which a script can be seen as linear is logically distinct from the linguistic level of the units that it encodes.   Alice Faber
>
> The genius of analysis that the Korean alphabet represents remains undiminished.   S. Robert Ramsey

Dissection and linearity

All writing systems incorporate linguistic analysis, and all writing systems are linear. This chapter deals with how these two universal properties interact. It will be shown that analyticity and linearity can be, and often are, manifest on different levels. Recognition of this fact helps to resolve a number of confusions about the proper classification of some writing systems, such as the Indian scripts discussed in the previous chapter. To say that writing systems incorporate linguistic analysis does not mean that first there was a proper analysis of speech and then there was writing. It just means that dissection of the stream of speech into constituent parts is indispensable for writing to occur. Only a few writing systems are the result of deliberate design and can accordingly be said to represent linguistic features that were found suitable for recording the language in question. More commonly, the interpretation of written signs and the analytic understanding of linguistic structure have advanced together, one contributing to the other. A linguistic fit thus evolved. This explains the great diversity of the world's writing systems, which tend to highlight different units, reflecting the linguistic environments in which they developed. But no matter how we answer the question of whether writing followed, preceded or accompanied the recognition of different levels of linguistic structure, it is clear that, by virtue of the fact that every writing system maps onto a linguistic system, it embodies and visibly exhibits the dissection of units of language and thus linguistic analysis.

However, since this analysis has in many instances evolved after the fact, it is not necessarily very systematic. Moreover, the breakdown inherent in the writing system may not reflect the salient units of the language very directly or very adequately because language change tends to disrupt the linguistic fit. Chinese offers a good example. When the Chinese writing system came into existence, Chinese words were predominantly one-syllable-one-morpheme units. This lexical structure is still reflected in today's Chinese writing, which treats individual characters rather than words as relevant units, although two-syllable words not necessarily consisting of two morphemes are very common in contemporary Chinese. Indeed, many Chinese characters do not make any sense but as part of a compound word. The lesson to be learned is that not every linguistic feature reflected in writing is always functionally relevant. More generally, a distinction has to be made between the unit of analysis – that aspect of linguistic structure encoded by the basic unit of a writing system – and the unit of interpretation – the constituent most relevant for processing a text and assigning it a linguistic interpretation. It is very common that there is no or only partial congruence between these two units.

Alice Faber (1992: 121), in the passage quoted at the beginning of this chapter, alerts us to a particular consequence of the disparity between the units of analysis and the units of interpretation. Scripts are linear. Spatial succession corresponds in one way or another to temporal duration. This is true in a very general sense and does not mean that all graphic components are interpreted consecutively, one after the other. The direction of a script, from left to right, from right to left, or from top to bottom, mirrors the temporal flow of connected speech, but this does not imply that the basic functional units of writing always appear in the same linear order as the linguistic units they encode. The extent to which there is agreement between the linear order of units of speech and units of writing is an index of the relative simplicity of the writing system. In English, for example, the phonetic interpretation of the graphic sequence <pop> is straightforward, [pɒp]. There is a one-to-one correspondence. By contrast, <pope> cannot be interpreted correctly as [pəʊp] unless <o-e> is recognized as a discontinuous graphic element that must be interpreted as the vowel [əʊ]. Two different principles are at work in the English orthography: (1) a simple direct mapping relation and (2) an organizational pattern of graphic units that deviates from that of phonetic units. This is one reason for the complexity of English orthography (see chapter 9 below).

There are many other writing systems where graphic elements encoding linguistic features are not arranged in the same sequential order of these features in continuous speech. Some have been discussed in the previous chapter, Devanagari, Tibetan and Thai among them. In each case, the level at which linear succession is expressed differs from the level of linguistic analysis embodied by the system. This is one reason why there is disagreement about the classification of certain writing systems and the use of hybrid terminologies such as 'alphasyllabaries'. These

Table 8.1. *The Mangyan syllabic alphabet*

ク (a)	ク̕ (i)	ろ (u)
フ (ba)	フ̄ (bi)	乙 (bu)
ド (ka)	ド̄ (ki)	乙 (ku)
↙ (da)	↙̄ (di)	↙ (du)
ら (ga)	ら̄ (gi)	ら, (gu)
V (ha)	V́ (hi)	V, (hu)
ム刁 (la)	ム̄刁 (li)	ム刁̄ (lu)
丸 (ma)	丸̄ (mi)	丸 (mu)
7ρ (na)	7ρ̄ (ni)	7乙 (nu)
K (nga)	K̕ (ngi)	K (ngu)
丸 (pa)	丸̕ (pi)	丸 (pu)
ム刁 (ra)	ıム刁 (ri)	ム刁, (ru)
乃 (sa)	乃̄ (si)	乃̄ (su)
W (ta)	W̄ (ti)	W (tu)
2ι (wa)	2ῑ (wi)	2ι̲ (wu)
7ι (ya)	7ῑ (yi)	7ι (yu)

systems seem to function like syllabaries, although the basic graphs of which they consist encode phonetic and phonological information beyond syllabic patterning. If we look at linearity they are syllabaries because the units that follow one another encode syllables. But if we look at the dissection they are alphabets operating as they do on the level of phonological segments.

Let us consider two other examples for further illustration, first the little-known Mangyan script and then the Ethiopic script. The Mangyan are a small minority people living on the Philippine island of Mindoro, and their script is a remote offshoot of the Brāhmī family of Indian scripts (Postma 1971). The basic signary is given in table 8.1.

The Mangyan script has one basic sign for the free-standing vowel /a/ and fifteen signs for consonants with inherent /a/. A diacritic mark called 'kulit' is used for expressing syllables with other vowels. It is a horizontal stroke which is read /i/ when placed above the basic sign and /u/ or /o/ when placed under it. The sign of the unmarked vowel /a/ functions as the base of the other vowel signs

154 *Analysis and interpretation*

in the same manner. Since consonant elements and vowel elements are clearly discernible in all of the characters, the analytic depth of the system can be said to reach the level of segments. Yet, linearity is expressed at the level not of segments but of syllables. Graphically each character forms an integrated unit. Further evidence for the functional salience of the syllable is the fact that the Mangyan language has closed syllables, which, however, the script has no means of expressing. There is nothing like the *virāma* vowel muting sign of the Indian scripts. Closed syllables like /bang/, /bal/, /bat/ and so on will all be written with the sign for /ba/. Each character is interpreted as a syllable whose appropriate form is contextually determined on the basis of a knowledge of the language. A Mangyan character is interpreted as a CV syllable or a CVC syllable, as the case may be, but there is no uncertainty about the linear order that progresses at the level of syllables.

ል ብ ስ

lə - əb - š(ə)

Figure 8.1 *Amharic* ləbəš *'cloak'*

The Ethiopic script, which is used for writing Amharic as well as some other languages such as Tigrinia and Somali, exhibits roughly the same general pattern, with the notable difference that the <Ca> graphs are systematically interpreted as encoding /Ca/ or /C/, thus allowing final consonants and consonant clusters to be written. The consonant base letters are modified for six 'orders' of vowels (table 8.2) by means of diacritics, which may be attached to the consonant sign on either the right or the left side. For example, the diacritic for /e:/ is a curly hook to the right side of the consonant sign, whereas /a/ is marked on the left. The Amharic word *lebeš* 'cloak' is spelt <lə-bə-š> as three syllable signs, but <l-ə-ə-b-š(ə)> if these were broken down into their consonantal and vocalic elements. Again, the implicit analysis is segmental, but the arrangement of segmental components is nonlinear. Linearity is realized at the level of syllables, which are the basic units of phonetic interpretation.

It is noteworthy that Amharic and its ancestor language Ge'ez, for which the Ethiopic script was first developed, are of Semitic stock because the alphasyllabic design of the script distinguishes it from all other Semitic writing systems. Yet, the Semitic consonant alphabets share with the Ethiopic script the feature under discussion here: the disparity of the units of analysis and the units of linear progression and interpretation. Since they do not encode vowels and consonants equally, vowel diacritics appearing above, below, within or on either side of the consonant letter, linearity only comes to bear with respect to consonants, or, as some would argue,

Table 8.2. *The Ethiopic syllabic alphabet*

	a	u:	i:	a:	e:	(ə)	o:
h	ሀ	ሁ	ሂ	ሃ	ሄ	ህ	ሆ
l	ለ	ሉ	ሊ	ላ	ሌ	ል	ሎ
ḥ	ሐ	ሑ	ሒ	ሓ	ሔ	ሕ	ሖ
m	መ	ሙ	ሚ	ማ	ሜ	ም	ሞ
s	ሠ	ሡ	ሢ	ሣ	ሤ	ሥ	ሦ
r	ረ	ሩ	ሪ	ራ	ሬ	ር	ሮ
š	ሰ	ሱ	ሲ	ሳ	ሴ	ስ	ሶ
q	ቀ	ቁ	ቂ	ቃ	ቄ	ቅ	ቆ
b	በ	ቡ	ቢ	ባ	ቤ	ብ	ቦ
t	ተ	ቱ	ቲ	ታ	ቴ	ት	ቶ
ḫ	ኀ	ኁ	ኂ	ኃ	ኄ	ኅ	ኆ
n	ነ	ኑ	ኒ	ና	ኔ	ን	ኖ
ʾ	አ	ኡ	ኢ	ኣ	ኤ	እ	ኦ
k	ከ	ኩ	ኪ	ካ	ኬ	ክ	ኮ
w	ወ	ዉ	ዊ	ዋ	ዌ	ው	ዎ
ʿ	ዐ	ዑ	ዒ	ዓ	ዔ	ዕ	ዖ
z	ዘ	ዙ	ዚ	ዛ	ዜ	ዝ	ዞ
j	የ	ዩ	ዪ	ያ	ዬ	ይ	ዮ
d	ደ	ዱ	ዲ	ዳ	ዴ	ድ	ዶ
g	ገ	ጉ	ጊ	ጋ	ጌ	ግ	ጎ
ṭ	ጠ	ጡ	ጢ	ጣ	ጤ	ጥ	ጦ
p	ጰ	ጱ	ጲ	ጳ	ጴ	ጵ	ጶ
ṣ	ጸ	ጹ	ጺ	ጻ	ጼ	ጽ	ጾ
ḍ	ፀ	ፁ	ፂ	ፃ	ፄ	ፅ	ፆ
f	ፈ	ፉ	ፊ	ፋ	ፌ	ፍ	ፎ
p	ፐ	ፑ	ፒ	ፓ	ፔ	ፕ	ፖ

syllables. If we look at the evidence of the examples discussed above, the coincidence of syllabic linearity and segmental analysis is by no means uncommon. Is there, perhaps, an advantage in this arrangement that is not easily perceived from the point of view of alphabets that encode consonants and vowels in the same way and that, on the face of it, appear to be segmentally linear? To answer this question we now turn to a writing system that features the disparity of unit of analysis and unit of linear progression and interpretation not as an accidental development, but as a deliberate design feature, Korean.

'Correct Sounds for the Instruction of the People'

The Korean script, which is now generally known as *Han'gŭl*, is a remarkable achievement. Its formal simplicity and systematic beauty cannot fail to impress linguists and students of writing alike, especially because these characteristics are the fruit of solid scholarship. For, unlike most other writing systems, the Korean script did not evolve gradually, but was created by a group of scholars under the enlightened leadership of King Sejong (reigned 1418–50). Literacy at the time was in Chinese, a foreign language to the Koreans of which only a small elite of literati had proficient command. King Sejong's purpose in providing a new writing system was threefold: (1) it should enable Koreans correctly to pronounce Chinese characters; (2) it should be easier to learn than the Chinese; and (3) it should be more suitable for the Korean language. Han'gŭl met these requirements admirably well. The script was introduced to the public in 1443 in a document called *Hunmin Chŏng'ŭm* 'Correct Sounds for the Instruction of the People'. A commentary with detailed explanations of the linguistic principles used in creating the characters, *Hunmin Chŏng'ŭm haerye*,[1] followed in 1446.

The very title of the original document highlights the crucial point. It was sounds that were to be encoded, and nothing else. The new system was to be a purely phonetic script. Chinese characters, as discussed in chapter 3 above, contain graphic elements for the interpretation of syllabic values, but if your knowledge of Chinese is limited your chances of getting the interpretation right are not too good. The characters that King Sejong wanted should leave no room for doubt as to the correct pronunciation both of Chinese and Korean words. This required a good knowledge of the phonological system of these languages. To this end, the creators of Han'gŭl built on the phonetic scholarship available at the time. They were familiar with Indian scripts, which treated consonants as syllable initials which were typically completed by a subsequent vowel. Chinese phonetics, too, was centred upon the syllable and, therefore, not quite sufficient for their purposes. In the Chinese tradition of rhyme dictionaries, a speech syllable was divided into an initial and a final. The Korean linguists discovered that syllables could be divided into three parts – initial, medial and final – and that the initial and final could be identical, as in a syllable of the type C_1VC_1. This paved the way for segmental analysis, but King

---

[1] An English translation of this document, which was written in Chinese, is given in Shin, Lee and Lee 1990.

Sejong and his scholars did not stop there. They identified a number of what in present parlance are called phonetic features and decided to take them into account in designing the new writing system, which to this day is witness to their ingenuity. Typologically the script is quite unique in that its graphic components are sensitive to subsegmental phonetic features. The argument has been made, most explicitly by Sampson (1985: 120–44) and Kim (1997: 145–60), that Han'gŭl is a feature-based system. But this is controversial. Before we examine some of the arguments for and against this view, let us take a look at the graphic design of the system. Two of the most outstanding characteristics are (1) the iconicity of basic letter shapes and (2) their arrangement in syllable blocks.

Iconicity

Like Chinese characters, Han'gŭl characters were originally written vertically from top to bottom in columns running from right to left, each character being allotted the same amount of space no matter how complex its internal structure (figure 8.2). The creators of the system were aware that the outer appearance of the new script was crucial for its acceptance and made an effort to deviate as little as possible from the Chinese model. Following the same rationale, they chose the syllable as the basic operational unit. On this level, then, Han'gŭl is a syllabary, since each character is interpreted as a syllable, just like Chinese. However, whereas the graphic complexity of the Chinese character is unrelated to the structure of the syllable it corresponds to, the complexity of the Han'gŭl character mirrors that of the syllable. A simple syllable of the V or CV type is graphically simple, and complex syllables such as CCVC are graphically complex, too. This is because the Korean linguists, as explicitly stated in the above-mentioned commentary, designed the characters 'according to the shape of the articulatory organs' (Lee 1990: 76).

We had already occasion in chapter 2 (see figure 2.7) to observe that the Korean script has certain iconic qualities. The designers actually tried to schematically visualize the process or position of articulation most salient in the production of the sound to be encoded. They first distinguished five classes of consonants, 'molar, lingual, labial, dental and glottal', choosing a basic letter for each.

Molar (dorsal, in modern terminology): ㄱ A right angle with the corner in the north-east depicts the shape of the tongue root closing the throat, which is what we do when uttering a [k].

Lingual: ㄴ A similar angle with the corner in the south-west represents the shape of the tongue touching the hard palate, a movement that helps to produce an [n].

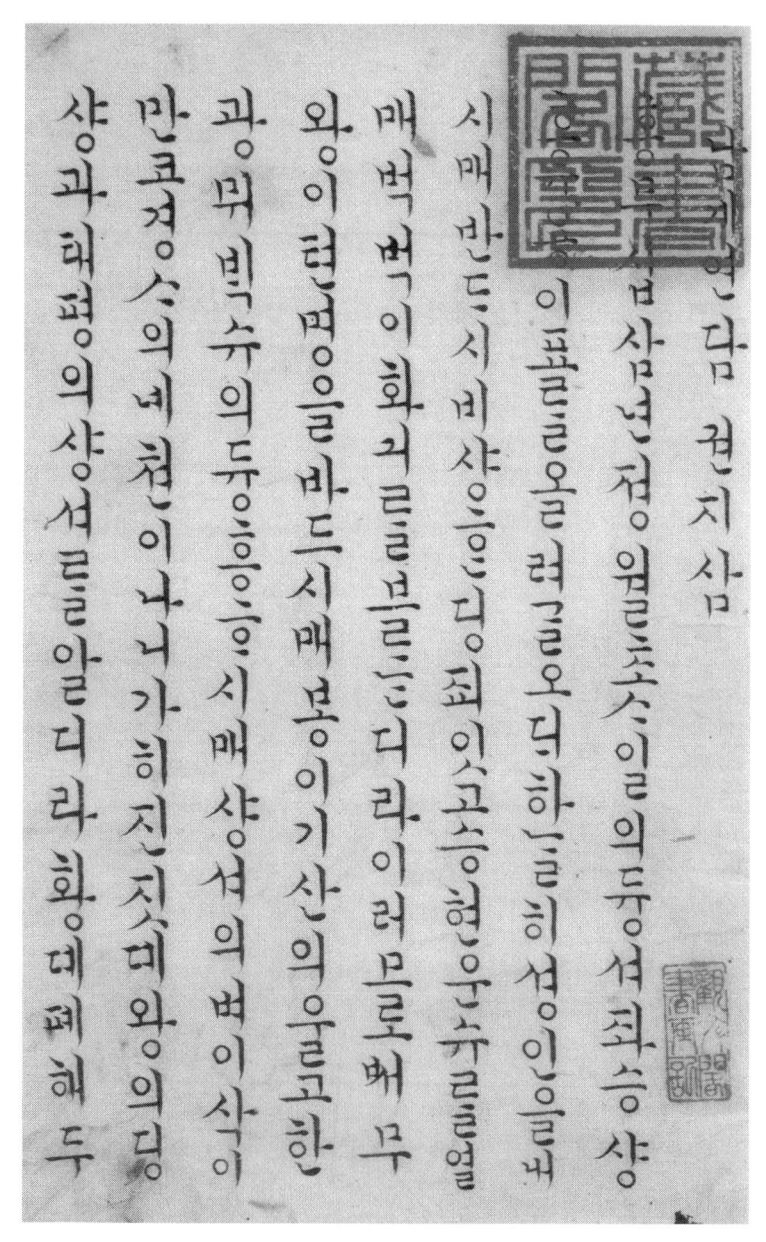

Figure 8.2 *Han'gŭl calligraphy by Kwon Ji-sam, seventeenth century*

Labial: ㅁ A closed square symbolizes closed lips, as when the bilabial nasal [m] is produced. This letter cannot really be said to be iconic, because closed lips do not look like a square, but a certain symbolism may be recognized when it is pointed out.

Dental: ㅅ A triangular shape without a base line is a pictograph of a tooth, the place where sibilants such as [s] are articulated. (In the original system there was a full triangle for the voiced counterpart [z] which is no longer in use.)

Glottal (laryngeal): ㅇ A circle or zero depicts the throat. It was written whenever a syllable started with a vowel.

These five geometric shapes provide the basis of the system of consonant letters. A second and third set of letters are derived by adding, respectively, one and two strokes to the basic letter shapes. The corresponding sounds were said to be 'harder' or 'stronger' by the creators of Han'gŭl. Modern scholarship converges on the view that 'hardness/strength' was the degree of aspiration (Kim-Renaud 1997: 164; Lee 1990: 77). In the case of the dental and bilabial nasals the stroke-added letters stand for sounds of a slightly different quality, turning /n/ into /t/ and /m/ into /p/, which makes good phonetic sense, as the point of articulation is the same, the difference being stop as opposed to continuant articulation. A stroke added to the letter of dental sibilant /s/ ㅅ yields a letter for /c/ ㅈ, an affricate whose aspirated counterpart is indicated by another additional stroke.

The strength hierarchy of the glottal series leaves some open questions. Originally there were four Han'gŭl letters based on a round shape, a circle with a top bar for /ʔ/, a circle with two top bars for /h/, and a circle with a dot on top for /ŋ/. As for the simple circle from which the other letters are derived, it has been variously suggested that it corresponds to a voiced velar fricative in fifteenth-century Korean (Ahn 1997: 91), a voiced laryngeal, or else has no phonetic interpretation at all, its function in writing being mainly aesthetic. If the addition of strokes is thought to systematically represent articulatory similarity, the empty-value hypothesis would seem to make more sense than the velar hypothesis, because the articulation of a glottal stop, which is represented by a one-stroke-added letter, is nowhere near the velar area. On the other hand, the letter of the velar nasal /ŋ/ is in complementary distribution with the zero letter, the latter being restricted to syllable-initial, the former to syllable-final position. In Western phonology it is usually assumed that complementary distribution of two sounds is a meaningful phonological fact only when these sounds are phonetically related. Now, clearly, /Ø/ cannot be considered phonetically related to /ŋ/ or any other sound, for that matter. A better candidate would be a voiced laryngeal /ɦ/, something like the unmarked initial sound of syllables not beginning with other consonants. It is conceivable that the Korean linguists considered this very weak sound related to /ŋ/ and therefore derived the

Table 8.3. *Han'gŭl basic and derived consonant letters*

Molar	ㄱ /k/	→	ㅋ /kʰ/			
Lingual	ㄴ /n/	→	ㄷ /t/	→	ㅌ /tʰ/	
Labial	ㅁ /m/	→	ㅂ /p/	→	ㅍ /pʰ/	
Dental	ㅅ /s/	→	ㅈ /c/	→	ㅊ /cʰ/	
Glottal	ㅇ /Ø/, /ɦ/	→	ㆆ /ʔ/	→	ㅎ /h/	→ ㆁ /ŋ/

Table 8.4. *Han'gŭl tense consonant letters*

/k'/	/t'/	/p'/	/c'/	/s'/	/x/
ㄲ	ㄸ	ㅃ	ㅉ	ㅆ	ㆅ

letter of one from the other, although this seems counter-intuitive from the point of view of Western phonology. We should keep in mind, however, that the categorization of speech sounds is highly contingent upon the linguistic system, and that what seems strange to contemporary Western phonologists, may have been a matter of course to fifteenth-century Koreans.

The proper interpretation of the zero letter is a question of continuing debate, but the common underlying principle of consonant letter formation is clear enough. A minimal graphic modification corresponds to a minimal phonological distinction. Notice, however, that the creators of Han'gŭl did not conceive of these distinctions as binary like the features of modern articulatory phonetics. Voiced sounds were regarded as weaker than voiceless sounds, which in turn were weaker than aspirated sounds. The resulting consonantal hardness scale yields the chart of fourteen letters shown in table 8.3.

Next, there is a series of six complex letters representing tense consonants. They were made by reduplicating the letters of the lax consonants /k/, /t/, /p/, /c/, /s/ and /h/. Again, a common phonological relationship is expressed by the same graphic device (table 8.4).

Turning now to the vowel letters, we notice that while the general graphic formation principle of the letters is similar to that of the consonants, the vowel letters are not intended to visualize articulatory organs or processes, but were designed to represent certain metaphysical characteristics. All vowel letters are derived from three basic shapes, which are said to correspond to the so-called Three Powers of Chinese cosmology: a round dot for Heaven, bright or *Yang*; a horizontal line for Earth, dark or *Yin*; and a vertical line for Man. Their phonetic values are [ʌ, ɨ, i], in this order. A first series of four derived letters consisting of the dot placed above and below the horizontal line and on either side of the vertical line, respectively, are for [o, u, a, ə]. According to *Hunmin Chŏng'ŭm haerye*, the design of these letters is meaningful with regard to the qualities of vowels in terms of tongue retraction and whether they are bright or dark. When the dot (Heaven) is placed above the horizontal line (Earth), it is bright, when placed under it, it is dark. The vertical line, Man between Heaven and Earth, is for a neutral vowel. Addition of a second dot yields another four signs for the glide onset vowels [yo, yu, ya, yə]. Kim-Renaud (1997: 174) argues that the glide onset was not considered a separate segment preceding the vowel, but a feature of the vowel. Hence its representation by a graphic element added to the basic vowel. These compound graphs are considered separate letters by the Koreans. The original dot was later transformed into a short line attached to the base line at a right angle.

Just as for the consonants, elaborate phonetic explanations are provided for the vowels and their graphic differentiation. ㅗ [o] is like · [ʌ] but with rounded lips. ㅏ [a] is like · [ʌ] but with unrounded lips. ㅜ [u] is like – [ɨ] but with rounded lips. And ㅓ [ə] is like – [ɨ] but with unrounded lips.

The original Han'gŭl system is traditionally regarded as consisting of twenty-eight basic letters. These were presented to the unsuspecting Koreans quite suddenly in the *Hunmin Chŏng'ŭm* as the new script that could accurately denote the sounds of all Korean words, and more than that. Chinese words, too, had to be written accurately. The creators of the system hence included several signs unnecessary for writing Korean including tone marks, which were more useful for Chinese than for Korean. Chinese, after all, was the unrivalled language of civilization. Yet, the idea of constructing a writing system on the basis of iconically representing articulatory traits and phonological alternations is entirely original, owing nothing to Chinese concepts of writing. Only in one respect did the designers of Han'gŭl honour the Chinese literary tradition, they decided to write in syllable blocks.

Syllable blocks

It is quite obvious from what has been said so far that King Sejong and his team of linguists had a sophisticated understanding of phonology as well as of the problem of how to symbolize the articulated sound stream with graphic means. They understood that articulation is a complex process, which can be analysed in terms of features that combine to form sound segments. But they also understood that analyticity does not imply sequentiality. Features that combine to form a

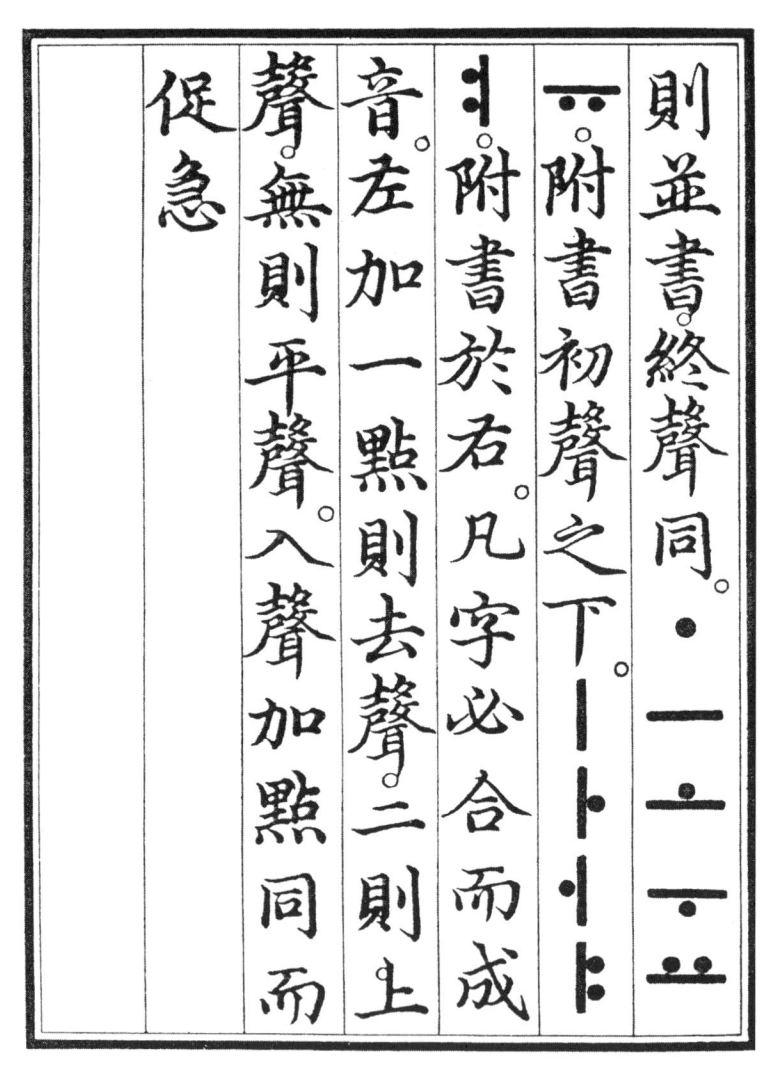

則並書終聲同。・ー丄ㅜㅛㅠ
附書初聲之下。ㅣㅏㅓㅑㅕ
凡字必合而成
音左加一點則去聲二則上
聲無則平聲入聲加點同而
促急

Figure 8.3 *A passage from* Hunmin Chŏng'ŭm haerye *explaining the vowel letters*

larger unit do not necessarily occur in linear succession, but often simultaneously. Recognizing the existence of features and segments is hence independent from handling these units for the purpose of writing. In their decision to group Han'gŭl graphs into syllable blocks the Koreans followed the Chinese practice of treating the syllable as the basic sound unit of encoding. But given the high level of their linguistic knowledge it is unlikely that they would have chosen a unit for encoding

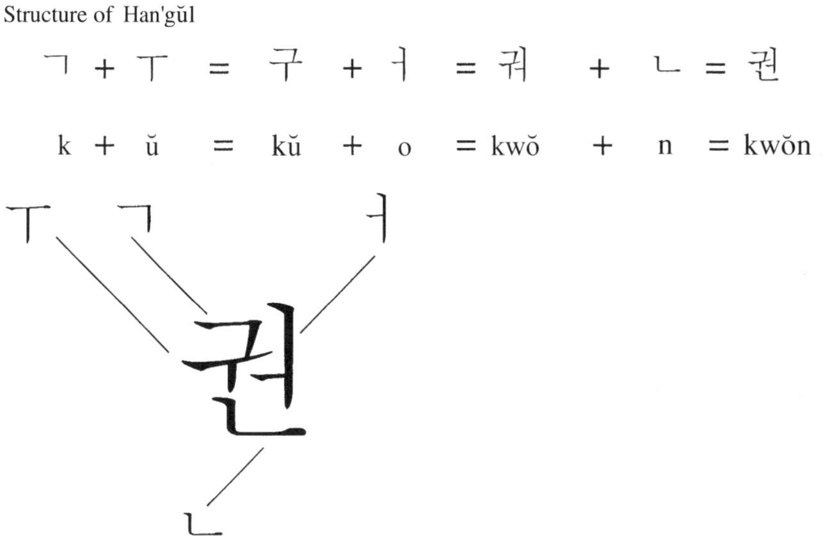

Structure of Han'gŭl

ㄱ + ㅜ = 구 + ㅓ = 궈 + ㄴ = 권

k + ŭ = kŭ + o = kwŏ + n = kwŏn

Figure 8.4 *Graphic composition of the syllable* kwŏn

and phonetic interpretation that would diminish the functionality of the new system. In the Chinese tradition, aesthetics has always been an important aspect of writing; for the designers of the new system it was an additional challenge.

The graphic building blocks of Han'gŭl stand for segmental and subsegmental units, but they are stacked together to form syllable blocks, each block being separated by a space. For illustration of how the individual graphs are arranged in an equidimensional square see figure 8.3. Table 8.5 provides examples of simple syllable blocks including syllables consisting of vowels and semivowels only. The rules of Han'gŭl orthography do not allow vowel graphs to stand alone. In the absence of an initial C they combine with the zero graph. The basic type of Korean syllable is CVC. In writing, the consonant graphs are grouped around the vowel nucleus. Two general formation principles are as follows: V graphs with a perpendicular main stroke have the C graph attached to the left side, and V graphs with a horizontal main stroke have the C graph on top. Stroke order in writing syllables is as in Chinese, from left to right and from top to bottom. Notice that there is yet another reason to concur with the graphical principles of Chinese writing. Arranging the basic Han'gŭl graphs in syllable blocks makes them easy to combine with Chinese characters. Chinese loanwords in Korean are abundant, and writing them with Chinese characters was considered natural. Hence a mixed style of writing evolved, much like in Japan with kana and Chinese characters.

Table 8.5. *Combinations of consonants and vowels*

Syllabic blocks beginning with /k/

가	개	갸	걔	거	게	겨	계	고	과	괘	괴	교	구	궈	궤	귀	규	그	긔	기
ka	kae	kya	kyae	kŏ	ke	kyŏ	kye	ko	kwa	kwae	koe	kyo	ku	kwŏ	kwe	kwi	kyu	kŭ	kŭi	ki

Syllabic blocks beginning with 'ㅇ' (not romanized)

아	애	야	얘	어	에	여	예	오	와	왜	외	요	우	워	웨	위	유	으	의	이
a	ae	ya	yae	ŏ	e	yŏ	ye	o	wa	wae	oe	yo	u	wŏ	we	wi	yu	ŭ	ŭi	i

Syllabic blocks ending with /a/

가	까	나	다	따	라	마	바	빠	사	싸	아	자	짜	차	카	타	파	하
ka	kka	na	ta	tta	ra	ma	pa	ppa	sa	ssa	a	cha	tcha	ch'a	k'a	t'a	p'a	ha

Syllabic blocks ending with /ŏ/

고	꼬	모	도	또	로	모	보	뽀	소	쏘	오	조	쪼	초	코	토	포	호
kŏ	kkŏ	mŏ	tŏ	ttŏ	rŏ	mŏ	pŏ	ppŏ	sŏ	ssŏ	ŏ	chŏ	tchŏ	ch'ŏ	k'ŏ	t'ŏ	p'ŏ	hŏ

Korean has a rather complex syllable structure, more complex in any event than Chinese. According to one estimate there are as many as 11,000 distinct syllables in Korean (Kim-Renaud 1997: 183). This has important consequences both at the graphic and at the systematic level. At the level of graphic encoding it means that each vowel and consonant graph appears in various positions and sizes because each syllable block occupies the same space. For instance, as part of a complex syllable such as /ppyō/ 뼈 the consonant ㅂ /p/ will be smaller in size than when part of the simple CV syllable 부 /pu/. For the designers of Korean text-processing software this was a bit of a problem at first, and it was they who suggested that the syllable blocks should be decomposed and Cs and Vs written in linear order. This is, of course, possible and has been tried experimentally, but it was found that reading the linearized script was slower by as much as two and a half times than reading in the syllabic mode (Kim and Sohn 1986). While Sejong did not conduct any experiments of this sort, he and his collaborators may well have been aware that the unit of analysis is not necessarily the most efficient unit of interpretation.

Systematically the large inventory of Korean syllables implies that the internal structure of the syllable blocks is psychologically active rather than having been frozen in the course of centuries of syllabic writing. To be sure, since the invention of Han'gŭl many phonetic changes have occurred as the language evolved. Certain distinctions such as those of the dental series have collapsed, and syllable-final consonants have weakened. These and other changes have contributed to making Korean spelling more phonemic as opposed to phonetic. Predictable phonetic alternations are ignored in modern spelling. For example, /k/ is pronounced [k] in initial position, but [g] in intervocalic position and as unreleased [k] in final position. The spelling for all three is the same (see table 8.6). However, notwithstanding the historical changes and notwithstanding quite a number of etymological spellings, Hang'ŭl still exhibits a close correspondence to the spoken language. The structure of each written syllable is transparent to Korean speakers. New syllables, as in foreign names, for example, can easily be read and written in accordance with the established combinatory principles. It has been argued that Koreans 'regard Han'gŭl symbols as separate individual letters rather than as partially identical components' (DeFrancis 1989: 197). In view of the large number of Korean syllables, this is likely to be true for high-frequency syllables only. And to the extent that it is true it certainly does not imply that the internal structure of syllable blocks is opaque. Evidence suggests, rather, that Korean readers rely both on syllable blocks and on their components as they need to (Kim and Sohn 1986).

Conclusion

In light of the above discussion it turns out that the question whether Han'gŭl is a feature-based writing system is not well conceived because it seems to require a yes-or-no answer. However, the ingenuity of the system is that it operates at different levels, and quite systematically so. The analysis of speech sounds encoded in the elementary graphs penetrates to the level of subsegmental features. At the same time, the syllable is recognized as the most functional unit of phonetic interpretation. Analysis and interpretation are independent. Both are assigned crucial roles in the Korean writing system. It is futile, therefore, to pursue the question of whether Han'gŭl should be considered a featural system or a syllabary. The question itself is informed by Western phonetic scholarship and Western alphabetic writing, which does not recognize the syllable as a unit encoded in its own right. The creators of Han'gŭl wanted it to be a script that is easy to learn and easy to read. These requirements are met by keeping the number of basic graphs – for segments and subsegmental features – very low to meet the requirements of the learner and writer, while creating enough graphic complexity – in the syllable blocks – to meet the reader's requirements for contrast and discernibility. Han'gŭl matches these two requirements in a unique way by systematically exploiting the functional and systematic independence of the unit of analysis and the unit of interpretation.

Analysis and interpretation

Table 8.6. *Han'gŭl letters and their modern interpretations according to the South Korean Ministry of Education*

A. Vowels

ㅣ	ㅡ	ㅜ
ㅔ	ㅓ	ㅗ
ㅐ		ㅏ

i	u	u
e	o	o
æ		a

Semi-vowels

ㅣ	y
ㅜ	w

B. Consonants

Korean letters	Ministry of Education ('84) Initial	Intervocalic	Final	Current use	Transcription of IPA into Korean: init./final	
ㄱ	k	g	k	g	g	ㄱ/그
ㄲ	kk	kk		gg	kʔ	ㄲ/끄
ㅋ	k'	k'	k'	k	k	ㅋ/크
ㅂ	p	b	p	b	b	ㅂ/브
ㅃ	pp	pp		bb	pʔ	ㅃ/쁘
ㅍ	p'	p'	p'	p	p, f	ㅍ/프
ㄷ	t	d	t	d	d, ð, θ	ㄷ/드
ㄸ	tt	tt	dd	tʔ		ㄸ/뜨
	t'	t'	t'	t	t	ㅌ/트
ㅈ	ch	j	t	j	dʒ	ㅈ/즈
						ㅈ/지
ㅉ	tch	tch		jj	dʒʔ	ㅉ/쩨
ㅊ	ch'	ch'	t	ch	tʃ	ㅊ/츠
					ts'	ㅊ/치
ㅅ	s/sh	s/s	h t	s	s	ㅅ/스
						슈/시
ㅆ	ss	ss	t	ss	sʔ	ㅆ/쓰
ㄴ	n	n	n	n	n	ㄴ/느
ㅁ	m	m	m	m	m	ㅁ/므
ㅇ	/	/	ŋ	ŋ	ŋ	ㅇ/으
ㄹ	r/s	r/l	l	r	r	ㄹ/르
						ㄹ/ㄹ
ㅎ	h	h	h	h	h	ㅎ

Questions for discussion

(1) What does it mean that writing systems are linear?
(2) How does English *past* differ from *paste* in terms of interpreting the order of written symbols?
(3) What is the analytic unit of the Ethiopic writing system, and what is its unit of interpretation?
(4) What is iconicity in writing? At which level does Han'gŭl exhibit iconic properties?
(5) What follows from the fact that components of Han'gŭl characters can be interpreted as phonetic features while the characters themselves stand for syllables?

9
Mixed systems

> We are like sailors who must rebuild their boat on the open sea without ever being able to take it apart in a dock and reassemble it from scratch.
>
> Otto Neurath[1]
>
> Scripts which have evolved over long periods as the everyday writing systems of whole speech-communities or nations are almost always something of a mixture.   Geoffrey Sampson

One of the many extraordinary features of Han'gŭl is its uniformity and systematic purity. Each Han'gŭl sign, that is, each unit of interpretation, relates to the same kind of linguistic unit, a syllable, in the same manner by building it up from smaller components, which in turn relate to parts and aspects of the articulated sound stream in a uniform manner. This makes Han'gŭl one of the most systematically coherent scripts ever invented and used. Most other writing systems are much less consistent, incorporating as they do a variety of units and relying on a variety of mapping relations for interpretation. The reasons for this lie in the principle of historicity, which, as pointed out in chapter 1, is common to all writing systems. From their inception to their mature form all writing systems have gone through an extended process of evolution, often retaining features of earlier stages. New features were added, others discarded, as the system evolved alongside, but not necessarily in close connection with, the language it was first used to write. As a consequence, the mapping relation with the language underwent changes, too, often getting more complicated. Most writing systems bear witness to these developments.

Otto Neurath, the philosopher with an interest in the problem of a universal character, whom we met in chapter 2, has likened scientists to sailors who, if they have to repair their boat, must rebuild it plank by plank while staying afloat in it on the high seas. The simile can be fruitfully extended to scribes who continue using their script while mending it to fit changed requirements. There is more to this comparison than a superficial metaphor, since writing systems

---

[1] See the opening quote of Quine 1960.

share a number of properties of science in that they dissect and describe certain phenomena. Entailing as they do a linguistic analysis, they can be viewed, among other things, as descriptions of a language. These descriptions are typically of a makeshift nature reflecting the fact that the scribes had to keep on making adjustments whenever they perceived the need to do so. Han'gŭl is the rare exception of a boat carefully designed and built to completion in the dry dock before it was launched. Its systematic consistency reflects this remarkable aspect of its genesis. In a like manner, other writing systems contain traits indicative of their history. Having absorbed influences of various sorts, they do not usually represent one type of writing system precisely but, to borrow Sampson's phrase quoted at the beginning of this chapter, 'are almost always something of a mixture'.

In most cases, if we compile a complete inventory of the graphemes of a writing system, that is, of all functionally distinct signs, we will find that they belong to several different categories involving different rules for their linguistic interpretation. Yet, as is so common with matters involving language, there is gradation. Granted that the textbook example of a logographic system or syllabographic system or a segmental system is the odd exception, it is still true that some are closer to the ideal type than others and, conversely, some systems are more mixed than others. Both the Chinese and the Japanese writing systems make use of Chinese characters, but the former is much more uniform than the latter, which has been derived from it. It will become apparent below that the rules that determine the interpretation of graphical units are more varied in Japanese than in Chinese. The same can be said about English and French, on one hand, and Spanish and Finnish, on the other. All four of them use the same alphabetic notation, but the interpretation of sequences of English and French letters is significantly more complex than that of Spanish and Finnish. Old Persian cuneiform comes close to a segmental script. Although its signary in addition to its thirty-six phonetic characters includes seven logograms, its basic modus operandi is phonographic. This cannot be said of other cuneiform systems such as Akkadian and its offshoot Babylonian, for example, which include logograms and syllabograms. In the event, the different kinds of signs are mixed in such proportions that it would be equally arbitrary to classify them as syllabic or logographic. Thus, in the absence of a predominant principle for the interpretation of their basic units, some writing systems cannot be assigned to a particular type. It is with mixed systems of this sort that we are concerned in this chapter. The question of typology is of some theoretical interest, but also impinges on the proper description and understanding of individual writing systems. In what follows we will, therefore, focus on a number of specific systems of a mixed nature: Egyptian, Akkadian, Japanese and English.

Egyptian writing

Until its decipherment by the French philologist Jean François Champollion (1790–1832) in the early 1820s, the nature of the Egyptian writing system eluded European scholars. The impressive naturalism of the pictographs as well as a number of misconceptions handed down from antiquity led them to believe that the script was symbolic and that each one of the so-called 'holy characters' – which is what *hieroglyph*[2] means – was to be interpreted as a word, if not an entire sentence. As it turned out, only few Egyptian signs are logograms. Champollion arrived at the conclusion that Egyptian hieroglyphs were a phonetic rather than a symbolic script when he analysed the Rosetta Stone, a stele dating from 196 BCE, which is inscribed in two languages, Greek and Egyptian, and three scripts, the Greek alphabet, and the hieroglyphic and demotic varieties of Egyptian. Counting Egyptian signs and Greek words, he found that there were 1,419 signs for 486 words. Since the 1,419 were made up of only 66 different signs, he correctly concluded that the script was phonetic, at least in part.

After Champollion's path-breaking discovery, the details of the system were worked out. It is a mixed system consisting of phonograms of various sorts and signs that are interpreted for meaning rather than sound. All in all some 700 signs were used to write the language during its classical period in the second millennium BCE, although the total number increased significantly in later periods. However, more than 400 signs were rarely needed at any one time. In addition to the pictorial hieroglyphs that are always used on monumental inscriptions, the Egyptians developed two more cursive script forms for manuscript writing, which allowed for greater speed and efficiency: the semicursive 'hieratic' and the cursive 'demotic', both so called by the Greeks. The iconic properties of the hieroglyphs were lost in these cursive scripts, but structurally they remained fairly close to the hieroglyphic model.

One important difference between the hieroglyphic script and the two cursive scripts has to do with the grouping and combination of signs. While hieratic and demotic writing is always linear from right to left, there is often no such clear correspondence between the flow of speech and the linearity of the hieroglyphic script. The arrangement of hieroglyphs makes more liberal use of the two dimensions of the writing surface, often closely integrating the written text with graphic images relating to its contents. Both the orientation of the hieroglyphs and their spatial arrangement in columns and horizontal lines is more varied and flexible than hieratic and demotic writing. Hieroglyphs are sometimes switched in their order for reasons of better spacing (Davies 1987: 13).

---

[2] Notice that the term *hieroglyph* is Greek and was coined by the Greeks, not by the Egyptians.

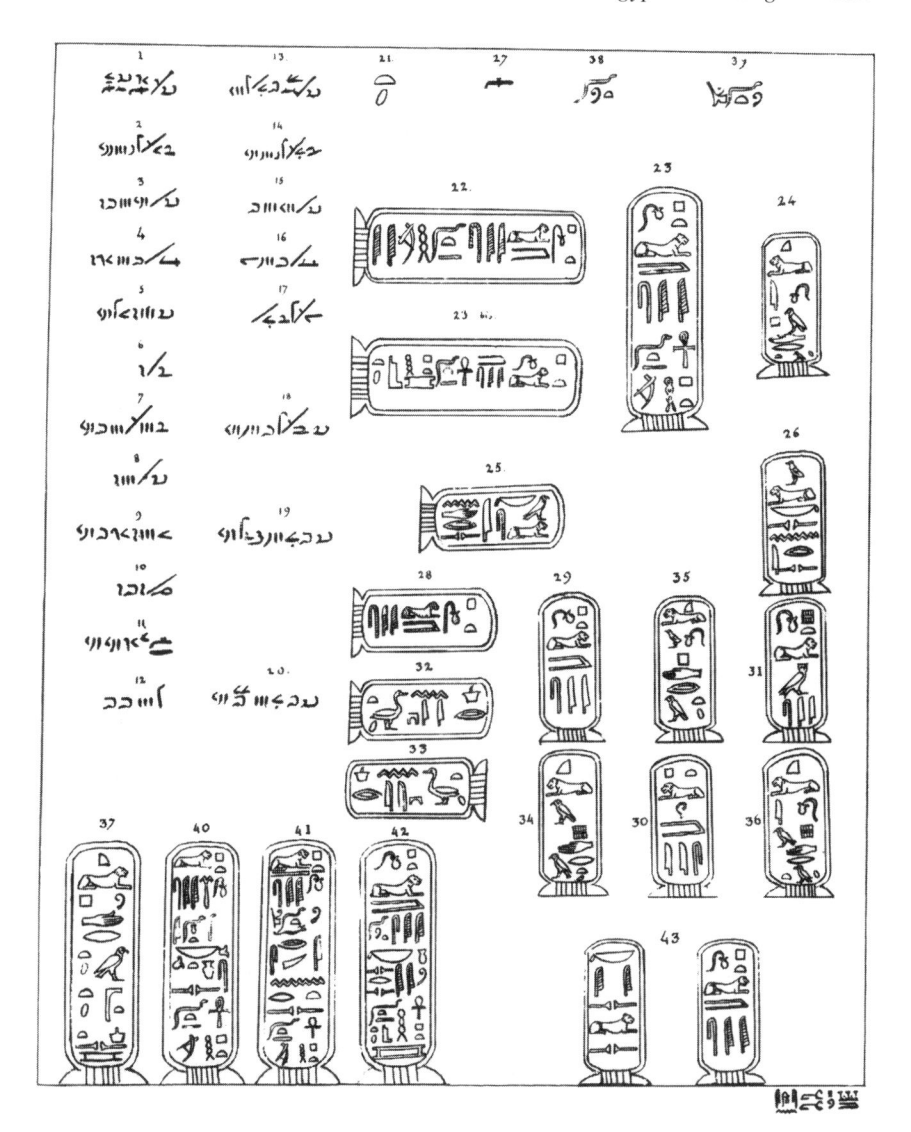

Figure 9.1 *François Champollion's decipherment of royal names: Ptolemaios (22, 23, 28, 29, 30, 31, 40, 41); Kleopatra (24, 34, 35, 36, 37); Alexander (25, 26); Berenice (32, 33)*

A defining feature of the Egyptian writing system is that it provides no overt cues for the interpretation of vowels (Schenkel 1984). Egyptian belongs to the Hamito-Semitic family of languages, which is characterized by triconsonantal word-roots. Other writing systems for Semitic languages also focus on consonants

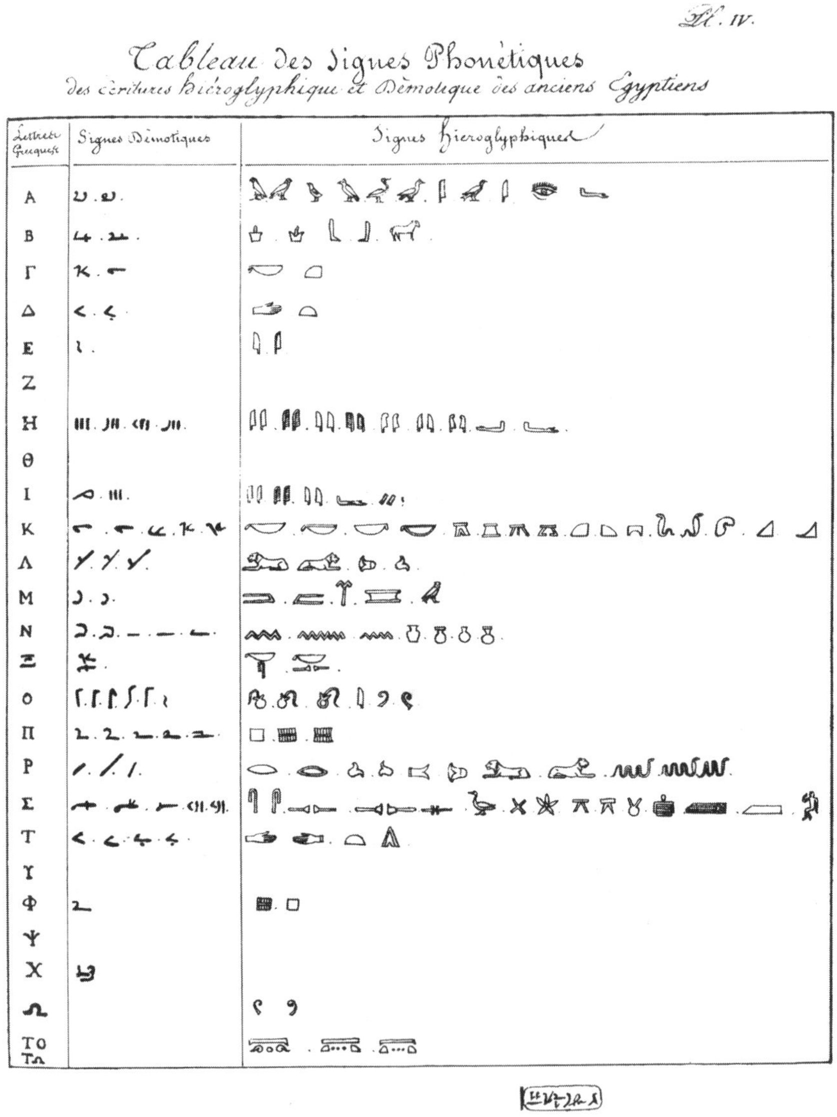

172 *Mixed systems*

Figure 9.2 *François Champollion's first list of Egyptian phonetic signs, columns from left to right: Greek, demotic, hieroglyphic*

(see chapter 6), but unlike both the North Semitic cuneiform systems and the consonant alphabets of the Phoenician family of scripts, the Egyptian script has no auxiliary means of vowel indication. On the basis of consonantal frames readers supply the contextually appropriate vowels to interpret the full body of the word.

👁 ĭr 'eye'

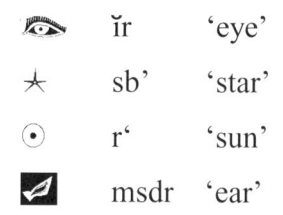

★ sbʾ 'star'

☉ rʿ 'sun'

🪶 msdr 'ear'

Figure 9.3 *Logographic hieroglyphs*

To this end they make use of three classes of signs that, as all available evidence suggests, were present in the earliest stages of the Egyptian script around 3000 BCE (Fischer 1989) and used continuously until the end of its long history in the tenth century CE. These three classes of signs are logograms, phonograms and determinatives.

Logograms, sometimes called 'ideograms', are the simplest and probably original hieroglyphs from which all others derive. Each logogram is memorized and interpreted as a whole on the basis of its pictorial iconicity. Depicting an eye, means 'eye' *ĭr*, depicting a star, means 'star' *sbʾ*, and depicting the ground-plan of a house, means 'house' *pr*. As these examples suggest, only words denoting concrete objects that are easily delineated can be written in this way, and indeed logograms constitute only a relatively small group of hieroglyphs. Their use was extended early on by semantic association. Thus, ☉, the glyph for 'sun', also means 'day' *hrw*, and 🖋, the glyph for 'writing equipment', also means 'to write' *sš*.

Phonograms came into existence when the Egyptian scribes exploited the homophony and near-homophony of many Egyptian words and used logograms in rebus fashion. Signs could thus be interpreted for their sound values only, irrespective of their meaning. They fall into three subsets: triconsonantal signs that are interpreted as groups of three consonants. About forty triconsonantal signs were commonly used, of which some are given in table 9.1.

The next set of phonograms, biconsonantal hieroglyphs, is the largest with some eighty signs. Constituting groups of two consonants, these signs have a wider application and are hence more frequently used than triconsonantal signs (table 9.2). Finally, there is a set of twenty-six monoconsonantal hieroglyphs of which twenty-four were used in the Classical language, a number that cannot but remind us of the Graeco-Latin alphabet. Not surprisingly, therefore, it is conventionally referred to as the Egyptian 'alphabet' (table 9.3). For obvious reasons these are the most flexible phonograms, lending themselves most easily to fully phonetic writing, but they never replaced the other groups. It would be possible, theoretically, to use the monoconsonantal signs much like a Semitic consonant alphabet and write Egyptian texts purely alphabetically. But in practice a mixed orthography was

Table 9.1. *Some common triconsonantal hieroglyphs*

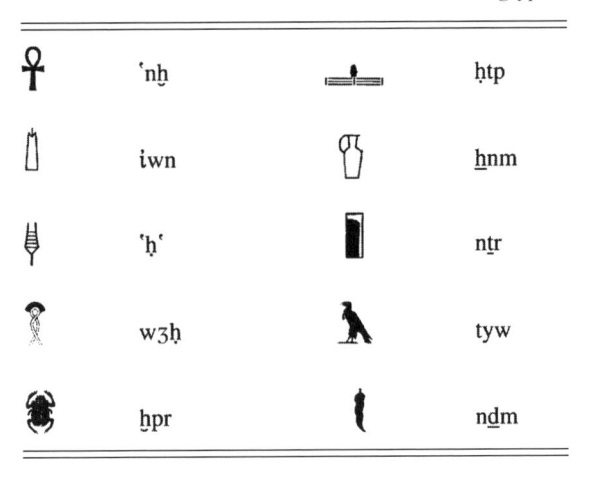

	ꜥnḫ		ḥtp
	iwn		ḫnm
	ꜥḥꜥ		nṯr
	wꜣḥ		tyw
	ḫpr		nḏm

Table 9.2. *Some common biconsonantal hieroglyphs*

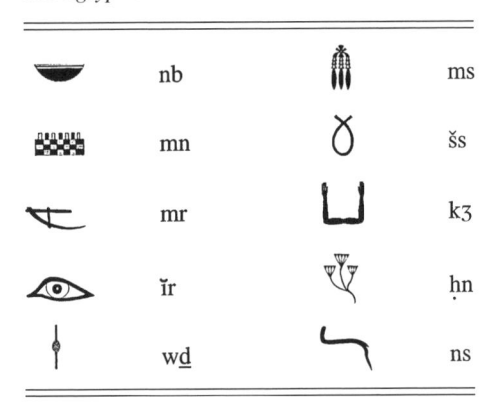

	nb		ms
	mn		šs
	mr		kꜣ
	ỉr		ḥn
	wḏ		ns

preferred (Ritner 1996). Monoconsonantal signs were used to write words for which no other signs were available. They were used for grammatical formatives, mostly left out in early texts, and they also served to write some very common words, which tend to be short in all languages. Yet another function was as a phonetic complement. Monoconsonantal signs were used to repeat the final consonant of words written by means of tri- and biconsonantal signs, probably to emphasize the fact that the word was written phonetically (Davies 1987: 33). Thus a word *mn* would actually be spelt *mn-n* where the second *n* is a monoconsonantal sign which only repeats the final of the preceding biconsonantal sign, and is not pronounced.

Table 9.3. *The uniconsonantal hieroglyphs of the Egyptian 'alphabet'*

Sign	Transliteration	Sign	Transliteration
	ꜣ		ḥ
	i		ḫ
	y		ẖ
	ꜥ		s
	w		š
	b		ḳ
	p		k
	f		g
	m		t
	n		ṯ
	r		d
	h		ḏ

Determinatives form the last category of hieroglyphs, functioning as semantic classifiers that help to specify the meaning of a word or to distinguish it from a homonym. Many of them are generic, indicating materials, actions, people, gods, body parts, animals, tools, as well as abstract notions such as movement, force, time and so on. Having no phonetic interpretation, determinatives improve legibility, since in addition to conveying semantic information they mark word boundaries. It is common that more than one determinative is used for a word, which makes for rather pleonastic writing.

Some hieroglyphs belong to all three classes of signs. For example, the sign of the ground-plan of a house is variously interpreted as the word *pr* 'house', as

176 *Mixed systems*

Table 9.4. *Hieroglyphic determinatives*

🧍	man	⌂	house
👤	woman	▭	sky
👤	god	⌒	desert, foreign land
👤	king	( )	hold, enclose
👤	enemy	×	break, tear
👤	death	⌇	book, abstract object

the biconsonantal phonogram *pr* used in writing various words, for example *prj* 'to edit', and as a determinative of the generic concept of space when attached to words like 'room', 'place', 'hall' and so on. Many hieroglyphs are polyfunctional in this manner. Since, moreover, logograms, phonograms and determinatives are not distinct in graphic appearance, the resulting writing system is quite complex. At its centre are conventionalized sign combinations interpreted as words.

Akkadian writing

The Old Akkadian writing system is the result of adapting Sumerian cuneiform to a Semitic language. Around the turn of the third millennium, the speakers of Akkadian migrated to Mesopotamia, where they first came into contact with writing. At the time, the Sumerians, whose language is of unknown extraction, had a full-fledged writing system consisting of both logograms and syllabograms. The former provided the nuclear content structure, while the latter were used supplementarily for grammatical formatives and other linguistic detail. Sumerian is an agglutinative language, which expresses grammatical relations by means of prefixes and suffixes. The earliest stage of Sumerian writing is limited to a 'telegraphic' style focussing on content morphemes only, but gradually rebus-derived syllabograms of the V, CV and VC type appeared, restricting the reader's choice as to the exact phonetic interpretation of the logograms. The fully developed system furthermore employs semantic determinatives that have no phonetic interpretation but help to determine the interpretation of other signs. According to one estimate (Civil 1973: 26), Sumerian writing consists of between 60% and 43% logograms, between 54% and 36% syllabograms, and about 3% determinatives.

All of these signs were shaped in the same manner as configurations of wedges impressed onto the plastic surface of clay tablets. When this tripartite system was applied to Akkadian it underwent certain changes, but it remained a mixed system. On one hand, the adaptation process led to simplification, since the proportion of syllabograms increased while that of logograms decreased. On the other hand, the system became more complicated, because many signs already polyvalent in Sumerian writing became even more so in Akkadian.

Logograms were most easily adapted to writing Akkadian. It was just a matter of reinterpretation. For instance, the sign for Sumerian LUGAL[3] 'king' was reinterpreted as Akkadian ŠARRU which also means 'king'. Translation thus was at the beginning of Akkadian writing. Where one-to-one translation equivalents were available this was a straightforward procedure. Yet, the result was not an Akkadian instead of a Sumerian reading of the word sign. In many cases the Akkadian interpretation supplemented rather than replaced the Sumerian word value, as Sumerian words were incorporated as loanwords into the Akkadian language. Since many logograms had more than one lexical interpretation in Sumerian already, they ended up having three or four readings in Akkadian. For example, by semantic extension the Sumerian logogram ⊢╪ for DINGIR 'god' was also interpreted as Sumerian AN 'sky'. In the course of the adaptation it came to be employed for both Akkadian lexical equivalents, ILU 'god' and ŠAMU 'sky'. In this manner quite a few logograms are polyvalent in Akkadian writing, which, of course, raises the question of how the intended interpretation can be determined. The answer lies in the combination of logograms and syllabograms in Akkadian writing.

Syllabograms were taken over from Sumerian unchanged, that is, the Sumerian phonetic interpretations of cuneiform signs were kept as they were. Signs interpreted in Sumerian as *bi, bu, ni, nu, zi, zu* were also interpreted as *bi, bu, ni, nu, zi, zu* in Akkadian. Still the complexity of the subsystem of syllabograms increased, basically for two reasons. One is that the Akkadian scribes had to augment their syllabary because the inventory of Sumerian syllabograms was insufficient for the Akkadian language. They did this by using the Akkadian reading of logograms for their sound value only or parts thereof. For instance, the Sumerian logogram ŠU 'hand' was first given the additional Akkadian reading QATU 'hand' from which the syllabic value *qat* was derived. In this manner, many new CVC syllabograms were introduced for which no Sumerian signs were available.

---

[3] Following conventional Orientalist usage, capital letters are used for transliterating logograms and italics for syllabograms in this section.

Syllabograms gained increased significance in Akkadian writing because the inflecting nature of the language made it difficult to interpret the grammatically correct form of a logogram without additional cues. Syllabograms thus were employed to enable an unequivocal interpretation of Akkadian texts. If the syllabogram *im* is appended to the Sumerian logogram LUGAL it is clear that rather than the Sumerian loanword its Akkadian reading is intended. The whole expression LUGAL-*im* must be interpreted as *šarrim*, the genitive form of Akkadian *šarru* 'king'. Alternatively, words can be spelt out entirely with syllabograms, which, however, does not necessarily make reading easier because, having been reinterpreted several times, many syllabograms are highly polyvalent. The sign KUR, originally a Sumerian logogram meaning 'mountain', acquired six different phonetic interpretations, *mad*, *nat*, *lad*, *sad*, *šad* and *kur*. To mitigate the ensuing uncertainty of interpretation yet more use was made of syllabograms. Akkadian has many CVC syllabograms, but CVC syllables are often broken up and written as CV_1-V_1C where V_1-V_1 is to be interpreted as a single vowel, *lu-um* is *lum*, *gi-ir* is *gir* and so on.

Determinatives, too, were taken over from Sumerian. Their frequency of occurrence in Akkadian is somewhat higher than in Sumerian, no doubt because of the higher level of polyvalence of both logograms and syllabograms. Determinatives precede or follow logograms, but also occur with words written with syllabograms.

As in Egyptian writing, the above three classes of signs are not graphically distinct, lending Akkadian texts a uniform appearance. Although the proportion of syllabograms increased significantly in comparison with Sumerian texts, the syllabographic subsystem was never standardized and streamlined to the extent that logograms and determinatives could be dispensed with. Rather than pushing the adaptation process further in the direction of a consistent and comprehensive syllabary, the Akkadian scribes apparently cherished the literary culture of the Sumerians and held on to some key features of the cuneiform system they had inherited from them. As we shall see in the next section, the Japanese showed a very similar attitude towards Chinese writing.

Japanese writing

When the art of writing spreads across language boundaries from literate to non-literate cultures, it is common that the written language is adopted along with the writing system. This is what the Akkadians did when they mastered Sumerian cuneiform, and this is what the Japanese did when they learned Chinese characters. Language and script cannot be separated easily at first. To both the Akkadians and the Japanese writing for a long time meant writing a foreign language, Sumerian in one case, Chinese in the other. Once they began to write their own language, they adapted the existing system rather than creating a new one. Yet, the resulting new system departs from the structural make-up of its model in fundamental ways. Although there are many differences in detail between the adaptation of Sumerian cuneiform for Akkadian and that of Chinese characters for Japanese, some basic parallels are also in evidence. Since, with the exception of a handful of original creations (cf. chapter 10), all writing systems past and present are adaptations, it is of general interest to see what these parallels are.

The scribes who first used cuneiform signs to write Akkadian, and Chinese characters to write Japanese adjusted a fully developed writing system to a typologically different language. Three mechanisms are involved in this process.

(1) Extant signs are reinterpreted. This is of some importance for the perspective on writing that informs this book. That is, the graphic sign precedes its linguistic interpretation. As we have seen in the previous section, the Akkadians took Sumerian logograms and assigned them an additional lexical interpretation, typically the Akkadian translation equivalent of the Sumerian word. The Japanese did exactly the same, providing Chinese characters with Japanese interpretations, while holding on to the Chinese interpretation, too. Notice that assigning an extant sign an extra interpretation is conceptually quite different from using a sign to represent a word. In the latter case the underlying question is, 'How do I write this word?' But this is not primarily what the Akkadian and the Japanese scribes asked themselves. Rather, their point of departure was the sign, which they changed by giving it an additional interpretation it did not have in the original system. As a result, Chinese characters have a Chinese reading, called Sino-Japanese, and a Japanese reading in Japanese, just as cuneiform signs have a Sumerian reading and an Akkadian reading in Akkadian.

(2) Signs are used for their phonetic interpretation only. Conditions are a bit different here, because the Sumerians were using cuneiform signs both as logograms and as syllabograms before the Akkadians adopted the system, while purely phonetic usage of Chinese characters was more limited in Chinese. Yet, like the Akkadians the Japanese used the adopted signs for their syllabic values only, disregarding their meaning in Chinese. But while the Akkadians left the form of Sumerian syllabograms unchanged, although they made some adjustments for their sound values, the Japanese gradually changed the graphic shape of the Chinese characters they used for their syllabic values only, eventually developing a set of signs immediately recognizable as syllabograms. These are the two kana syllabaries discussed in chapter 4. Once again it is clear that extant signs were reinterpreted and subsequently graphically modified so as to mark them off as a functionally distinct set of signs not to be confused with Chinese characters.

180   *Mixed systems*

Table 9.5. *Kokuji, Japanese native characters*

Kokuji	Reading	Meaning	Kokuji	Reading	Meaning
凧	tako	kite	垈	nuta	anvil
栂	tsuga	hemlock spruce	娚	meoto	married couple
凪	nagi	a calm	枠	waku	a frame
噺	hanashi	story	畑	hatake	field
峠	touge	mountain pass	笹	sasa	bamboo grass
凩	kogarashi	wintery wind	栃	tochi	horse chestnut
椛	momiji	Japanese maple	籾	momi	unhulled rice
躾	shitsuke	upbringing	辻	tsuji	crossroad
鑓	yari	spear	辷	sube-ru	to slip

(3) New signs modelled on those of the adopted system are created. There are some cuneiform logograms in Akkadian that do not exist in Sumerian. They were created by the Akkadians and are sometimes called 'artificial' Sumerograms (Krebernik and Nissen 1994). In the same manner, the Japanese created some new characters, applying the principles of graphic composition of Chinese characters. In contradistinction to the Chinese characters that were reinterpreted, these *kokuji* or 'native characters' have no Chinese reading (although there are some exceptions where a pseudo-Chinese reading was invented). Many *kokuji* were created for Japanese words that lack obvious Chinese translation equivalents, thus bearing witness to the writer's need to adapt the system to the Japanese language. Obviously, the same words can be written syllabically, but in many regards logographic writing was more appealing to the Japanese scribes, as it was to their Akkadian colleagues. Some examples of *kokuji* are given in table 9.5. Notice that readings consist of two to four syllables, as is typical of Japanese words, whereas Chinese characters are consistently interpreted as one syllable in Chinese.

These are the basic adaptation mechanisms, but in actual fact the polyvalence of signs brought about in the process is even more complex. In Akkadian texts many cuneiform signs have multiple Sumerian and Akkadian interpretations. Similarly, Chinese characters have multiple Chinese and Japanese readings in Japanese usage. The signs of both donor systems were doubly adopted, for sound and meaning. A difference between the Mesopotamian and the Far Eastern case is that Sumerian was superseded as a spoken language by Akkadian, while Chinese was unaffected

明 **MEI, MYŌ, MIN**

a-, aka-, aki-, saya-

明月	*meigetsu*	bright moon
明日	*myōnichi, ashita, asu*	tomorrow
明	*min*	Ming (Dynasty)
明かし	*a(kashi)*	proof
明るい	*aka(rui)*	light
明らか	*aki(raka)*	bright
明けし	*saya(keshi)*	pure
明がね	*ake(gane)*	a bell at dawn
明明	*meimei, akaaka*	brightly, very clear

Figure 9.4 *Polyvalence in Japanese writing*

by the fact that Japanese adopted the Chinese script. The Chinese language thus continued to change with the obvious consequence that the phonetic interpretation of Chinese characters also changed. Since the Chinese written language was used and held in high esteem by the Japanese for more than a millennium after they had begun to write Japanese, these changes made themselves felt in Japanese usage as well (Seeley 1991). Moreover, the Japanese adopted Chinese loanwords not only over a period of many centuries, but also from different parts of China, and sometimes they would adopt the same word more than once. The result is a proliferation of interpretations associated with a given Chinese character. For example, 明, *ming* in Chinese, has three different Sino-Japanese readings, *myō*, originating in sixth-century Chinese, *mei*, reflecting eighth-century Chinese, and *min*, based on fourteenth-century speech of the Hangchow region. In addition, the character is given several Japanese interpretations, *a-* and *aka-* among them. Some of the most common characters are also the most polyvalent. The character 日, whose semantic interpretations include 'sun', 'day' and 'Japan' has two Sino-Japanese readings, *nichi* and *jitu*, and as many as twelve Japanese readings.

In addition to these readings that can be traced to particular Chinese words or Japanese translation equivalents, Chinese characters have many haphazard and obscure readings in Japanese that cannot be predicted or reconstructed. Some are used to write non-Chinese loanwords, which thus lose their conspicuousness. Before any measure of standardization was achieved, writers took many liberties assigning characters peculiar readings at will. In its present form the system is streamlined and regulated. The official 'List of Chinese Characters for General Use' (*Jōyō kanji hyō*) of 1981 contains 1,945 characters with a total of 4,087 readings. In technical literature many more characters are in use. The industrial standard list of characters for computers JIS X"0H-1990 includes 6,353 characters.

This raises the question of how the correct reading of a character can be determined. Regularization and standardization notwithstanding, it is still difficult to design a foolproof algorithm to this end (Unger 1984). Context plays an important role, as compounds tend to have Sino-Japanese readings, but compounds with Japanese or mixed readings also exist. In some cases compounds have more than one reading, as for example 昼飯, which can be read *chūhan*, in Sino-Japanese, or *hiromeshi*, in Japanese, both words meaning 'lunch'. Nothing in the script itself indicates which is the intended. The Japanese, therefore, rely to a large extent on memorizing written words rather than their components. Grammatical information also helps. Grammatical formatives written in kana usually reduce the choice of possible interpretations of the preceding character to one. The character 歩 has several interpretations, the Japanese readings *ayumu* 'to step' and *aruku* 'to walk' among them. By writing the final syllable of the verbs in kana it becomes clear which is intended.

   歩く to walk 歩む to step
   ARU-ku   AYU-mu[4]

Where the reader cannot be expected to figure out the intended reading, kana in small type (called *furigana*) can be attached as reading aids to the character in question. A writer may also use this device to indicate that a reading that deviates from the standard is intended. For instance, by adding *furigana* to the first two characters of the following sentence, Natsume Sōseki indicated that he wanted them interpreted as *yamamichi* 'mountain path' rather than the standard near-synonymous *yamaji*.

   やまみち
   山路を登りながら、こう考えた。
   YAMAMICHI
   YAMAJI -o NOBOrinagara, kou KANGAeta
   Climbing the mountain path I thought this.

The Japanese writing system, then, is a mixed system on two levels. One is the subsystem of Chinese characters. Unlike the Chinese model, where each character is interpreted as a syllable-cum-morpheme in a relatively straightforward manner

---

[4] Small capitals for Chinese characters, small letters for kana.

(chapter 2), the Japanese adaptation is polyvalent in nature, most characters allowing for two or more interpretations that may be meaningless syllables, syllable-cum-morphemes or entire words. The Japanese interpretation of Chinese characters cannot be properly described as homophony, where several phonetic units of the same kind are assigned to a single character. Rather, it is a matter of assigning characters functionally quite different units. At another level, the Japanese is a mixed system in that it employs two functionally distinct subsystems, Chinese characters and kana. The fact that roman letters, usually with a phonetic interpretation approximating English pronunciation or English letter names, have also become a regular part of Japanese texts further adds to its syncretistic nature (Saint-Jacques 1987). All this points to the primacy of the written sign, which is to be assigned its proper interpretation. Since the Japanese writing system lacks a defining unit common to all elements of its signary, this has to be done in accordance with a variety of strategies.

English writing

In contradistinction to Japanese, the English writing system has a defining unit, or so it would seem. On the face of it there is just one class of signs, alphabetic letters. But this is deceiving, because an analysis of English writing gets nowhere if it starts out with the assumption of individual letters having uniform canonical interpretations. In fact, the English writing system has long been recognized as a mixed system, although this has only rarely been pointed out explicitly (Stubbs 1996). It is mixed in the sense that there are units of different kinds and that the conventions for their interpretation are diverse. Albrow (1972), for example, identifies three sets of rules that operate in the English orthography: basic, romance and exotic. Chomsky and Halle's (1968) important work on the sound pattern of English is often quoted as hailing English writing as a near-optimal morphophonemic orthography, but building on this research Klima (1972) argued that there are at least six ways of analysing the English writing system, ranging in abstractness from phonetic to morphophonemic. Thanks to the multifaceted history of English writing (Scragg 1974) several different sets of rules combine, and sometimes compete with each other. And when all rules are exhausted, a considerable area of unpredictable spellings remains. This is not the place for a comprehensive account of the English writing system, which has been intensively researched and written about in recent decades. Several monograph-length studies are readily available (see, e.g., Haas 1969; Venezky 1970; Dewey 1971; Vachek 1973; Carney 1994; Cook 2002). Suffice it for present purposes to point out some of the characteristics that expose the mixed nature of English orthography.

Since the English writing system makes use of the Latin alphabet, the most common approach to its analysis is to figure out how these letters are to be interpreted. Attempts at compiling a comprehensive list of correspondences between sound and spelling of English have yielded various results. According to Dewey (1971), the typical vowel can be spelt around twenty different ways. Later researchers such as Nyikos (1988) have found that the forty-odd phonemes of English correspond to 1,120 different graphemes. That is, on average twenty-eight different letters and letter combinations are given the same phonetic interpretation. It is often assumed that letter-to-sound correspondences and sound-to-letter correspondences are mirror-image processes. Yet, once again we must ask whether 'How do I spell this word?' and 'How do I pronounce this word?' are really analogous questions equally suitable as a point of departure for the analysis of a writing system. Intuitively, it seems to make more sense to say that <-ough> in *through* is interpreted as [uː] than to say that [uː] is represented by <-ough>. The difference is in perspective and not just terminology because, surely, nobody ever thought of representing [uː] by <-ough>. Rather, this peculiar correspondence, as many others, results from certain changes in the language, in this particular case the loss of a final velar fricative in certain words (compare *rough*). Both the autonomy principle and the historicity principle come to bear here and must be referred to if such correspondences are to be explained. To make this point more explicit, we should say that in most varieties of twenty-first-century English [uː] is one possible interpretation of <ough> in word-final position.

As a general rule, spelling conventions, once established, are more resistant to change than speech, which is another way of saying that written words tend to have an autonomous existence and phonetic interpretations are adjusted. Since sound changes, though regular, are contextual, not all words in which a certain sound occurs are affected in the same way. Individual letters are, therefore, bound to become more polyvalent in the course of time. Graphic autonomy is, indeed, quite important in English spelling where morpheme constancy is often given priority over phoneme constancy. Two or more words are thus identified as incorporating the same root morpheme, for example *critic – criticize* (<c> – [k, s]); *elect – election* (<t> – [t, š]); *tyrannical – tyrant* (<y> – [ɪ, aɪ]; *bomb – bombard* (<b> – [ø, b]). In these as in many similar cases the semantic relationship of the word pairs would be obscured if the spelling were adapted to the pronunciation. A related mechanism that also weakens the unequivocal grapheme-phoneme link is homophone differentiation. *For, four, horse, hoarse, morning, mourning* are common examples. It accentuates the independent existence of graphic words, the price for more distinctness at this level being a higher degree of complexity at the level of grapheme-phoneme correspondence.

Table 9.6. *English consonants*

	labial	dental	alveolar	palato-alveolar	palatal	velar	glottal
stop	p b		t d			k g	
fricative	f v	θ ð	s z	ʃ ʒ			h
affricate				tʃ dʒ			
nasal	m		n			ŋ	
liquid			r l				
glide					j	w	

Table 9.7. *English vowels and diphthongs*

	front	central	back
high	i ɪ		ʊ u
mid	e ɛ	ɚ ʌ	ɔ o
low	æ	a	

Diphthongs

| aj | aw | oj |

The highest degree of irregularity is in the vowel system. Written <a> has eleven different interpretations (Carney 1994), and the back vowel [u] can be spelt eighty different ways if names are included (Nyikos 1988). This high degree of polyvalence in both directions is due to a combination of internal and external influences. By the eleventh century, English had something like a standard orthography, which was much more regular than it is now. But then two things happened:

```
                         phonemes

                 /eɪ/    c_ake
                 /ɑː/    _arm
                 /e/     m_any
                 /ɔ/     equ_ality
         <a>     /ɔː/    _all
                 /æ/     _adult
                 /i/     vill_age
                 /ei/    p_atient
                 /ə/     comp_any
                 /ɸ/     dist_ance
```

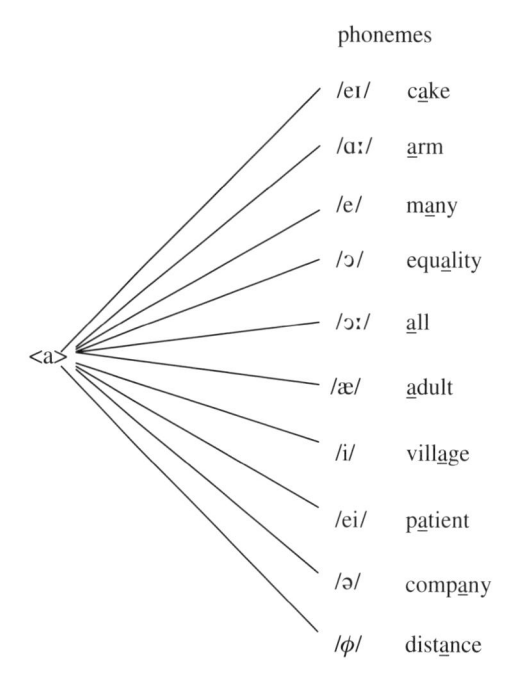

Figure 9.5 *English <a> and its phonemes*

the Norman Conquest, which brought many Romance loanwords and their spelling conventions in its wake; and the Great English Vowel Shift whereby, for example, [eː], [iː] and [uː] became, respectively, [iː], [ai] and [au]. These changes were only inconsistently observed in writing with the result that the interpretation of Modern English vowel letters is both irregular and deviates markedly from other European languages, although individual spellings can be explained. For instance, that [iː] is spelt <ee> in some words such as *deed* and *greed* but <ie> in others such as *grief* and *thief* is due to the fact that Middle English conventions are followed in the former and French in the latter words.

Many spellings were introduced following the principle of etymology. The idea that the correct way to spell a word should lead back to its origin won wide acceptance, especially regarding the actual or assumed Latin origin of French loanwords. Hence, French *dette* (from Latin *dēbitum*) and *samon* (from *salmōnem*) were respelt *debt* and *salmon*, reflecting Latin spelling rather than French pronunciation. Again, there were many inconsistencies giving rise to modern spellings such as *honour* and *hour*, but *ability* from the French models *honneur*, *heure* and *habilité*, which were all pronounced with initial vowel when they were borrowed into English. In a similar fashion, <th> and <ph> spellings came into the language with Greek-

English writing 187

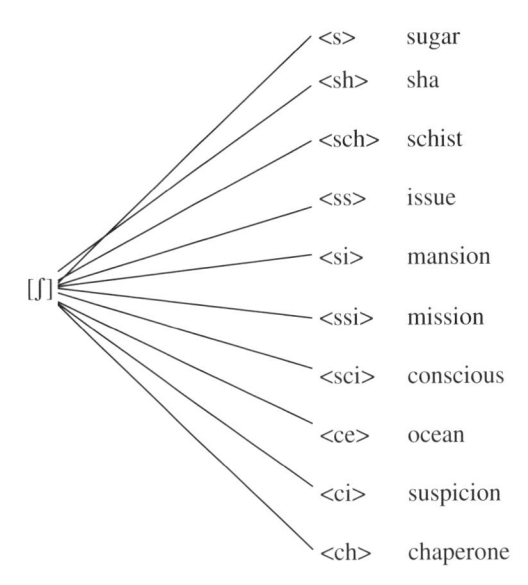

```
              <s>    sugar
              <sh>   sha
              <sch>  schist
              <ss>   issue
              <si>   mansion
[ʃ]
              <ssi>  mission
              <sci>  conscious
              <ce>   ocean
              <ci>   suspicion
              <ch>   chaperone
```

Figure 9.6 *English [ʃ] and its graphemes*

or Latin-origin words, sometimes reflecting false etymologies, for example *author* from Latin *auctor*. There is, however, consistency in that <ph> for [f] is tolerated only in Greek-origin words like *alphabet* and *orthography*, but not in Anglo-Saxon words such as **phrank* and **phree*.

There are several other principles at work in English orthography, some of which have been identified with logographic writing (Sampson 1985). Venezky (1970) points out that two-letter words are likely to be grammatical words, whereas homophonous lexical counterparts, which could have been spelt with two letters, add a consonant or vowel letter. Pairs such as *be/bee*, *by/buy*, *or/oar* suggest that grammatical and lexical homophones are held orthographically distinct. Short content words such as *egg* and *eye* seem to confirm the tendency to reserve two-letter spellings for grammatical words, but *ox* is an obvious counter-example. Groups of words such as *right, rite, write, Wright,* and *cove, love, move*, as well as nonce spellings such as *have, people, psalm, said, do, done, egg* and the matchless *women* also exemplify a logographic component in the English writing system. It is further reinforced by unphonemic spellings that are not motivated by morpheme constancy, such as *debt, knight, science*, where letters with no phonetic interpretation serve to make the word more distinct. Many other idiosyncratic words of English cannot be derived by sound-letter correspondence rules, however limited in application. The <h> in *ghost*, for example, reflects Dutch usage, which had a certain influence when printing was introduced to England from the continent in the fifteenth century. Clearly, then, there are subsystems in English writing, if indeed systems they are, which are more sensitive to lexical distinctions than they are tied to morphophonology or phonology.

In sum, English writing makes use of different units. At least three levels must be distinguished: (1) individual letters and digraphs and trigraphs, which are regularly interpreted as phonemes, allophones often being ignored; (2) letter sequences interpreted as morphemes; (3) orthographic words that cannot be reduced to grapheme–phoneme correspondences or morphophonological alternations. In addition, there are strata of the written lexicon that are held distinct by virtue of different spelling conventions or the absence thereof. Anglo-Saxon words, Romance (and Greek-origin) words, and etymological cognates follow different rules. Even though a sizeable part of the English lexicon – estimates vary between 50 per cent and 70 per cent – consists of words that are spelt regularly in one way or another, English orthography cannot be reasonably assigned to one type of writing system. It is a mixed system.

Conclusion

The writing systems discussed in this chapter are very diverse in almost every respect: their histories, their languages and their basic units. But there is one characteristic they have in common: they are all mixed systems. In Egyptian writing words make use of more or less standardized sign combinations, just like in English. Both the Akkadian and the Japanese systems require multiple interpretations of signs in terms of different lexical strata reminiscent of the orthographic marking of Romance words in English. All four systems employ many signs that can be interpreted unequivocally only in context. The main lessons to be learned from these examples are threefold. (1) Mixed systems exhibit a high degree of polyfunctionality of signs. (2) Words are spelt in conventional ways whereby lexical (morphemic) identity often overrides straightforward phonetic interpretability. (3) Most importantly, the basic graphic units, no matter whether they belong to one system only, as in Egyptian, or several distinct systems, as in Japanese, do not allow a reasoned classification of the writing systems they serve. The crucial difference here is that between a **notation** – Egyptian hieroglyphs, cuneiform signs, Chinese characters, roman letters – and a **writing system**. As all four examples clearly show – Egyptian and Akkadian could be fully phonetic, but are not; Chinese characters are not the same in Japanese as in Chinese; alphabetic letters do not make for a phonemic writing system in English – the notation does not determine the nature of the writing system.

Questions for discussion

(1) What is the function of determinatives, and why are they used in Egyptian and Akkadian writing?
(2) In what respect can Akkadian and Japanese writing be said to be similar?
(3) The letters of the Latin alphabet are conventionally interpreted as phonemes. English uses the Latin alphabet. Yet its orthography has logographic tendencies. How can we explain this?
(4) Explain the difference between a notation and a writing system, discussing specific examples.

10
History of writing

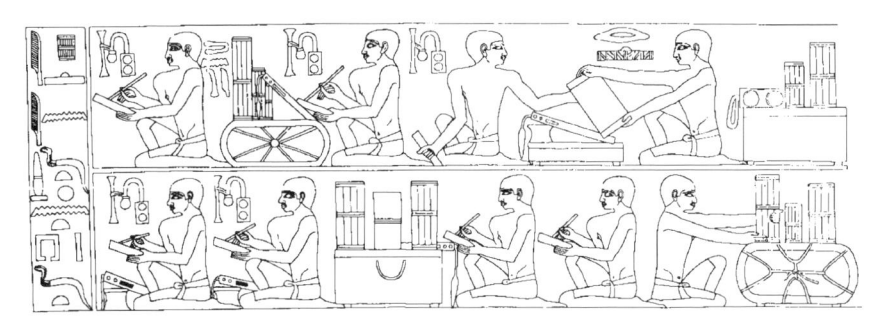

Figure 10.0 *Egyptian office. Mural relief in the tomb of official Ti in Saqqara (fifth dynasty). Mémoires publiés par les Membres de l'Institut Français d'Archéologie Orientale du Caire.*

> Inventions usually represent responses to particular needs and result from gradual improvements upon previous achievements. This is certainly true of writing.   Asko Parpola

> There is a direction in the growth of knowledge related to changes in the means of communication and, specifically, to the introduction of writing.
> Jack Goody

Three major issues in the history of writing are the following:

(1)   How did writing come into existence?
(2)   How did writing develop?
(3)   How did writing spread?

If these were just factual questions, they could be dealt with independently, one by one. But this is not so. The meaning of the first question is, of course, dependent on the definition that we have in mind of what writing is, making it hard to avoid a theoretical commitment. The advent of writing by definition marks the transition from prehistory to history, but in the initial stages it is by no means easy to determine whether a visible mark or image should count as writing or some other form of graphic expression, whether a linguistic interpretation is intended and, if so, to what extent it can be conventionally realized. The idea of writing emerged bit by bit, only gradually revealing its potential as one of the most powerful tools of civilization builders. The second question, similarly, presupposes a point of departure for the development to take off, and, to make things even more complex, it defies neat separation from the third question, because the spreading of scripts to other language areas is a major factor in their development. For instance, the addition of vowel letters to the Semitic consonant alphabet was effected when it was applied to a non-Semitic language, Greek.[1] The adaptation of the Chinese script to Japanese led to the reduction of meaningful characters to meaningless syllabic signs. These are two of the most prominent examples illustrating the interaction of the dispersion and development of writing systems.

As in the history of language, things are quite involved in the history of writing, and I will not pretend otherwise. It would be nice, for example, if we could study the history of writing just in terms of structural developments. However, since system-internal and external factors interact, it is not so easy to distinguish the history of writing from other aspects of the history of civilization. What appear to be superficial material aspects of writing – the surface, the implements, and the mechanics of the hand – have contributed to determining the form and through it the structure of writing systems. The cuneiform writing system, for instance, would never have become what it was had not clay been available in abundance and used as building material in the ancient cities of Mesopotamia. What is more, writing answers certain needs and serves certain functions, which must be assumed to influence the history of its development. This is not to say that causal links can easily be established between structural features of writing systems and literacy practices. Certainly attempts to tie literacy rates or functions to particular types of writing systems, or, conversely, to demonstrate that certain social conditions favour the development of certain types of writing systems have not been very successful. Yet, few would deny that writing grows out of, and has important consequences for, economic, social and cultural developments. Some scholars have viewed the advent of the written word as the watershed between traditional and modern societies (e.g. Ong 1982; Goody 1986). Subsequent researchers have been more cautious, arguing that writing played less a causal role than an ancillary one in social and psychological change (Olson 1994; Christin 2001). That these changes were too profound to fathom within the confines of a single scientific field is, however, generally agreed. In what follows I will, therefore, not

---

[1] Writing in 440 BCE the Greek historian Herodotus explains that 'the Phoenicians... introduced into Greece upon their arrival a great variety of arts, among the rest that of writing, whereof the Greeks till then had been ignorant' (*The History of Herodotus*, Book V, translated by George Rawlinson). He was right about the Phoenician source of the alphabet, but apparently was unaware that writing had been present in Greece in the form of the Minoan scripts earlier (cf. Woodard 1997).

hesitate to venture across disciplinary boundaries where such excursions promise to help us better to understand that part of the unfolding of human communication systems that consists of visual marks of some durability interpreted as language.

Origin

Most scripts would not have come into existence if others had not spread. This much can be said with certainty, since the vast majority of all scripts past and present can be traced back to a handful of original creations. In the past, from the nineteenth to the mid-twentieth century, the question of a single or multiple origin of writing dominated the discussion. The monogenetic theory enjoyed a certain support which was not always grounded in disinterested research. Religious notions of humanity as a divine creation and a hierarchy of peoples closer or further removed from God were allowed to contaminate scholarship. The Sumerians whose Gilgamesh epic, rediscovered in the 1870s, speaks of the deluge, casting new light on the Bible, were commonly credited with inventing the ancestor script from which all others derive. In the meantime, however, evidence for the independent origins of writing in Mesopotamia, China, Mesoamerica and elsewhere has been piling up. No connections with other scripts can be established for some undeciphered scripts such as Proto-Elamite (Damerow and Englund 1989), developed around the end of the fourth millennium BCE in Susa, western Iran, Linear A (Palaima and Sikkenga 1999), used by the Minoans in Crete (ca 1800–1450 BCE), and the Indus script (Parpola 1994), which came into existence around the middle of the third millennium BCE in the Indus Valley. Monogeneticism is, therefore, no longer considered a viable theory. Everything in present knowledge points to the fact that writing was engendered independently by several relatively advanced sedentary civilizations characterized by urbanization, division of labour, and a surplus economy. Although, since the first spectacular decipherments of ancient scripts early in the nineteenth century, progress in the historiography of writing has been considerable, the tapestry that tells the whole story is still full of holes and ragged spots waiting for reconstruction.

The origin of Mesopotamian cuneiform is well documented by a wealth of clay tablets. Little doubt remains that accounting and administration of the temple economy were the primary functional context of this writing system (Nissen, Damerow and Englund 1990). At its beginning were crude pictures scratched into wet clay. Their referents were natural objects and artifacts, cattle, sheep, bushels of wheat, clay vessels. When these pictorial signs were given a linguistic interpretation, writing was born. From archaeological evidence we know that this happened in the Uruk Period, late in the fourth millennium BCE. Pictures, then, are at the root of Sumerian writing, but there was another accounting system consisting of variously shaped clay tokens, which were used in many parts of the Middle East for thousands of years prior to the appearance of writing. Several correspondences between clay impressions of these tokens and early Sumerian inscriptions have been discovered (Schmandt-Besserat 1992), opening up the possibility that there was another input into the formation of the Sumerian writing system. To what extent this was the case is still a matter of debate.

The pictorial basis of another ancient writing system that emerged at the western end of the fertile crescent, Egyptian, is even more striking because it was never lost. The significance of the pictorial signs, that is, the underlying semiotic relationship, changed much like in the Sumerian case when they came to be interpreted as signs of names of objects rather than as signs of objects (figure 10.2). But unlike cuneiform signs, which lost all iconic features, the ornate pictorial appearance of hieroglyphics was as clear when the Egyptian writing system finally fell into disuse in the fourth century CE as in the earliest stages. This is precisely what makes the origin of Egyptian writing more enigmatic than that of cuneiform, because it commences suddenly in full bloom without any precursors or primitive stages. The earliest Egyptian hieroglyphs appear around 3000 BCE, a bit later than Sumerian writing. Since there *were* influences of the advanced Mesopotamian culture upon Egypt, and since it seems unlikely that a major innovation such as writing should not be adopted by a budding civilization, it has been suggested that the Egyptians adopted the idea of writing from the Sumerians by 'stimulus diffusion'. However, this is no more than speculation, for Egyptian hieroglyphics show no similarity with the Sumerian system (Fischer 1989). What is more, cult and the creation of a centralized state rather than economic imperatives seem to have precipitated the creation of writing in Egypt.

Egypt's importance for the history of writing is not limited to its being the birthplace of hieroglyphics and one of the world's greatest literary cultures. It is also a strong contender for the ultimate honour of being the homeland of the Semitic consonant alphabet that, through its Greek and Latin descendants, has spread to more languages than any other writing system. Hard proof is still scanty, but since the great British Egyptologist Alan Gardiner first suggested it in 1916 in a famous article, 'The Egyptian Origin of the Alphabet', evidence has been accumulating to support the theory that there is an Egyptian inspiration behind the invention of the Semitic alphabet. The first traces of alphabetic writing were discovered in the Sinai desert, where early in the second millennium BCE turquoise miners at Serabit el-Khadim left behind a number of short inscriptions in an unknown script. The number of distinct signs in these inscriptions was less than thirty, too small for a syllabary. Since the Egyptians had a set of pure phonograms embedded

Figure 10.1 *Sandstone sphinx from the Middle Kingdom temple at Serabit el-Khadim with inscriptions in Egyptian hieroglyphs, 'Beloved of Hathor, [Mistress] of turquoise', left, and in the Proto-Sinaitic script, 'Ba'alat', right.*

in their writing system, which they used for writing foreign names, Gardiner[2] surmised that the Sinaitic signs were modelled on these hieroglyphs. He further assumed that the signs were pictographic and that their phonetic interpretation, like that of phonographic hieroglyphs, was acrophonic, the initial sounds of the names of the depicted objects being the sound values of the letters. For a group of four recurrent signs that along with a hieroglyphic inscription referring to Hathor, goddess of turquoise, appear on a little sandstone sphinx (figure 10.1), he suggested the reading b- ' -l-t which could be interpreted as Ba'alat, the Semitic equivalent of Hathor. Gardiner's analysis was carried on by American orientalist William Albright, who called the script 'Proto-Sinaitic' and suggested that the language it encoded was West Semitic. Albright identified the Egyptian models of twenty-three Proto-Sinaitic letters and their Semitic interpretations (table 10.1), lending further credence to the hypothesis that there is indeed an Egyptian-Semitic link, which could very well explain the origin of Semitic consonant writing. Where exactly the Proto-Sinaitic script originated – in Sinai, in Egypt or in Palestine – is, however, uncertain, and further epigraphic discoveries are hoped for to resolve this question.

Turning next to the Far Eastern cradle of writing, the origin of the Chinese script, too, is uncertain and waiting to be elucidated by further archaeological findings. The pictorial source of Chinese characters is uncontested, but new artifacts keep coming to light, forcing history to be rewritten. A small stamp seal excavated by Fredrik T. Hiebert, archaeologist of the University of Pennsylvania, at Anau depe close to the Iranian border in Turkmenistan in the summer of 2000 has been carbon-dated to about 2300 BCE. It bears an inscription of four characters

---

[2] See Gardiner, Peet and Černý 1952, Albright 1948, and Sass 1988 for details of the Proto-Sinaitic decipherment.

Table 10.1. *Proto-Sinaitic signs. From Sass 1988, Table 4.*

Sign (with variants)	Transliteration
	ʒ
	b
	g(?)
	d
	h
	w
	ḏ
	ḥ
	y
	k
	l
	m
	n
	ʿ (?)
	p
	ṣ
	q
	r
	š
	t
	signs with unknown value

of an unknown system, which, some Sinologists (Victor Mair (2001) among them) claim, look very Chinese. Since the first appearance of Chinese writing, in the form of 'oracle-bone inscriptions' and bronze moulds, known so far dates from the Shang dynasty (from the seventeenth century BCE to about 1025 BCE), this finding is very puzzling. For if the new finds prove to be Chinese, they hold the potential of pushing back the origin of Chinese writing by as much as a millennium. What is more, the discovery may lead to a reappraisal of writing in China for which Chinese scholars have always claimed an indigenous origin. The inscription on the little stamp seal makes the question of whether there was a Western connection worth pursuing. Rare as discoveries such as the Anau inscription are, they remind us that the early history of writing is still very much work in progress.

This is certainly true of the dozen or so autochthonous writing systems of Mesoamerica. The earliest monumental inscriptions were made by the Zapotec in the seventh century BCE (Coe 1992). But they already represent a sophisticated culture with stone monuments, massive buildings and a complex dating system that has much in common with the Maya calendar. Little is known of the early forms of this civilization, how it relates to the Olmec and the Maya (Justeson and Kaufmann 1993), and what caused visible signs to be transformed into writing. It seems that pictures and iconographic signs were gradually given linguistic interpretations as logographic signs with phonetic components being added as the script developed. But this is no more than a most general enumeration of logical steps, while the particulars of the origin of Mesoamerican scripts lie in the dark. 'The relationships between the scripts is not well understood, and there is lack of agreement about which is the earliest' (Macri 1996: 172).

Two points, then, can be noted here about the origin of writing: (1) it is rooted in pictures, and (2) it happened several times. Writing grew out of drawing. In addition to the recognizable imagery of the earliest written symbols, indirect evidence for this can be seen in the fact that several ancient languages, such as Egyptian, Chinese and Greek, had only one verb meaning both 'writing' and 'drawing'. Yet pictures do not become writing naturally. A major conceptual transformation is necessary to turn a picture, more generally, a visual sign of a natural object, into a sign of the name of an object (figure 10.2). Present evidence suggests that this remarkable reinterpretation was effected independently at least four times in different parts of the world, Mesopotamia, Egypt, China and Mesoamerica. However, many details of the full story remain to be filled in, details as to how this was brought about, how things and their names were conceptually separated, and how Sumerian, Egyptian, Chinese and Zapotec draughtsmen reinvented themselves as scribes, replacing objects by words as the primary referent of the visible marks they inscribed on clay, stone and bone.

Development

Once pictorial signs are conventionally linked with a linguistic interpretation, the foundations of writing are in place. Then begins its development from a

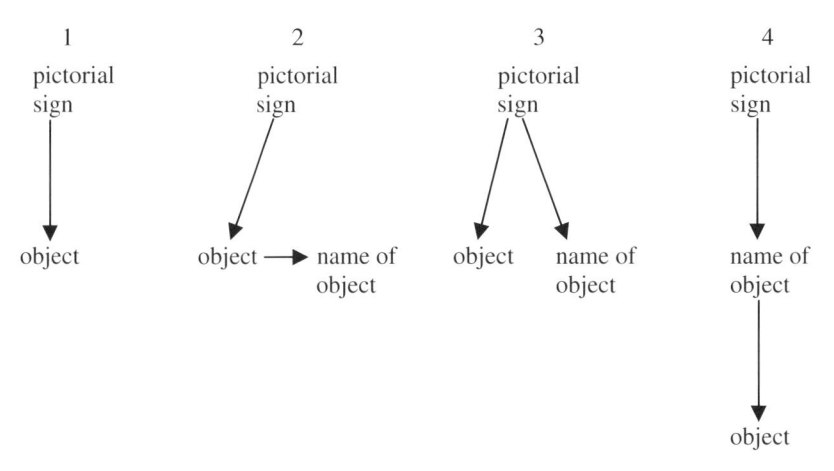

1	2	3	4
pictorial sign	pictorial sign	pictorial sign	pictorial sign
↓	↙ ↘	↙ ↘	↓
object	object → name of object	object name of object	name of object
			↓
			object

Figure 10.2 *Sign system to writing system: changing semiotic relationships. (1) A picture refers to an object; (2) a picture refers to an object and its name, the object being the primary referent; (3) a pictorial sign can refer to either an object or its name; (4) the primary referent of the pictorial sign is the name of an object which in turn refers to the object.*

rough recording system to a flexible instrument of visual communication, accurate, unequivocal and capable not only of expressing every nuance of human language, but also, and more significantly, of opening up new dimensions of linguistic expression. Some essential features and tendencies common to the development of all ancient writing systems are the following: pictographic origin, linguistic interpretation, the rebus principle of exploiting homophony, graphic stylization, normativism and historicity. The question is whether a general theory of the development of writing can be derived from these commonalities. Gelb (1963) made a first attempt to provide such a theory based on the quasi-Darwinian notion of 'unidirectional development'. He was convinced that development meant progress, that writing evolved not only in a particular direction but also toward a particular goal, the roman alphabet.

'What this means in the history of writing is that in reaching its ultimate development writing, whatever its forerunners may be, must pass through the stages of logography, syllabography, and alphabetography in this, and no other, order' (Gelb 1963: 201). Gelb's outstanding service to the study of writing was that by advancing a clearly formulated theory he gave a highly complex and diverse field a common direction. His theory provided a basis for the comparative analysis of writing systems, a hypothesis that could be tested, a model that could be checked against the available evidence. He assumed two underlying principles that have driven the development of writing: economy of effort and the 'natural' desire to reduce complexity. As he saw it, the history of writing led inevitably to, and culminated in, the twenty-six letters of the alphabet.

Modern scholarship has not confirmed the unidirectional theory of writing unconditionally. The real picture is more muddled, and certain aspects of Gelb's teleological evolutionism must be rejected. Harris (1986) speaks of 'the evolutionary fallacy', while others have criticized Gelb's theory as an expression of alphabetocentrism, if not Western supremacism. These allegations are not entirely groundless, because Gelb viewed the evolution of writing as paralleling that of culture. Three stages followed one upon another: the Sumerians accomplished the first breakthrough, the linguistic interpretation of visual signs, called 'phonetization' by Gelb; by extensively applying the rebus principle the Northern Semites created syllabographic writing; and the Greeks crowned the development by differentiating consonant and vowel letters, treating both as units of the same kind. That this perspective was informed by cultural Darwinism is clear from Gelb's contention that 'this sequence of the stages of writing reflects the stages of primitive psychology' (1963: 203).

Quite apart from the questionable precepts of cultural Darwinism, there are a number of obvious problems with the unidirectional theory of writing and its underlying principles. As we have seen, the Egyptians had incorporated in their writing system a subsystem of, depending on the time period, twenty-four or twenty-six monoconsonantal signs that came pretty close to being an alphabet. Nevertheless, they stuck to their highly complex mixed system of logograms, phonograms and determinatives until the very end of their literary tradition. If anything, the Egyptian writing system grew more complicated as the centuries went by. Changes can be observed in the history of Egyptian letters, but hardly progress in the sense of economizing effort and reducing complexity. Why? The obvious answer is that the Egyptian writing system was more functional than it seems to the alphabetic mindset of decipherers and readers, none of whom ever *heard* the Egyptian language spoken. The Chinese, too, knew at an early stage of their literary history that characters could be interpreted for their sound values alone and that by using them as syllabic signs their number could be drastically reduced. Yet not only did they continue to interpret characters for both meaning and sound, they also allowed them to proliferate. In stability and continuity Chinese writing is unique. The Japanese reduced Chinese characters to a syllabary, but strangely refused to climb the last step of the evolutionary ladder to reach the alphabetic peak. Not only that, they did not even take advantage of the new system to alleviate the burden of Chinese characters but used it side by side with them. Should we regard the resilience of the Egyptian script and the more than two millennia of Chinese and Japanese literacy, as malformations, as evolutionary blind alleys and remnants of primitive psychology? Something is obviously wrong with this perception.

Looking at the purported evolutionary ascent from the top end, the Greek and Latin alphabet, can only reinforce our doubts about unidirectional development. Notice that 'the alphabet is neither a revolutionary type of writing system, nor a uniquely efficient one' (Parkinson 1999: 183), and it surely is not the ultimate destination of development. If Man (2000: 42) says, a bit tongue in cheek, perhaps, that 'Sumerian writing matches English in complexity', he implicitly makes an anti-evolutionist statement. Greek and Latin alphabetic writing was relatively simple, English is complex. Citing examples such as the many spellings of /ʃ/, as in *nation, shoe, sugar, mansion, suspicion, ocean*, among others, which can be pronounced correctly only if recognized as part of a syllable, he argues that 'English is, in part, a syllabary' (2000: 97). According to Gelb's developmental stages of logography, syllabography and alphabetography, this is not supposed to happen, because 'there is no reverse development' (Gelb 1963: 201). Part of the problem lies in the sequence of Gelb's stages, because alphabetography is not of the same order as the other two. The elementary signs of logography are interpreted as words, those of syllabography as syllables, but those of alphabetography are not interpreted as alphabets. The unwieldy name itself suggests that it is not easy at all to say what the elementary signs of the alphabet should be interpreted as. This is so because, as I have noted, the alphabet is not a writing system but a notation that serves a potentially infinite variety of writing systems. To call the often-stated principle that the optimal alphabet represents every sound of a language by a single sign and that each sign has only one sound an idealization hardly does justice to the confusion that inspired it. It is a fundamental fallacy because it sees polyvalence in both directions as an aberration rather than a functional operating principle. It is moreover based on the erroneous premise that the complexity of writing systems can be measured along a single dimension, the number of elementary signs. The binary code has only two elementary signs, 1 and 0. Is it easier to handle than codes with more extensive signaries?

Let us pursue the idea of linear evolution a bit further. How is evolution carried forward? We can lean on George Kingsley Zipf here, who has worked out a theory of the Principle of Least Effort as it applies to language. Zipf (1949) compares language to the tools on a carpenter's work-bench. Over time, the carpenter will adapt his tools and arrange them on the work-bench in such a way as to minimize work expenditure. The Principle of Least Effort will make him find the right balance between the number of tools he needs and the number of jobs he can perform with each. There will be a few small multipurpose tools within close reach and many specialized tools used only occasionally, which will end up at the far end of the work-bench. Eventually a functionally ideal arrangement of tools for the carpenter's work will emerge. In like fashion, Zipf argues and demonstrates with a wealth of statistical data that the Principle of Least Effort governs the speakers' communicative work expenditure, a process that is reflected through perpetual change in the linguistic system. Length of time is too crude a measure for work expenditure. Instead, every instance of using a tool and, by analogy, a language, counts as a work unit. In a meticulous study of the impact the mechanics and control of the hand had on the development of writing, van Sommers (1989) has shown the reduction of permissible wedge positions in early cuneiform writing to be the result of principles of economy. At the level of graphic design features the idea of an evolution driven by economy of effort seems to work, but this is not the only level of complexity of writing systems. Van Sommers also points out that further simplification of the cuneiform code was probably halted as a concession to readers, that is for the sake of legibility. For an efficient graphic code to be developed the countervailing demands of encoding (minimizing manual work) and decoding (maximizing visual discrimination) must be taken into account. And this is of course only one of several levels of complexity. Another is the system of linguistic interpretation. If we assume that evolution is propelled by work units defined as instances of use, then written English should be the most advanced system, because more written material has been produced in English than in any other language. If by 'advanced' we mean simple and efficient, this is plainly wrong. Not even the most committed alphabetocentrist would deny that systems simpler than English spelling can be conceived of and actually exist. Are we forced, then, to conclude that English is exceptional or that unidirectional development has run afoul when English spelling was codified?

It seems more reasonable instead to discard the unidirectional theory. Present-day English orthography constitutes the latest stage of more than two and a half millennia of alphabetic writing, but it is not alone. French is a close rival when it comes to involved spelling rules. In both cases, as in many others, many intervening factors have thwarted an undisturbed linear development towards simplicity and systematic stringency. Just like the long life of Egyptian writing and the persistence of Chinese characters in the face of allegedly more advanced alphabetic writing, so the complicated application of the alphabet in English spelling shows that the aim to align all writing systems in one evolutionary hierarchy is too ambitious. Evolutionism is based on two tacit assumptions: (1) that writing is nothing but representation of speech, and (2) that there is one optimal way to do this. The history of writing in the real world rather than that of abstract ideas teaches us that both are wrong. It is a mistake to see writing systems as quasi-natural organisms governed in their development by natural laws. Every script is a cultural implement subject to human ingenuity and error, created under certain circumstances for certain purposes and a certain language. To be sure, there are common traits, and economy of effort clearly is one of the guiding principles of human behaviour. Yet there is plenty of room for waste, extravagance and manifestations of the human mind defying bare utility. Cultural inertia and conservatism (we've always spelt it this way) and normativism (there must be a correct spelling) are strong forces at work in every literate community. They have little to do with writing systems as such or with their efficiency, yet they exercise a strong influence on their formation. Writing is a cultural product *par excellence*, and its development must be understood as such rather than in quasi-naturalistic terms.

Spread

Nowhere is the cultural embeddedness of the world's writing systems more apparent than in their dissemination. Writing spread with trade and religion. Phoenician traders carried their letters westward (Cross 1989), along the North African coast (where they still live on in the form of the Tifinagh script of the Berberphone people in Algeria (van den Boogert 1997)), and to Greece where the Greeks adapted them to their needs and passed them on, through the Etruscans, to the Italian peninsula. There a number of Italic or Tyrrhenian alphabets evolved (table 10.2). One of them, the Latin alphabet, eventually spread further afield as the script of the Roman Empire and the Holy See. The consequences of this expansion are still visible today. The present distribution of scripts[3] testifies to the close link between writing system and religion. Boundaries defined by scripts largely coincide with those of faith.

That the Latin alphabet has been adapted to write so many languages is a direct result of the Christianization of Europe. Using the Latin script to provide many hitherto unwritten languages with an alphabet, the Summer Institute of Linguistics, an aggressive Protestant missionary organization, continues to prove the validity of David Diringer's (1968) much-quoted dictum that 'alphabet follows religion'. The distribution of the Greek alphabet and its Cyrillic extension corresponds to the realm of the Orthodox Church, Cyril (827–69 CE) having been a Greek missionary who converted the Slavs. To this day, the division between catholic Rome and orthodox Constantinople runs right through the erstwhile Serbo-Croatian language area, the catholic Croatians using the Latin alphabet, the orthodox Serbs the Cyrillic. Many other branches of Christianity had earlier developed their own alphabets, Coptic in Egypt, Serto in Syria, Nestorian in Iran, among them. The establishment of the Armenian and Georgian churches resulted in the creation of the Armenian and Georgian alphabets. The Arabic alphabet, an offshoot of the Aramaic-derived Nabataean script, issued from the Arabian peninsula in the wake of the Islamic conquest and now serves as many as one hundred languages in largely Islamic

---

[3] For a good map of the contemporary distribution of major scripts, see Murawiec 2001: 95.

Table 10.2. *The Etruscan and Latin alphabets*

Tyrrhenian	Etruscan	Archaic Latin	Classical Latin
A	A A	A A	A
B		B B	B
⟨ C	⊃ ⟩	⊃	C
D		◁	D
ᛖ	⇃	⇃	E
ᛖ		⇂	F
I	I 千 ⼟	I	(G)
⊟	⊟ ⊟	⊟	H
⊕ ⊙	⊗ ⊙		
l	l	l	I
k	⼅	⼅	K
レ	↓	↓	L
⋈	⋈ ⋈	⋈	M
N	⋈ ⋈ h	⋈	N
⊞			
⊙ O		O	O
P	⇃	⇃ ⌐	P
⋈ M	⋈		
◁ ϙ	ϙ ϙ	ϙ ϙ	Q
P	◁ ⋈	⋈	R
⟨	⟨ ⋈ ⟨	⟨ ⟨	S
T	✝	T ✝	T
Y Υ	Y V Y	V	V
+		X	X
ϕ			
Y	⊕ Y ⋈ 8 8 8 ⼅		

countries on three continents, Africa, Asia and Europe. Each one of the original letters of the Arabic alphabet is revered as a creation of God himself. For many languages texts in Arabic script are the only source of information on the diachronic development. Other branches of Aramaic are linked with other religions, such as the Manichean script, which is said to have been invented by Mani, the Iranian founder of the Manichean religion. The Chinese script spread to regions beyond the Chinese empire, such as Vietnam, Korea and Japan together with Buddhism and Confucianism. Travelling along another route, from India through Sri Lanka to South-east Asia in the period 100 CE to 800 CE, Buddhism also helped to spread the Brāhmī-derived Pali script. And in the north another Brāhmī-branch, the Tibetan script, developed as the vehicle for the Lamaist variety of Buddhism. The Hebrew square script, too, is a holy script serving Jewish communities both for Biblical and modern Hebrew and their respective local languages, for example Yiddish, Ladino and Judeo-Arabic.

Of course, religion was not the only force behind the dissemination of writing systems. Trade and empire also played major roles, as exemplified, for instance, by the spread of cuneiform from Assyrian/Babylonian to other languages in the region, the wide dissemination of the Aramaic script as the clerical medium of Imperial Aramaic, or, in modern times, the promotion of the Russian alphabet in the Soviet Union. Many languages, such as, for example, Korean, Mongolian, Persian, Romanian, Turkish and Vietnamese have been written in different scripts, reflecting changing political alignments. However, in the early history of writing, when secular and spiritual authority was not sharply differentiated, cult was the paramount catalyst of collective identity. The powers to be were by the grace of God and truth was found in The Book, which, of course, came along in a particular script one had to master in order to gain access to sacred and liturgical texts. Conversion, in the usual sense of the word, therefore, depends on holy scriptures: Buddhist sutras, the Torah, the Bible, the Qur'ān. Writing systems not associated with a proselytizing faith, like oral religions, usually remained local.

As scripts spread, they change, both in outer form and linguistic interpretation. Structural adaptations are necessary whenever a script is transferred to another language, sometimes resulting in a change of type (e.g. syllabomorphographic Chinese characters > syllabographic Japanese kana). But even where no change of type is brought about, the transformations associated with the diachronic development of languages and the diffusion of scripts across linguistic boundaries pose an intriguing theoretical problem. Consider first the outer form. In handwriting every instance of a letter differs slightly from every other. In the early days of writing this vicissitude was even more pronounced with letter orientation, size and junction often lacking uniformity. Rotation, mirror image, compression, stretching, skewing and truncation are only some of the graphic transformations of letters, for which descriptive terms are readily available. Such transformations exhibit collective tendencies, much like dialects, which coalesce to form 'national hands', as school-induced standardization takes effect. These aspects of writing, that is, interpersonal and collective differences in the form of written symbols, are often disregarded as not belonging to the study of writing *systems*. But this is wrong, as Watt (1994) has most cogently argued.

Upon closer inspection, the distinction between writing system and script and, since Gutenberg, that between script and font, are less clear than the different terms suggest. We say that both French and English are written with the same script, roman. However, there is no <ç> in English, to mention but one obvious example. Hence, there is no complete congruence of the English and French scripts, a fact that can be analysed at the graphic level alone, although it obviously relates to differences between the two writing systems, that is, linguistic correspondence rules. Clearly, French <ç> is there for a reason. The reason is that a roman *c* in French is interpreted as [s] before <e> and <i>, as in *cent* [sã] and *civil* [sivil], but usually as [k] before <a>, <o> and <u>, as in *café* [kafe], *code* [kɔd] and *culte* [kylt]. A cedilla is added where *c* is to be interpreted [s] even though it precedes <a>, <o> or <u>, hence *face* [fas], but *façade* [fasad]. This would not be absolutely necessary, because no native speaker of French would pronounce *facade* [fakad]. Dutch, for example, also has a *c*-spelling with similar [s, k] phonetic interpretations and no cedilla to mark the difference. But this is how the French system works. The point at issue here is that formal and systematic differences evolve together, gradually differentiating one system from another. From a systematic point of view, a French <c> is not quite the same as an English <c>, or a Dutch, German or Spanish one, for that matter, let alone a Chinese Pinyin <c>, because its phonetic interpretations are different and because it contrasts with <ç> which it does not in English.

This raises the non-trivial question of the c-ness of <c>. Is it possible to identify the essence of <c>, both in terms of graphic form and linguistic interpretation? Does it help to go back to the roots? Roman <c> derives from Greek Γ, gamma, which in turn goes back to Semitic ג, gimel. G and C were not differentiated in Greek and archaic Latin, which means that a Latin C/G was a far cry from an English *c* or any other contemporary *c*. There is no prototype *c*.[4] This argument applies, *mutatis mutandis*, to other letters of the alphabet and to the alphabet as a whole. Conceptually, this is very remarkable because what we are left with is not a small set of definite letter forms and equally definite phonetic interpretations. Rather, what the alphabet does is to match two jerry-built fuzzy sets in such a way that we get the impression of definiteness and exactitude. This has important implications for the more general question of how to differentiate one system from another. The theoretical problem, much like that of a dialect chain and diachronic periodization, is how to subdivide a continuum into non-arbitrary phases and units. It is the problem of where local variation and temporal shift turn into distinction.

There are, of course, clear cases. For example, the Old Hebrew alphabet and the Mongolian alphabet are two distinct systems (table 10.3). Whatever similarities

---

[4] Hofstadter (1982) presents convincing arguments that no set of parameters can capture the essence of an abstract category such as a letter form.

Table 10.3. *The Old Hebrew and Mongolian alphabets*

Transliteration	Old Hebrew	Transliteration	Mongolian Initial	Mongolian Final
ʼ		a		
b		e,ö,ü		
g		i		
d		o,u		
h		ö,ü		
w		n		
z		ŋ		
ḥ		x		
ṭ		g		
y		b		
k		s		
l		š		
m		t,d		
n		l		
s		m		
ʽ		ts,dz		
p		dž,j		
ṣ		x,g		
q		r		
r		w		
š		p		
t		dz		
		h		

between letter forms one may detect do not seem to go beyond chance, and phonetic interpretations are radically different. Old Hebrew has twenty-two letters, while Mongolian has twenty-three, which, moreover, come in initial and final forms. Old Hebrew is written horizontally from right to left, while Mongolian texts run

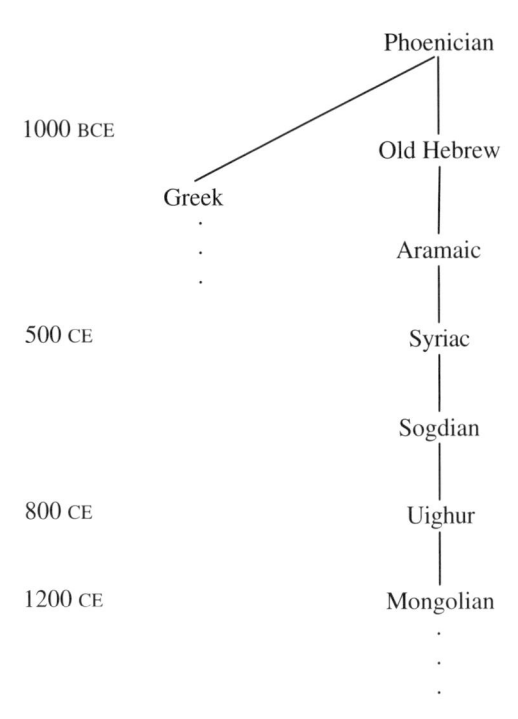

```
                              Phoenician
 1000 BCE                    /    |
                            /  Old Hebrew
                        Greek     |
                          .       |
                          .    Aramaic
                          .       |
  500 CE                       Syriac
                                  |
                               Sogdian
                                  |
  800 CE                       Uighur
                                  |
 1200 CE                      Mongolian
                                  .
                                  .
                                  .
```

Figure 10.3 *Schematic derivation of the Mongolian alphabet*

from top to bottom in vertical columns shifting from left to right. Except that both systems consist of visible symbols with more or less canonical phonetic interpretations, they do not seem to have much in common, and I have to stress the 'more or less'. Yet we know that the Mongolian alphabet of the thirteenth century CE derives from the Old Hebrew, which antedates it by more than two thousand years.

Thanks to the great spatial and temporal distance separating Old Hebrew from Mongolian it is not difficult to decide that these are two different scripts and two different writing systems. The story of transmission from Palestine to the Far East is long and involved. Old Hebrew was transformed into the Aramaic script, which spread to Persia first where it was taken over by the Sogdians, an Iranian people, who in turn bequeathed it to the Turkic Uigurs from whom eventually the Mongols obtained it. This is roughly how it went, in hindsight a straightforward development, a distinct number of steps, as summarized in figure 10.3. However, if we could reconstruct in minute detail the line that connects the two ends it would not be so easy to cut it up into discrete portions each of which constitutes a separate system. Certain changes are sudden, making it easy to draw a line. The rotation of the script by 90° was effected abruptly in the eighth century CE by

Table 10.4. *Phoenician and Greek sibilant letters*

	Phoenician			Greek	
name	sign	phonetic value	name	sign	phonetic value
zain	I	[z]	zeta	Z	[ds], [sd]
samek	⟂	[s]	xi	Ξ	[ks]
sade	↑	[ts]	san	M	[z]
shin	W	[š]	sigma	Σ	[s]

the Uigurs rather than gradually, and so was the addition to the alphabet of five Tibetan-derived letters by Lama Tsorji Osir. But many other changes were gradual, especially those bearing on letter forms. The early history of the Semitic consonant alphabet is fragmentary, attested in occasional and scattered inscriptions. What is often called the Canaanite alphabet was used by various peoples, such as the Ammonites, Arameans, Edomites, Israelites, Moabites and Phoenicians, whose writings can be described with equal justification as different historical phases and regional variants of the same script or as different scripts. Giving them different names suggests different systems, even though there really is an unbroken chain.

The great continuity of the alphabetic tradition is attested by a feature often disregarded as trivial, the order of letters. Actually, it is a most remarkable fact that the letters of the Semitic alphabet have been handed down to us through roughly 140 generations in the form of the same canonical list, give or take a few additions and omissions along the way.[5] However, fragmentary epigraphic records often do not allow us to perceive continuity. It is difficult, therefore, clearly to distinguish the spread of a writing system from its evolution, derivation and transmutation into a new system.

Nevertheless, certain discontinuities do justify the postulation of distinct systems. Whenever a writing system is transmitted to a typologically different language we can expect it to undergo drastic adaptations. The syllabic component of cuneiform quickly increased when the script was transferred to Akkadian from Sumerian in the second half of the third millennium BCE. The adaptation of the alphabet to Greek from its Semitic source around 800 BCE, at the latest, likewise was a far-reaching break, evidenced, for example, by the peculiar mismatch of the phonetic interpretations of the Semitic sibilant letters zain, samek, sade and shin and their Greek derivatives zeta, xi, san and sigma (table 10.4, cf. Woodard 1997, ch. 6). In conjunction with the innovation of letters for vowels, this clearly

---

[5] Notice that Watt (1989) has argued that the alphabetic letter order is not arbitrary but originates in an organized matrix reflecting phonological knowledge.

makes for a different system. The adaptation of the roman alphabet to Vietnamese necessitated the introduction of a whole layer of diacritics to mark tonal and so-called suprasegmental features unknown in Semitic and Indo-European languages. It would be premature, however, to conclude that the boundaries of language families and scripts coincide. The Brāhmī-derived Indian scripts have spread from Indo-European to Dravidian languages without a change of type, and Chinese characters have been used for Korean and Japanese, which are genetically unrelated to Chinese and structurally very different. Since writing systems are artifacts, they are subject to deliberate manipulation. Tolerance for complexity and the desire to have a writing system that looks like, or, on the contrary, differs from, another are variable factors not easily captured by general laws. The history of writing, therefore, cannot rely much on universal tendencies, but has to investigate the spread and transmutation of every script in its own right.

Notice that this holds true, in particular, for the relationship between writing and language. Although historical linguists have been slow to incorporate influences of writing on language into their theories, it can hardly be denied that such influences exist. To a considerable extent historical linguistics consists in determining the phonetic interpretations of ancient written records and in explaining changes in the relationship between spelling and sound. The historical study of the Indo-European, Semitic and Sino-Tibetan language families has profited greatly from the availability of such records, but it has generally been taken for granted that writing is a representation of speech, however imperfect. Little attention has been paid to writing as an agent of linguistic change. Writing as a channel of language contact, especially loanwords (e.g. Sumerograms in Akkadian and other cuneiform languages such as Hittite and Elamite; Chinese character words in Korean, Vietnamese and Japanese; a Greek stratum of lexemes and morphemes in Latin and modern European languages), spelling pronunciation, and language standardization are three areas calling for more systematic and comparative study in this regard. Virtually nothing is known about the differential potential of specific writing systems to influence linguistic development, and much remains to be explored about how writing has shaped linguistic activities, attitudes and concepts, that is, how language in our highly literate societies differs from what it was in oral societies. Changes in the way we perceive language and theorize about it must also be understood as an aspect of the history of writing.

Conclusion

The history of writing is incomplete, in many respects. It continues to unfold as we write, nowadays on computer screens rather than clay tablets, and so do our insights into the development of human communication and information storage by means of visual signs from the beginnings of history itself to the present. Since the great decipherments of the nineteenth century, especially of Egyptian hieroglyphics and Assyrian cuneiform, and their twentieth-century successors, Proto-Sinaitic, Linear B, Hittite hieroglyphic and Maya, the known universe of writing has expanded. Of several sign systems that were not formerly recognized as such we now know that they are writing, notably those of Mesoamerica. Our view of the history of writing has been affected by these insights. Monogeneticism is dead, and so is unidirectional evolutionism, assuming we do not allow history to end with the appearance of the Greek alphabet. As we have seen in this chapter, writing was invented more than once: to the best of our knowledge, at least four times, in Mesopotamia, Egypt, China and Mesoamerica. Caution is in order, though, because the Indus script, Linear A, the new finds of Turkmenistan and some other systems still hold many unresolved questions.

In this brief overview we have also seen that the development of writing systems must be explained in terms of how visual signs are interpreted, as much as in terms of what they are meant to encode. And this holds true of the dispersion of scripts from one language to another as well. The reinterpretation of signs plays a crucial role in the adaptation of scripts. (For example, Phoenician *'*, *h* and *j* were reinterpreted as Greek *a*, *e* and *i*, respectively.) All this points to the shortcomings of the representational approach, which views writing as a representation of speech and tries to explain its history as an approximation towards this ideal. But writing is an artifact. Writing systems are highly complex instruments shaped by the interaction of material and systematic factors, which relate to, but are not the same as, those of speech. Both speech and writing are subject to diachronic change, but there is no simple dependency here. It is the task of the history of writing to explain the interaction between the two.

Questions for discussion

(1) Is evolution theory a suitable model for the history of writing?
(2) Why is the transmission of scripts across linguistic boundaries of special significance in the history of writing?
(3) What is the historical significance of the order of the letters of the ABC?
(4) Why is English spelling a problem for the theory of unidirectional development of writing?
(5) How and why does the history of writing differ from the history of language?

11
Psycholinguistics of writing

> When he was reading, his eye glided over the pages, and his heart searched out the sense, but his voice and tongue were at rest.   Augustine
>
> Writing requires deliberate analytic action on the part of the child. In speaking, he is hardly conscious of the sounds he produces and quite unconscious of the mental operations he performs. In writing, he must take cognizance of the sound structure of each word, dissect it, and reproduce it in alphabetic symbols, which he must have studied and memorized before.   Lev S. Vygotsky
>
> Foreigners always spell better than they pronounce.   Mark Twain

In the previous chapter we noted that the introduction of writing implies a cognitive reorientation and a restructuring of symbolic behaviour. Names of objects are conceptually dissociated from their denotata, as signs of physical objects are reinterpreted as signs of linguistic objects, names. In a second step, signs of names are recognized as potentially meaningless signs of bits of sound, which are then broken down into smaller components. This cognitive reorientation first happened five thousand years ago, and philosophers have speculated about the human capacity to produce and process visible signs since antiquity. The scientific investigation of the literate mind is, however, of relatively recent origin. Yet, testifying to the importance of writing in modern times, it has grown into a vast field of research dealing with the psychological differences between *Language by Ear and by Eye*, to quote the title of a seminal book by James Kavanagh and Ignatius Mattingly. The general questions pursued in this field are (1) What happens when readers read and writers write?, and (2) How are these processes different from what happens when listeners listen and speakers speak?

Reading and writing are extremely complex processes that are subject to scientific study on at least three different levels. First, there is the external hardware, the physiologies of eye and hand, which are to writing what the auditory and articulatory systems in human beings are to speech. There is obvious correspondence – eyes and ears are for input, while the hand and vocal tract are for output – but no isomorphic parallelism. Eye movements directed towards a fixed input signal are essential for reading, whereas ears are fixed input channels directed towards an evanescent input signal. On the production side, both vocal tract and hand execute coordinated movements controlled by, respectively, auditory, visual and kinaesthetic monitoring and feedback loops. But activating this process while simultaneously engaging in other activities, chopping onions, for example, is more natural in the former case than in the latter, because hand and eye do not seem to be adapted for language processing in the same way that vocal tract and ear are (Tzeng and Hung 1981: 241). In this sense, too, written language is more of an artifact than speech.

At the other end of the reading and writing process is the brain, the internal hardware, which controls both monitoring and muscular activity as well as the conversion of physical signals into linguistic and cognitive units and structures, and vice versa. The scientific investigation of the relationship between brain and language since the mid-nineteenth century has focussed on pathological language disorders, attempts at localizing linguistic functions in the brain being at the forefront. Since certain kinds of brain damage were found to result in distinct reading disorders and others where subjects retained the ability to read but could not spell, theories have been developed trying to understand the neuropsychological specifics of language-processing disturbances in speaking, comprehension, reading and writing, as well as writing system-specific disturbances (see, e.g., Paradis, Hagiwara and Hildebrandt 1985). The question thus arises whether *written* language, a historically recent invention and ontogenetically usually acquired after speech, has any implications for the organization of language in the brain. This is the proper territory of aphasiologists and neurolinguists.

The psycholinguistics of writing is concerned with the middle ground between the mechanics of the external hardware and the ways in which the brain works when dealing with written language. At issue are the mental processes involved in reading and writing, the linguistic knowledge that is necessary, the cognitive consequences of manipulating written symbols for thinking, and the acquisition of written language production and reception skills. It is impossible to present a review of even the most important enquiries and theories that have been advanced in this area. This chapter instead discusses some of the key problems that have occupied research about reading and writing in recent years.

Reading

The bulk of all reading research is concerned with writing systems that make use of the alphabetic notation. This is hardly surprising, given the wide distribution of the roman alphabet and its unassailable dominance in Western countries, which are at the forefront of psychological research. It should be kept in mind, however, that this focus on the alphabet has implications for the questions that are asked, how they are pursued, and eventually for theory formation. To mention but one striking example, recognition of the word as the primary processing unit of fluent reading was an important step in developing a theory of reading (Henderson 1982). But suppose Chinese character literacy were the default case. In the event, the assumption that it is words, rather than other units, that are processed in reading would be the most intuitive pretheoretical point of departure. Although the reading process in Chinese, Japanese and Korean has been investigated intensively by experimental and cognitive psychologists (Cheng and Yang 1989; Taylor and Taylor 1995; Yamada 1997), it is safe to say that most research on reading has been informed by explicit and implicit assumptions about alphabetic writing systems and their scientific descriptions, if only because it has been carried out by researchers who are proficient readers of alphabetic scripts. Notice, further, that linguists and philologists have described and classified writing systems variously as logographic, ideographic, morphosyllabographic, syllabic, phonemic and so on. These classifications are one thing; but how writing systems work in terms of actual perception, processing and production is another. Psycholinguistic research into reading can shed new light on classifications derived from structural descriptions, and lead to a reassessment of how meaningful they are.

Word superiority

As I have indicated repeatedly, no writing system is 'pure' in the sense that its units are interpreted as linguistic units of one type only: words, morphemes, syllables or phonemes. What does this imply for the reading process? Typically, alphabetic writing systems recognize units of various structural levels of language. In antiquity, texts were commonly redacted in *scriptura continua*, without word boundaries (Saenger 1991). The reader had to do then what the writer does now, in modern print literacy; he had to divide the string of letters into words. At the time, reading was usually aloud and for shared consumption. Manuscripts were recited over and over again, the message of the text being recovered through oralization. Silent reading was exceptional, and even to medieval observers such as Augustine, whom I quoted at the outset of this chapter, still a matter of astonishment and wonder. If letters were so obviously meant to be interpreted as sounds, how was it possible to read them and 'search out the sense', while 'voice and tongue were at rest?' Rephrased in modern terminology this is still one of the central questions of reading research. It revolves around what is known as the problem of phonological recoding to which we will turn presently. But first a few more words about words, for words, unlike speech sounds, are meaningful, and this is what reading is all about. We read not to intone, but to understand.

The minimal coding unit of alphabetic writing systems is smaller than the word, but modern alphabetic texts consist of words divided by spaces, reflecting the intuitive insight that word separation facilitates reading. The reader's general task is to 'search out the sense' that is linguistically encoded. How then is a mental representation of the message of the text reconstructed on the basis of processing visible signs? Written words consist of sequences of letters. Are these read sequentially one after another from left to right, or, in Semitic scripts, from right to left? This assumption could be corroborated if pronounceable sequences of letters (pseudowords) were read as readily as words, but this is not the case. The 'word superiority effect' (Cattell 1886; Reicher 1969), discovered in the early days of psychological reading research, falsifies the sequential processing hypothesis. Letters are recognized more quickly and more accurately when presented within words (e.g. *input*) than in isolation or within pseudowords (e.g. *inpat*). This finding leads to the concept of a lexicon or mental dictionary against which the visual input is matched. In fluent reading, a visual input is linked to a lexical entry that contains morphological and semantic information such as the part of speech of the word and its meaning. Early evidence of automatic (i.e. uncontrolled) access to word meaning was found in a famous experiment by Stroop (1935). He discovered that naming the colour of the ink in which a word is written is delayed when that word is the name of a different colour. It is assumed that the delay is caused by the interference of the meaning of the word. However, if this assumption is correct we still do not know how word meaning is accessed. Word recognition is accordingly a major issue in reading research. One of the most intensely debated questions is how graphic words and letters relate to each other. To what extent does lexical access depend on the recognition and interpretation of the component letters of graphic words?

Phonological recoding

Letters somehow map onto the phonological code of the language in question. The qualification 'somehow' is necessary, because this is done in different ways, as the alphabet holds various structural possibilities for the link between print and speech. Alphabetic writing systems such as Spanish and Finnish are often called 'shallow' or 'surface' systems because grapheme-phoneme correspondences are relatively simple. In 'deep' systems, the relationship between spelling and phonology is complex, involving deeper levels of linguistic structure, especially morphology. English spelling, which in fact is a mixed system (cf. chapter 9 above), is often regarded as the paradigm case of a deep orthographic system. Somewhat paradoxically it has been called 'not a pure alphabetic writing system' (Treiman 2001: 666). Since English *does* make use of the alphabet, this presumably means that in English the alphabet is not applied properly, namely as a one-to-one phonological mapping code. This, of course, testifies both to the representational view of writing and to the idea that a 'pure' alphabetic orthography is something like a transcription system. In the preceding chapters I had occasion more than once to criticize these notions, which, however, have been dominant in reading research as they have in other fields of the study of writing. The possibility that writing, rather than being derived from speech, is at least partially autonomous, embodying other aspects of language than speech, has rarely been seriously considered. Hence, the process of recovering a word's linguistic form is generally seen as a decoding operation where letters are 'somehow' linked to sounds. In reading aloud this is obvious, although it is by no means clear at what point of the reading process the phonological code comes into play. Both in shallow and deep orthographies, it is assumed, printed words are mapped onto speech, and this holds for silent reading too, the only difference being that actual vocalization is suppressed. Silent reading, in this view, is accompanied by a flow of phonetic imagery through the mind.

The question many researchers have tried to resolve is whether the phonological form of words is accessed as part of the recognition process or as a result of it. Are letter sequences phonologically recoded, that is, transformed into mental interpretations of phonological forms before the word is recognized, or is the graphemic form assigned a phonological interpretation after it has been recognized as a word? Research in cognitive psychology converges on the view that fluent readers have two routes available for word recognition: one that is mediated by the phonological code, and one that leads to the lexical entry directly, bypassing the phonological code. There is little agreement, however, about how these two routes are put to use in the process of word recognition. Some researchers hold that phonological coding is always involved in word recognition in silent reading (Rubinstein *et al.* 1971; Pollatsek *et al.* 1992). Others suggest that the phonological code is not always functional in lexical access (Taft 1982) and claim that there is no conclusive evidence that phonological recoding occurs prelexically (Günther 1988: 146). Research with deaf children has demonstrated that written language can be acquired as a first language by very young children (Steinberg and Harper 1983). No speech recoding occurs in these readers whose mental dictionary, one has to assume, contains templates of sight words rather than templates of phonic words. This suggests that reading does not depend on phonological skills and that, accordingly, it may not be necessary to assume a phonological recoding operation for lexical access to occur. Although it is not clear that conclusions can be drawn from deaf or hearing readers, this notion is supported by reading research on morphographic and semantically oriented writing systems where individual speech sounds are not graphically encoded, as in Chinese. It has been conjectured that morphographic readers use the graphemic form and, when necessary, the meaning as a means to obtain the phonological codes through memory retrieval. Lexical access thus precedes access to the phonological code (Kaiho and Nomura 1983). It has been argued that this is also true of English. 'All fluent English readers eventually learn to identify whole words as if they were Chinese characters' (Steinberg, Nagata and Aline 2001: 97).

Reading acquisition

The conflicting views about the role of phonological recoding in fluent reading are mirrored in a long-standing controversy that pervades reading teaching methods. On one hand, the phonics and decoding method views reading as a process that converts written forms of language to speech forms and then to meaning. A teaching method, consequently, should emphasize phonological knowledge. As one leading proponent of the phonics/decoding approach puts it, 'phonological skills are not merely concomitants or by-products of reading ability; they are true antecedents that may account for up to 60 per cent of the variance in children's reading ability' (Mann 1991: 130). On the other hand, the whole-word method sees reading as a form of communication that consists of the reception of information through the written form, the recovery of meaning being the essential purpose. 'Since it is the case that learning to recognize whole words is necessary to be a fluent reader, therefore, the learning of whole words right from the start may be easier and more effective' (Steinberg, Nagata and Aline 2001: 97).

The dispute between the two approaches to the teaching of reading, as that about the role of phonological mediation in lexical access, has attracted a great deal of attention (for a review, see Pollatsek and Lesch 1996), but it is unlikely that its outcome will be a clear victory for one side or the other (Adams 1990). Phonics and decoding advocates do recognize that learning sight words may be functional in reading acquisition, and, by the same token, whole-word advocates do not deny that the teaching of sound values of letters can serve a useful purpose in reading instruction. Fluent readers rely on different strategies for word recognition: matching sight words with templates stored in memory; predicting words from context; applying grapheme-phoneme correspondences to reconstruct phonological words; guessing unknown words by analogy to others already known (e.g. reading *mat* [mæt] like *cat* [kæt]). Moreover, from research that focussed on the reading of longer words it follows that lexical access is not a process involving only letters and words. Subword units, especially morphemes, are also functional (Taft 1987). In English orthography, which pays a great deal of attention to morpheme constancy, this is particularly important. The dichotomy between whole-word sight reading and letter-oriented phonological recoding thus turns out to be quite artificial. It is not likely that, in performing a complex task such as reading, the human mind applies a single strategy. As indicated above, writing systems are not pure and orthographies are typically made up of several subsystems. To what extent readers adapt their reading strategies to the various subsystems is not clear, and the question of how phonology and morphology fit into word recognition continues to be on the research agenda. Some studies (e.g. Butterworth and Yin 1991) suggest that both sound-oriented and meaning-oriented reading strategies are universally applied. However, cross-linguistic, or rather, writing system-specific tendencies remain another important issue to be further explored.

Research methods

It seems that so far reading research has produced more questions than answers. This impression is partially correct, and there are two main reasons for it. One is that the full complexity of what happens between the stimulus of a piece of text hitting the retina and its meaning being interpreted in the brain is only gradually becoming apparent. The other has to do with the enormous difficulties of devising experiments from which conclusions can be drawn about this process. For on conclusions we have to rely, because direct observation is impossible. The construction of suitable psycholinguistic experiments to elucidate specific aspects of the reading process has, consequently, evolved into a scientific subdiscipline in its own right (for a review, see Smith 1996). Methodological research has focussed on four main areas: (1) presentation technologies, (2) presentation material, (3) choice of subjects, and (4) measurement of reading performance.

(1) Since the eye takes in information in little jumps (saccades) which take about 150 milliseconds to initiate and since visual stimuli can be identified accurately only when presented to the central area of the retina, precision instruments adapted to the visual system such as eye cameras and presentation projectors are needed for well-controlled experiments. (2) In selecting suitable presentation material the physiological and technical frame conditions cannot be ignored. It was found, for example, that the retinal region to which stimuli are presented can be wider for words than for random sequences of letters. The stimuli must be carefully chosen to examine certain variables and not others. For instance, the effects of morphology and evidence about decomposition have been investigated by comparing processing times of stimulus word pairs where one item is prefixed, while the other only

appears to contain the same prefix (e.g. *refill*, *relish*). The effect of context has been researched by measuring detection rates of mistakes inserted in various positions of words and clauses. (3) It can be expected that a professional proofreader and a firstgrader will perform error detection tasks and most other tasks involved in reading differently. Careful selection of subjects is necessary to obtain sound results. Many experiments are intended to learn more about certain groups of subjects, such as people who are particularly good at speed-reading or people whose below average reading abilities are not attributable to external factors such as late initial exposure to reading material or brain damage. The 'normal reader' too is much sought after. (4) This implies the need to develop reliable measures of reading performance. In order to test reading skills you need to know what and how to measure, which means that you need to know quite a few things about the reading process to begin with. Hence, the four aspects of developing methods for reading research are tightly interconnected and feed into reading theory, which is now a sophisticated field of research where cognitive and perceptual psychology and linguistics overlap.

Writing

Psycholinguistic research into writing is not nearly as developed as reading research, perhaps because more people read than write, and perhaps because as a mental and linguistic process writing is even more intractable than reading. Experimental techniques are few, and introspection is notoriously unreliable. What happens when people, literally, put pen to paper is difficult to discover. Empirical graphotactics, the would-be counterpart of the highly sophisticated field of articulatory phonetics, is still so much in its infancy that it does not show up in the indices of even the most comprehensive general reference works of linguistics or psychology, although the production of letter forms and their integration into larger units is no less intriguing than that of speech forms. A letter is not easier to define than a speech sound, a grapheme just as abstract a unit as a phoneme. But writing is less natural than speech, which may be another reason that research into writing skills lags behind. The muscle and coordination control necessary for manual writing develops later than that for articulatory organs, and unlike the control of the articulators the acquisition of sequences of manual muscle movements that produce an output that is unmarked with respect to the norms of the reference community typically requires conscious guidance. Without deliberate effort people do not learn to write. Yet once internalized, the routines of writing cease to involve conscious control. This does not mean that monitoring and feedback control become unnecessary (Try to write more than a few words in the dark!), but conscious attention is no longer required. Fluent writers do not pay more attention to the physical aspects of production than do fluent speakers.

However, this is only the end of the story. The physical writing process, by hand, keyboard, spray can, alphabet soup or any other output modality, is the observable surface of a multilayered process connecting ideas with traces of ink (or pasta). We distinguish writing from calligraphy, font design and lettering for good reasons. The latter, however abstract, have to do with the graphic side of visual symbols, which are thought to be conceptually independent of spelling, capitalization, hyphenation, punctuation, sentence-level grammatical planning, as well as the linguistic and cognitive organization of coherent text beyond the level of the sentence. Or this is the most prevalent view in the West. In some Asian cultures, calligraphy has been the essence of writing instruction for centuries and thought to be indivisibly interconnected with composing. Most modern writing research is, however, concerned with cognitive and linguistic aspects of composition. Hayes and Flower (1980) proposed an influential analytic model of the composition process based on protocol analysis, that is, self-observation, of adult writers. This model consists of three recursive processes that are at the centre of competent writing: planning, transcribing and reviewing. Subsequently the model has been modified and elaborated (e.g. Scardamalia and Breiter 1986; Newell and Winograd 1989) to include an initial problem identification stage, conceptual processes, inner speech processes, evaluation processes, motor processes and editing processes. Cognitive processes during composition, such as the integration of world knowledge – what do writer and reader know, what knowledge do they share? – and contextual knowledge – what has been 'said' before – are to be specified and converted into linguistic strategies such as devising sentence plans, selecting suitable lexical items, keying text-referential and deictic elements to the context and to the situation, where applicable (e.g. *No left turn here*). Finally, spelling routines must be recalled from memory. Connecting them with internal representations of specific movement patterns is where internal planning is externalized and eventually translated into physically executed gestures.

The writing process can be disrupted at any of the above stages, as testified by a range of problems in developing and mature writing. At opposite ends of the writing process, both writer's block and writer's cramp prevent the would-be writer from realizing his or her intention, and many other difficulties encountered between mental planning and physical execution can interfere with the process of composing. Incoherent text organization, syntactic deficiencies at the sentence level, deficiencies in spelling, and deficiencies in letter-forming routines can all be observed independently, suggesting that skills of very different sorts are involved.

By far the greatest number of studies have focussed on spelling disorders, precisely because they often result from specific deficiencies, sometimes summarily labelled 'dyslexia', which, however, is a very mixed bag of problems (for a review, see Kay 1996). At the very least, it should be distinguished from agraphia or dysgraphia, that is, acquired writing deficiencies. Developmental difficulties by children who are slow to master spelling rules must be distinguished from spelling disorders caused by brain damage. The linguistic nature of spelling disorders is also variable and can be very specific. For example, some patients were found to have deficiencies in writing vowels but not consonants, leading to the assumption of distinct mental subsystems (Cubelli 1991). What the various observable deficiencies in spelling suggest is a specific mental skill, or mental skills, responsible for spelling.

A large number of children have difficulties learning to read and spell, but spelling is clearly the more problematic. This is not just because active productive skills are generally more difficult to master than passive receptive ones, but because different skills are involved. The investigation of spelling and reading errors has revealed that spelling and reading are not mirror image processes and skills (Frith and Frith 1980). Mark Twain's observation quoted at the beginning of the chapter that foreigners are better at spelling than pronouncing lends further support to the insight that reading and spelling do not necessarily develop together and involve different skills. For second language learners the threshold of acquiring perfect spelling competence may be lower than that of acquiring perfect pronunciation competence because the learning process is focussed on the written language from the beginning. Although we know little about the interaction of reading and spelling in the acquisition of these skills, it is clear that progress in one is not automatically transferred to the other. There are children who can read quite well but not spell and, more significantly, some children whose spelling performance is superior to their reading. One of the reasons why spelling should be more difficult than reading can be inferred from cases such as the inability to spell vowels. Vowels are less important than consonants, not just in Semitic languages. In reading, a particularistic deficit concerning a class of letters such as vowels can be more easily compensated for and thus go undetected than in writing. Relying on contextual cues, readers with specific deficiencies, such as a weakness in processing vowels, may still recognize the word. Guessing is more successful as a strategy in reading than in writing, because the number of possible spellings for a given phoneme is larger than that of possible phonetic interpretations of a given grapheme. In writing everything must be spelt out in linear sequences of letters. Uncertainties cannot be covered up. In reading, word recognition is central. In spelling, however, both visual memory for graphemic words and phonological awareness are involved. There is much individual variation, and much remains to be learned about how these faculties interact, but good spellers apply both, and, as Russian psychologist Lev Vygotsky noted many years ago, consciously so.

Cognitive consequences of writing

Vygotsky was one of the first psychologists to take an active interest in the cognitive consequences of writing. Working in the 1930s, he was intrigued by the question of how awareness of the properties of speech is affected by writing. In the meantime, numerous studies ranging from the flow of ideas and the level of discourse planning (Chafe 1987) to that of speech-sound segmentation abilities (Morais 1987) have lent support to the notion that people's knowledge about language and their actual language use are influenced by literacy. According to Givon (1979), preliterate speech communities prefer loose, coordinated constructions over condensed, subordinate sentence patterns. Kalmár (1985) has shown how literacy promoted the emergence of syntactic subordination devices in Inuktitut, a language almost never used in writing until recently. Several studies have demonstrated that the notion of what a word is depends on writing (Homer and Olson 1999). Another cognitive effect of writing is to enhance awareness of speech sounds. Readers, as Vygotsky already noted, were much better at identifying individual speech sounds than illiterates. Once again, alphabetic writing has been at the centre of attention, and it has been hypothesized that an analytic understanding of speech sounds develops largely as a result of reading instruction in an alphabetic script. However, Japanese children trained to read kana but not the alphabetic transliteration of Japanese were shown also to acquire speech-sound segmentation skills (Mann 1986). Thus, for speech-sound awareness to occur, mastery of a *phonographic* writing system seems to be the key factor, rather than of an alphabetic script.

People have reported that they 'write things down in order to understand what they want to say'. This is less unreasonable than it might seem at first, for in order to write a thought down it must be lifted out of the realm of the vague and amorphous, and, being given a definite externalized form, it becomes more accessible to conscious reflection. With respect to all of the subsystems involved in writing, the act of composing and transcribing a message requires deliberate analytic reasoning. It is in this sense that Vygotsky regarded writing as a separate linguistic function. Anticipating many more recent studies, he described it as 'speech in thought and image only, lacking the musical, expressive, intonational qualities of oral speech' (Vygotsky 1962: 98). Vygotsky thought that mastery of written language, even at a minimal level of development, required a high level of abstraction. The detachment of written language from the utterance situation necessitates a more consciously analytic attitude. Learning to use language in the written mode, he concludes, is of paramount importance for the mental development of the child. Few developmental psychologists would argue with this today, and many agree that learning to read and write is more than a technical skill. It is a cognitive operating mode, which, thanks to the many empirical studies that have been carried out since Vygotsky's pioneering work, we are beginning to understand as the defining feature of the literate mind.

Conclusion

A great deal of knowledge about the organization of language in the mind has been gained as a result of perceptual and cognitive psychological research of reading and writing. Reading a word correctly is not the inverse of spelling it, the underlying cognitive and motorsensory processes are not complementary. It has become apparent that both faculties involve a number of very specific mental and physical operations that must be synchronized and coordinated for reception and production of written language to be performed successfully. Far from being mere technical extensions of natural faculties, reading and writing have lasting effects on cognitive development. So much so that the notion of the literate mind has gained currency among cognitive psychologists. Language in the written mode is handled differently from speech, both because different physical and mental skills are involved and because written language is not just speech written down. Written language, once mastered, takes on a life of its own, influencing the way we speak and conceptualize language. The investigation of the acquisition and (acquired and congenital) disturbance of written language skills yields many insights into the working of the human mind and continues to occupy a great deal of scientific energy. Research about how the human mind works hardly requires any justification, but in addition to this motivation, there are specific expectations. One of the reasons why reading research and, more generally, psycholinguistic research on written language has flourished in recent decades is that illiteracy is increasingly seen as a problem, both in the highly literate societies of the northern hemisphere and in societies with substantial illiteracy rates in the southern hemisphere. The question 'Why can't Johnny (or Mary) read?' has lost nothing of its urgency, and it is hoped that the psycholinguistics of writing will provide answers, if not *the* answer. The great importance that is attributed to writing and literacy is not a psychological issue but a social one to be dealt with in the next chapter.

Questions for discussion

(1) What is phonological recoding and how does it relate to Augustine's remark about silent reading?
(2) What can we conclude from the fact that literate subjects recognize letters more accurately and faster when they occur within words than in random sequences?
(3) There are two major methods of teaching reading, phonics/decoding and whole-word. What is the gist of the dispute between their respective proponents?
(4) Why is spelling more difficult than reading?
(5) Discuss some of the cognitive and linguistic consequences of writing and try to think of experiments to study them!

12
Sociolinguistics of writing

> For a long time, writing was a secret tool. The possession of writing meant distinction, domination, and controlled communication, in short, the means of an initiation. Historically writing was linked with the division of social classes and their struggles, and (in our country) with the attainment of democracy.
> Roland Barthes

> Literate societies are characterized by a literate environment which promotes extensive and regular use of literacy in all communicative domains. In such societies, illiteracy is considered to be a stigma by both the literate and the nonliterate sections of the society.   Chander Daswani

Illiteracy, says the Indian linguist and educationalist Chander Daswani, is a stigma. This is not the whole story, but it says a lot about writing and society, indeed, about literate society. If it is appropriate to speak of written language and the literate mind, it is certainly no less so to speak of the literate society. We are living in a literate society, which is to say in a modern society. For universal literacy is a recent accomplishment brought about by general education. As late as a century ago, large sections of the most advanced countries could not read or write. In former times, literacy used to be a specialized skill mastered only by a small elite of professionals. Writing was always associated with power and social distinction, as the French philosopher and media theoretician Roland Barthes pointed out. But in a society where the vast majority were unable to read and write, illiteracy was not an embarrassment and did not offer itself easily as an attribute for discrimination. This is different today where illiteracy is a manifest sign of insufficient education, failure or economic disadvantage. Illiteracy can exist only in a literate society. It is precisely the premise of universal literacy that turns illiteracy into a stigma. Even the most advanced countries have illiteracy rates that many find surprising. An OECD report of 1995 revealed that up to 20 per cent of adults in some rich European and North American countries have low literacy skills. Illiterate individuals typically belong to socially disadvantaged and marginalized groups. Illiteracy is a strong predictor of poverty, both domestically, for social strata, and internationally, for GNP (Adiseshiah 1990).

A stigma is a stereotyped expression of social attitudes. Such attitudes manifest themselves in various ways ranging from tacit assumptions to openly discriminatory language. They are proof that writing is not an immutable value-neutral technology, but a socially embedded practice associated with social and cultural values, which, accordingly, changes in content over time and from one culture to another, and which has a profound impact on the society and language to which it is brought.[1] Recent research has stressed the social aspects of reading and writing and the varying cultural and linguistic conditions of creating and sustaining a literate society (e.g. Coulmas 1984; Goody 1986; Heath 1983; Rafoth and Rubin 1988; Street 1995; Wagner, Venezky and Street 1999). In what follows we will take a closer look at attitudes directed at literacy and social evaluative meanings of writing relating to (1) social **practices** of reading and writing; (2) the **people** who use written language and are affected by literacy practices; (3) the **code** of written as opposed to spoken language.

Attitudes towards social practices of literacy

The acquisition of writing is a social accomplishment of great importance. Already in ancient Egypt where literacy was limited to as little as 1 per cent of the population (Parkinson 1999: 127), the social power of writing was clearly recognized. Scribes enjoyed high prestige and a comfortable standard of living and the cultural significance of writing was publicly celebrated as in this passage inscribed on the exterior wall of a temple in the second century BCE.

> These mighty ones created writing in the beginning
> in order to establish heaven and earth in their moment
> ... lords of the art of acting exactly,
> a mooring post for those who travel on mud,
> craftsmen of knowledge,
> leaders of teaching,
> nurses of the person who fashions perfect words,
> lords of the standard, rulers of accounts,
> whose true work is everything that ensures the well-being
> of the entire land.   (quoted from Parkinson 1999: 194)

Obviously composed by one of those who are praised here for their work that 'ensures the well-being of the entire land', such accolades may not be regarded as

---

[1] Notice that, with new literacies such as keyboard and computer literacies emerging, the term has acquired a plural form, reflecting diversifying skills and a more differentiated understanding of them. Cf. Verhoeven 1994, Olson and Torrance 2001.

entirely disinterested, but clearly the modern feeling that sophisticated civilization owes much to writing was already present in Egypt. Of particular importance is the explicit recognition of the essential functions of writing for knowledge creation and systematic schooling ('craftsmen of knowledge, leaders of teaching'), language cultivation ('perfect words'), standardization ('lords of the standard'), and book-keeping ('rulers of accounts'). These four themes can be subsumed under the general heading of the authority of writing, which has characterized attitudes toward the written word since antiquity and wherever literacy-based cultures emerged.

It seems that the authority of writing is an unpremeditated by-product of literacy resulting not from deliberate choice but from the physical properties of the medium. In contradistinction to sound waves carried by air, graphic traces on a stable surface are permanent, taking on a life of their own. Repeated inspection, verification, and comment become possible and hence the codification of linguistic meaning: knowledge, belief, law and language. The authority of writing is thus enshrined in encyclopedias, scriptures, legal codes, and grammars and dictionaries. Literate society is based on institutions that function as the wardens of these repositories of cultural capital: libraries, temples, courts of law and schools. Though present in non-literate societies, too, worship, jurisdiction and tutelage take on a different character once a society has adopted writing. Several other institutions come into existence solely as a consequence of literacy, of which copyright is perhaps the best example. It certifies and protects ownership of a product that does not and cannot exist in the absence of writing. Copyright is paradigmatic for the social attitudes toward literacy practices in modern society. Authorship is recognized as worth protecting and the written word as having authority, credibility and certainty.

Attitudes towards (non)literate people

The social value of writing that finds expression in the institution of copyright is the counterpart of the stigma of illiteracy. In modern times, there is no place for the noble illiterate, such as Charlemagne and other medieval kings who had their scribes but were themselves unable to read and write (although the CEO unable to surf the Internet is a counterpart of sorts). Worldwide, illiterates still number in the hundreds of millions, but what was once a normal state of affairs is now considered a disadvantage and an obstacle to human and social development. There is wide agreement that illiteracy is something to be eradicated, although there are differing opinions as to how this can be accomplished (Wagner 1995). On one hand, it has been held that 'the industrialized countries achieved economic development because of universal literacy' (Daswani 2001: 289). Accordingly, literacy campaigns in developing countries are expected to be conducive to, and speed up, development. On the other hand, it is well known that few literacy campaigns have achieved their stated goals, leading to the double insight that the success of mass literacy programmes depends on complex linguistic and social conditions obtaining in the society in question, and that the demand for a literate workforce brought about by economic development may be driving the diffusion of literacy rather than the other way around. However, one thing is certain. There is a complex interaction between literacy and economy that is yet to be fully explored (Coulmas 1992: 209ff.).

Although a general correlation between literacy rate and prosperity can be observed, relatively poor countries with high literacy rates, such as Vietnam and Sri Lanka, and very rich countries with residual illiteracy, such as the United States, do exist. Hence, the socioeconomic value of literacy cannot be measured on a scale with linear progression. Affluence does not imply general literacy, and the most literate man is the wealthiest man no more than the country with the lowest illiteracy rate has the highest per capita income. Illiteracy in wealthy countries is indicative of unequal distribution of per household income, whereas high literacy rates in poor countries would seem to suggest that cultural development is not altogether a function of economic development. Expected economic payoff is certainly a major incentive for acquiring the art of writing, but as it is an intellectual tool, its uses are not limited to obtaining material benefits. Moreover, mass literacy has consequences for society and its languages that are quite beyond individual insight. Yet, no matter what the exact nature of the relation between literacy and affluence, humanity appears to be moving in the direction of a fully literate world where illiteracy is confined to ever smaller pockets of forgotten peoples, the socially excluded, and individuals with pathological learning disabilities. Already the cultural divide between oral and literate has been turned almost completely into a social divide, and the illiterate will, accordingly, become ever more deviant and marginal. Participation in the modern world requires literacy.

Attitudes towards the written code

Universal literacy does not of course imply that all languages will be written or that the difference between oral and written language will disappear in the near future. But the influence of writing on language and on attitudes towards it is pervasive and has made itself felt for many centuries.[2] Of particular importance for the sociolinguistics of writing is the process of language standardization. Every

---

[2] Modern linguistics has been criticized for paying too little attention to this influence, failing to admit that 'standardization, prescription, and pedagogy are basic sources of its data' (Gray 1981: 219).

language is a self-regulated system governed by rules and conventions that evolve quasi-naturally, guided by an 'invisible hand'. Standardization is the process of consciously intervening in the development of a language in order to determine a norm and secure compliance with it by means of a 'visible hand' in the form of institutions, such as academies, schools and reference works. Standardization presupposes graphization and a literate section of the speech community.

Standardization

An early well-documented case in point is the Carolingian reform at the turn of the eighth century CE. As part of a wide-ranging reform in education, Alcuin of York, on behalf of Charlemagne, demanded that the corruption of the language of the church, Latin, should be checked. By that he meant that Latin should be pronounced not in its various local varieties that had evolved as a result of language spread in the wake of Roman expansion, but in a unified way throughout the empire: it should be pronounced *ad litteras*, to the letter (Bullough 1991). This reform was a first deliberate attempt at standardization and at establishing written Latin as the model of the language. No longer should the written form of Latin be open to a variety of local phonetic interpretations. Instead, the phonetic interpretation was fixed and limited to one. To illustrate, before the reform Latin <cantare> 'to sing' could be pronounced [kantārə] or [ʃāter]. The reform had the effect that [ʃāter] was no longer considered a permissible interpretation of <cantare>. Since literacy was restricted to a minority at the time, the written standard thus defined could provide guidance to the pronunciation of a very small section of the speech community only. A measure of standardization of the pronunciation of Latin was achieved, but this could not arrest change in the unwritten vernacular speech of the largely non-literate speech community. As a result, the gap between written and vernacular Latin widened. The evident difference between the *ad litteras* pronunciation, for example [kantārə], and what were branded as corrupted local pronunciations of the same written form, for example [ʃāter], led to the realization that these 'corrupted' forms, too, could be written. To mark the difference, a new written form was introduced, <chanter>, a different word rather than a variant of another. Hence, Latin split up into what became the Romance languages whose independence became a fact once they were given a written form in their own right.

The *ad litteras* reform did not spawn the family of Romance languages, but it served as a catalyst for the process of language divergence. In the event writing proved to be an indispensable instrument for language cultivation, that is, consciously articulated language attitudes that are implemented by means of specific directives concerning the observation of stated rules. Both linguistic conservatism and claims for linguistic independence rely on writing, which in either

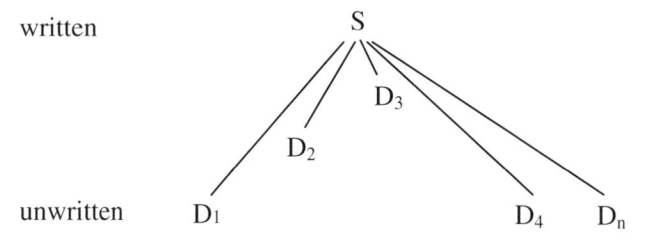

Figure 12.1 *Standard and dialects: some dialects are closer to the standard than others*

case functions as a model rather than an image. Writing thus introduces a functional differentiation into the overall linguistic situation of a speech community that finds expression in various ways. It can foster both language divergence and language convergence. The Romance languages diverged from their Latin source developing into separate entities by virtue of the fact that they became written languages. But these new written languages were not monolithic. Rather, the dialect that was reduced to writing became the focus of standardization and the gradual affiliation of other local varieties, the dialect of Tuscany for Italian, the dialect of the Ile-de-France for French, and so on (Wright 1991). Similar processes have been repeated many times in the Germanic and Slavonic language families. On the Indian subcontinent, four distinct language families, Indo-Aryan, Dravidian, Tibeto-Burmese and Austro-Asiatic, are represented with estimates of the number of living languages varying between a record number of 1,652 and more moderate 96 (Mahapatra *et al.* 1989). This enormous variance must be attributed to the still unresolved question of what constitutes a language in its own right and what a variety of a language. Counting languages is easy only when we count written languages. In India, the idea that a language with a credible claim to its own identity must have a written form is firmly rooted. Eleven scripts with a much larger number of different orthographies are visible proof of the status of separate languages. Sanskrit diversified into local languages known as Prakrits, from which the modern Indo-Aryan languages derive: Bengali, Marathi, Gujarati, Oriya, as well as Hindi and Urdu, each with its own script.

Various criteria have been proposed that must be satisfied for a language to be accorded the status of a written language. It is not sufficient that linguists have transcribed it for analysis, devised a practical alphabet, or even published texts in it. Rather it must be used in writing by native speakers (Wurm 1994: 255) and used as the medium of instruction in primary school (Daswani 2001: 286). Notice that without further qualification the first criterion would exclude a number of languages that may be regarded as prototypical written languages. These are languages that exist first and foremost in writing: Sanskrit, Latin, Old Church Slavonic, Ge'ez,

Classical Arabic. In these and some other cases, writing has led, on the basis of a rich, authoritative literature, to the highest level of standardization and the emergence of a generally respected norm resistant to change. Hence **classical languages** came into existence. It is the systematic analysis of these languages that has laid the groundwork of grammar as a field of scientific inquiry. Through them writing has had a pervading influence on language development and on the conceptualization of language in popular and scientific thought. This is attested very clearly by a sociolinguistic phenomenon that is hard, if not impossible, to explain without reference to writing: diglossia.

Diglossia

Since its seminal description by Charles Ferguson (1959) the sociolinguistic situation known as diglossia has prompted a vast number of case studies.[3] It consists in the coexistence of two distinct varieties of what their speakers recognize as one language. These varieties or registers, which are called 'high' (H) and 'low' (L), are functionally complementary, being reserved for formal vs. informal usage, respectively. Diglossia shares many features with a standard cum dialects situation from which it differs, however, in that H is no speaker's first language, while a standard variety may be one dialect among others, which implies that some speakers' speech is closer to the standard than that of others. By contrast, the norms related to H and L are more general than those of standard and dialect and less subject to a social gradient. H is used by no members of the speech community for all communicative functions, and this function-specific distribution of varieties is stable over a long time. How does a diglossia situation come about? To consider this question, let us briefly return to the above example of the Romance languages.

From a theoretical point of view and disregarding speaker awareness of language distinctness, we could say that Latin is still alive, albeit in the guise of different local varieties, which have been formed over the centuries, absorbing various influences of adjacent languages. At no point in time was the death of Latin diagnosed, or the birth of Italian, French, Castilian, Catalan, Portuguese and so on. Yet, when Dante Alighieri composed his *Divine Comedy*, he chose not to write it in Latin, at the time the language still most commonly used for literary purposes by other writers. He, too, wrote many of his works in Latin, especially theoretical tracts, but great poetry, he felt, should be closer to the vernacular he heard people speak in Tuscany. This was at the beginning of the fourteenth century CE, five hundred years after the Carolingian reform. What had happened in the meantime? The process that differentiated the Romance languages from Latin and from each other was long

---

[3] Britto 1986 offers a monograph-length theoretical discussion focussing on Tamil. For more recent reviews of the literature see Hudson 1992, 2002.

and complex. The initial state, Latin, and the outcome, Italian, French, Castilian, Catalan, Portuguese and so on, are clear, at least in a schematic description. But the long period in-between is rather muddled. Language identity is a normative notion, that is, one that refers to speaker awareness as much as to observable linguistic facts. For many centuries people spoke Latin in the sense that this was what they thought they spoke. They were quite aware, however, that 'real' Latin was different. That was the language of educated people who could read and write and knew of all the inflectional endings that had long disappeared from their speech. (Latin had six morphologically marked noun cases, in Italian this system collapsed almost completely.) Still, in a vaguely defined sense they understood the 'real' Latin (H) and their Latin (L) to be the same language. This is what we now call diglossia, a relatively stable functional distribution of varieties held together by a general awareness in the speech community that they are part of the same diasystem. Medieval Romance diglossia came to an end when the various vernacular Ls were reduced to writing and eventually given a standard in their own right.

From this example it should not be concluded that H is an archaic variety of L or, conversely, that L is an advanced state of H, for the coexistence of the two varieties endures for many generations of speakers. While it is H rather than L that is the object of linguistic conservatism, H does not cease to change. In Germanophone Switzerland, for instance, standard German (called *Schriftdeutsch* 'written German' by the Swiss) and Swiss-German have coexisted in diglossia for centuries. If the written norm had a restraining effect on change in standard German, it surely has not arrested change altogether. Rather, in diglossia both H and L keep changing, but not necessarily simultaneously. That is what distinguishes an H from a classical language that has lost all communicative functions in everyday life and is reduced to a written language only. H is used both in writing and speech.

Notice, however, that writing is crucial for diglossia to be occasioned and terminated. Not surprisingly, therefore, in discussions about diglossia, H is commonly equated with written language, as in this description of Sinhala diglossia where H and L are given as: '(1) *Literary Sinhala*. The chief defining characteristic is Literary main verb forms, particularly the subject-verb agreement.... And (2) *Spoken Sinhala*, lacking Literary verb agreement' (Gair 1986: 324). It should be noted that writing is a necessary but not a sufficient condition for diglossia to emerge. Creating a literary variety does not automatically lead to diglossia. Two additional conditions conducive to diglossia are restricted literacy[4] and the conservation of a literary variety that takes its orientation from a classical or high-prestige language. These conditions imply that H cannot exercise a strong influence on L

---

[4] Diglossia and restricted literacy have been conceptualized as a chicken and egg problem. Indian linguists in particular have, however, argued convincingly against the notion that diglossia is an impediment to mass literacy.

$$S = H$$

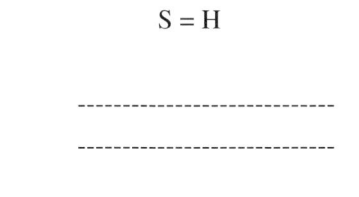

$$\{D_1 \quad D_2 \quad D_3 \quad D_4 \quad D_n\} = L$$

Figure 12.2 *Diglossia: a functional divide allows no influence to be exerted by H, the standard (S), on L, the vernaculars ($D_1 - D_n$)*

and that L will not typically be used in writing. A wide and relatively stable gap between H and L is the result. Diglossia is a widespread phenomenon. Some of the better-known cases include Classical and vernacular Arabic, literary and vernacular Tamil, and French and Haitian Creole. The varietal distinction in diglossia relates to several other conditions having to do with, among others, the functional distribution of H and L (formal vs. informal), the mode of their acquisition (schooling vs. spontaneous acquisition) and the degree of their structural disparity (more than stylistic differentiation, less than separate languages). They cannot be discussed here. In the present context most significant is the uncontroversial fact that the written/spoken contrast is essential, and that diglossia is one of the most noticeable and theoretically important manifestations of the deep-reaching influence writing exerts on the structure and use of languages.

Language is a social fact, which implies that it is a mental phenomenon. Its written form speaks to the mind in its own way, shaping the language users' awareness of their language and hence its identity. Yet another sociolinguistic situation where the nexus between writing and language identity is in evidence is known as digraphia.

Digraphia

Though reminiscent of the term diglossia, the notion of digraphia is conceptually unrelated (Grivelet 2001). It refers to the use of two different scripts, writing systems or orthographies for the same language. This looks like a simple definition, if it were not for the fact that a language's orthography is one of the subsystems of its overall system. Substitute 'phonology' for 'orthography' and it is immediately obvious that we land in hot water: 'one language, two phonologies' is not a descriptive proposition many linguists would let pass in a term paper without comment. What digraphia thus brings to light very clearly is that writing does not leave languages unaffected. To say the very least, writing is a part of a language's identity and, as it happens, literally the most, even only, visible one. It therefore has an impact on language that cannot be ignored. Consider some examples.

Are Hindi and Urdu different languages? No matter which reference work we consult, the answer is yes. Yet, no Indologist would argue with King (2001: 43) that 'Hindi and Urdu are so similar in their marketplace spoken forms that no linguist would hesitate to classify them as near dialects of the same language'. It is writing that pulls them apart. The Brāhmī-derived Devanagari script written from left to right gives Hindi its visible authenticity, while Urdu is embodied in the Perso-Arabic script brought to India by Muslim invaders. The two scripts always had political and cultural implications, which left their mark on the language(s). Until the early decades of the nineteenth century, Persian served as the administrative language of the Mughal dynasty. Using the same script, Urdu was drawn into the Persian cultural orbit. It was only natural that its speakers would turn to Persian and Arabic for lexical enrichment, especially in writing. Hindi, by contrast, drew on Sanskrit, India's classical language from which it derives and with which it shares the same script. Since the British Raj made Urdu the administrative language in the 1860s, the social dimension of Hindi-Urdu digraphia became more pronounced, because Devanagari Hindi was more popular among the common people than elitist Perso-Arabic Urdu. Religious associations added to the rift, since the Arabic alphabet has always been the script of Islam, while the Hindu revival movement in the latter half of the nineteenth century promoted Devanagari as the script of India and its native religion, Hinduism. Writing in 1981, a noted Indian linguist comments, 'At one time [Urdu] was cultivated by Hindus and Muslims alike. With the passing of time it became a symbol of Muslim identity and now it is a reason for political and social tensions' (Pattanayak 1981).

Without the twofold graphization this situation would not have come about, but the split is more than a matter of two different graphic forms. The cleavage between Hindi and Urdu is experienced so strongly by many speakers that they deny intercommunicability. In the wake of the partition of India in 1947, the link between religion and script was further reinforced and spilled over to other languages. To cite another case in point, the British rulers had decreed in 1853 that Sindhi, mostly spoken in the province of Sind in what is now Pakistan, was to be written in the Perso-Arabic script. However, in 1948 Hindu speakers of Sindhi in India resolved to write their language in Devanagari, only to be challenged in court. The Indian government then decided to allow the use of both scripts for Sindhi (Daswani 1979).

Another well-known case of digraphia goes back to the creation in the ninth century of the Cyrillic and Glagolitic alphabets for missionary work among the Slavs, sowing the seed of language divergence. The Cyrillic alphabet has been consistently used ever since by the Serbs, while the Glagolitic was used by the

Croats who, however, later replaced it with the Latin alphabet. Eventually, the scriptual division came to coincide with a religious division, the Orthodox Church controlling the Serbs, the Roman Catholic the Croats. In 1850, under Hapsburg rule, linguists and literary scholars of both groups met in Vienna to decide 'on fusing their variants into a common language with two alphabets' (Magner 2001: 18). Subsequently, compound language designations such as Serbo-Croatian gained some currency, but the continuation of digraphia always held the potential of linguistic secession, which was promptly turned into official policy when Yugoslavia disintegrated in the 1990s and Serbia and Croatia became independent republics. The two alphabets for which a straightforward one-to-one conversion had been accomplished through deliberate orthography planning were highlighted as symbols of ethnonationalism. Serbo-Croatian gave way to Serbian and Croatian.

For a language to be written in two or more scripts is not uncommon. What instances should be subsumed under the notion of digraphia is a question of definition. DeFrancis (1984a), for example, calls the availability of the romanized Pinyin orthography for Chinese digraphia, although Pinyin is little used by the Chinese themselves. Hannas (1997: 299) wants to include Korea and Japan (see also Unger 2001) as well, because in both cases it is possible to dispense with Chinese characters, writing Korean in Han'gŭl exclusively, as is actually practised in North Korea, and Japanese in kana, as is common in certain texts, such as children's books. Japanese writing is more commonly described as a mixed system (see chapter 9 above), but it is true that heavily sinicized varieties replete with Chinese characters coexist with others that include few or none at all. There is also a social aspect to Japanese literacy, as there is to Korean, since character literacy puts a heavier burden on the learner than kana and Han'gŭl. In the Japanese case it is hard to see the potency of causing language divergence, which is very real in Hindi/Urdu and Serbian/Croatian digraphia. In the two Koreas, however, linguistic divergence is taking place, largely as a result of two different orthographies and orthography-based standards (Sohn 1997). Other examples of digraphia include roman Romanian vs. Cyrillic Moldavian; roman Finnish vs. Cyrillic Karelian; Greek and Latin alphabets for Albanian; Javanese, being written in the Javanese and roman alphabets; Swahili in Arabic and roman letters; Mongolian in Mongolian and Cyrillic, among others.

Differing orthographic standards such as British vs. American and Swiss vs. German spelling or simplified characters in China vs. traditional ones in Taiwan may also be mentioned, although a different term, 'diorthographia', has been proposed for such cases (Zima 1974). Obviously, the visible difference between British and American English is nothing in comparison with that between Hindi and Urdu. Yet even minor differences such as *centre/center*, *defence/defense*, *favour/favor* and so on are noticeable and hence hold the potential of symbolic

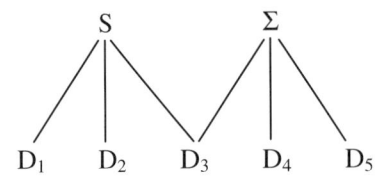

Figure 12.3 *Digraphia.* Twofold graphization with different scripts fosters the development of two standards and linguistic divergence or split, as in the Croatian (S)/Serbian (Σ) dialect continuum.

instrumentalization. As a matter of fact, symbolic interpretations of digraphia, however petty, are hard to avoid because writing systems, scripts and orthographies are not perceived by their users as value-neutral instruments. Their symbolic potential comes to bear most strikingly when reforms are planned and implemented.

Writing reform

Some digraphia situations eventuate from writing reform projects, an old and a new system being used side by side during a transition period. Only rarely are such reforms perceived with indifference by the speech communities concerned. Given the political and cultural significance attached to scripts and in view of the potentially consequential effects a language's writing system has both on the language and on its speakers' metalinguistic concepts, the public interest that writing reform proposals usually arouse is not surprising. An established written standard is associated with authenticity and time-tested ways and, therefore, not easily altered or abandoned. Three cases must be distinguished, which are here exemplified in order of decreasing impact.

Reform of the writing system

The romanization of Vietnamese was a reform of the writing system, as Chinese characters, a completely different system, were abolished and a new system was specially designed for Vietnamese, roman letters augmented by a set of diacritical marks. In the event the Vietnamese adopted a new script along with the new writing system, although they are not coterminous. Remember that script and writing system are distinct notions. It is conceivable to keep the script, while changing the writing system. A spelling reform for English leading to a phonemic orthography would be a case in point. Notice, however, that, since the number of English phonemes exceeds that of roman lower case letters, digraphs such as <sh, th, ou> and so on would have to be augmented and systematized to achieve strict one-to-one phoneme-grapheme correspondence with the present script. This brings us back to the theoretically interesting question of how scripts and writing systems relate or, to put it differently, how we can determine the restrictions a script places on a writing system.

Script reform

One script is replaced by another without any change in the writing system. An example is the shift from Cyrillic to roman in Moldova following the demise of the Soviet Union. Under Soviet rule the Cyrillic alphabet was intended to underscore the distinction from roman-written Romanian, which the reversion to roman was intended to deny. Similar examples marked the history of language planning in the USSR where several languages were provided with a roman orthography first, which was later replaced by a Cyrillic one.

Spelling reform

Some orthographic rules are changed in order to make adjustments necessary to preserve the basic underlying principles and accommodate historical changes. Alexandrian grammarians of the Hellenistic period introduced three different pitch accent marks into Greek orthography. In the 1980s this threefold graphic accentual system was replaced by a single accent mark because in Middle Greek the three accents had collapsed into one, leaving the orthography with more distinctions than warranted phonetic interpretation. No changes in the writing system or the script were involved. Notice, however, that a spelling reform may border on, or combine with, a reform of the writing system.

Reforms of all three kinds are more likely than not to meet with resistance. As we have seen in the discussion of digraphia, courts and other government institutions tend to get involved whenever changes in the written norm are planned or executed, pitting the proponents of innovation and improvement against the preservers of the proven and reliable. In one example, no less than twelve German district courts had to rule on a spelling reform commissioned in 1996 by the governments of Austria, Germany and Switzerland. Five areas of the spelling system were at issue: letter/sound correspondence, capitalization, spelling of compounds, punctuation and hyphenation. All in all, the proposed changes were quite modest. Yet, the matter had to be referred to the Constitutional Court, Germany's highest court. In one of the federal states, the anti-reformists initiated and won a plebiscite against the reform. Although it is invariably linguistic arguments that are advanced by both sides in such a struggle – evidently, *Fluss* is far superior, on systematic grounds, to *Fluß*, or vice versa – the goodness of the system is not the real issue, if only because it has always been possible, sobering though it is, to find expert witnesses who testify one way or the other. The real issue is whose language it is and who should be entitled to make any prescriptions about it. A common language is after all the potentially most democratic institution we have. Why should an authority be allowed to meddle with it?!

It is a telling sign of modernity that the state is charged with the task of codifying a writing system and acting as the sealkeeper of the written language, protecting it from lawlessness, decay or hijacking by linguistic terrorists. This was not always so. Until late in the nineteenth century, orthographic conventions evolved by and large without official sanction. That the government cannot allow its people to spell as they see fit is a modern notion closely linked with compulsory education. The free-marketeers who trust that a spelling system can perpetuate itself as a self-regulating system are an endangered species, for it has become doubtful that the rules of a written language can be reformed effectively without government intervention. Over the decades, statist thinking has gained ground as writing is increasingly conceived of as not just being similar to law, but as providing its very foundation. There is an apparent desire in many speech communities, fostered not least by communication industries such as printing and software development, to legalize the written language. Language, especially in its written form, is turned into an instrument of social engineering and forging political allegiance. 'Linguistic unification is a key to the recovery of national identity and the reunification of Korea' writes Korean linguist Sohn who, therefore, argues that 'there is no reason why a unified spelling system cannot be legislated' (1997: 212f.).

China provides another illustration for the indispensably of government involvement. Since the early decades of the twentieth century, China has grappled with the problem of a writing reform (DeFrancis 1984b). This project has always been understood as a linguistic and social endeavour, because the traditional written language, far removed from speech, in the form of an unlimited number of characters was seen as an impediment to mass literacy and hence education and hence development. All aspects of written communication were, therefore, put to the test: script, spelling, writing system, and the relationship of spoken and written language. Far from being considered a mere technicality that should be judged and mended on pragmatic grounds alone, the reform of the Chinese written language was a political issue from the start. Various options were discussed, ranging from romanization, the most radical solution, to moderate character simplification. Different romanization schemes were developed and tried out (Chen 2001) but for decades came to nought because, afflicted by wars and revolutions, China had no effective central government. Lasting results were accomplished only after the People's Republic of China was founded in 1949 whose leaders made writing reform one of their earliest priorities. A first reform scheme was worked out by the Chinese Committee on Writing Reform and ratified by the State Council in 1956. Characters in common use were limited in number and simplified by reducing composite strokes, and a roman orthography, Pinyin, was designed, which

門 → 门   無 → 无
 8   3   12   5

Figure 12.4 *Chinese characters,* mén *'gate' and* wú *'without', in full and reduced form (index ciphers = number of strokes)*

was formally adopted in 1958. In 1964, a list of 2,238 simplified characters was issued, followed by a second list published in 1977.

These are practical matters, but in this case, too, it has proved impossible to reduce writing reform to a question of utility detached from vested interests. Taiwan did not accept the reform, avoiding every sign of submitting to Beijing's authority. Some Western scholars are convinced that Chinese characters are on their last legs (e.g. Unger 1987). Their chief argument is that 'Chinese characters have put people using them at a competitive disadvantage vis-à-vis users of alphabetic scripts in the speed and facility with which information can be processed' (Hannas 1999: 279). This may be so, but practical criteria of efficiency have never been the sole determining factor of the success or failure of writing reforms. As Fishman (1988: 280) put it, 'replacement of a writing system threatens to dislocate indigenous intellectual authority structures. The longer the prior writing system has functioned as an indigenous marker of authenticity and status ... the less likely it is that this established system will be completely replaceable without extreme dislocation.' The Korean writing system promulgated by King Sejong took some 500 years to take hold, although there could be no doubt that it was superior to Chinese characters in every conceivable utilitarian respect, unless we consider the use of Chinese characters as a means of protecting elite privileges an advantage. It was only when Han'gŭl became a symbol of Korean nationalism and resistance against Japanese colonial domination in the first half of the twentieth century that it achieved universal acceptance as the proper writing system of the Korean language. This is not to say that the Chinese and the Japanese will keep the characters forever, but it is an indication of the complexities involved in writing reforms. Conditions in contemporary East Asia are not the same as those obtaining in fifteenth-century Korea. Literacy rates are much higher today and the functions and requirements of literacy are more demanding. But the social forces inflamed by, and affecting, writing reforms seem to be as powerful as ever. Even if it is true that, in the long run, time works against Chinese characters, which is by no means certain, I would not take any bets on how long this may be.

It seems that politics and other vested interests just cannot be left out of consideration where writing reform is at issue. Unless the political constellations are right, the best reform programme is bound to miscarry, because simplicity, elegance and linguistic fit are only one part of the equation and one, furthermore, that is not at all easy to evaluate on objective grounds. In China with its long literary tradition it took a revolution to initiate a reform. Similarly, in one of the most widely discussed reforms, Mustafa Kemal Atatürk successfully replaced the Arabic with the roman alphabet for Turkish in 1928. Wielding dictatorial powers over a largely illiterate speech community, he made the reform of the writing system an integral part of a quasi-revolutionary scheme of westernization. As for the English language, it is no coincidence that the only spelling reform ever to be effected coincided with the independence of the United States, conceived and launched by American nationalist Noah Webster who in 1789 declared:

> As an independent nation, our honor requires us to have a system of our own, in language as well as government. Great Britain, whose children we are, and whose language we speak, should no longer be *our* standard; for the taste of her writers is already corrupted, and her language on the decline. (Webster 1992: 34)

Whatever the merits of *honor, labor* and *color*[5] as tokens of the honour of an independent nation, Webster's sentiments concerning the needs of a self-respecting nation for an orthographic standard of its own are shared by many throughout the world. This way of thinking about written language exemplifies an attitude that expects the state to accept political responsibility for the linguistic wellbeing of the nation. With the spread of literacy it has taken root in many speech communities and helped to turn a select number of languages into national languages. There is no shortage of reform proposals for English spelling, about which many lament much as Hannas, quoted above, laments about Chinese characters, namely that it has 'put people using [it] at a competitive disadvantage vis-à-vis users of [other] alphabetic scripts in the speed and facility with which information can be processed'. But an entrenched system is not easily dislodged, and notwithstanding their evident appeal, schemes such as those by Mark Twain or Jonathan Keitz, inventor of Kånådån and editor of *Dhe Taim ův Toronto*, have no better chance to succeed than all the other designs for an improved English spelling advanced over the years (Haas 1969). The stigma of illiteracy makes itself felt here, too. For if you write like Jonathan Keitz, chances are you will be discriminated against as someone who cannot spell.

---

[5] Webster also recommended many more extravagant spellings such as *bilt* for *built*, *giv* for *give*, *laf* for *laugh*, among others. He also proposed several new diacritics, such as a cross bar for <th> to distinguish [θ], as in *thin*, from [ð], as in *then*. For a review of Webster's influence on American spelling, see Clark 1965.

> **Dhe**
> # Jeinerål Rules
> ův **kånådån**,
> dhe fiinål långweij !

Dhe folloing rules ar dhe jeinerål rules ův dhe internåsionål kånådån. It iz probåbel dhåt dher will bi futurål alterråsiones in sum ův dhiiz rules.
(Notaiz: Al rules will můstaiz tu bi kompleitikli rijidik, totålli imfleksåbel, ånd strinjensikli enforsaized.)

A. **Dhe Alfabet: 31 letteres** (In inggliš 4 ův dhe 5 vokales (80 %) håv **imkorrektik** neimes ! Dhe reizult : kontiinuål, universål problemes.)

Iic kånådånål foneim iz reipreizentaized bai å distingktik, alfabetik letter, or bai ådifthongål diigråf.

Vokales(8): a, å, e, **ii / i**, i, o, u, ů;

Konsonantes(23): b, c, d, dh, f, g, h, j, k, l, m, n, ng, p, r, s. sh→š
t, th, v, w, y, z.

Difthongos(4): ai, au, ei, oi.

Vokales
1. **A, a:** kaled aa [inggliš: ah/aw/aa/a]: Ek.: alfabet, tak, lak, Jan, Pal, Årabia, Astralia, ets.
2. **Å, å:** Dhe seiparatik å-sond [inggliš: a]: Åfrikå, åfrikål, glås, klås, ets.
3. **E, e:** kaled e: ekzaltůs, essei, Estonia, letter, better, pensil, ets.
4. **I, I:** kaled ii [inggliš: **(32 variåsiones !)** ee, i, ets.]: iit (eat), hiit (heat), sliip (sleep), diip, piip, obviůs, Italia, violiin, ets.
5. **I, I:** kaled ii-shortik (i-šortik): it, hit, slip, dip, pip, ets.
6. **O, o:** kaled o: dor, glamor, glori, ror, mor, Ohaio, dherfor, ets. Shorter-o (not ån aa-sond): Sk*o*tlånd, ets.
7. **U, u:** kaled uu (not yu): tru, nu, yu, thru, tu, tuu, mu (kau), myu (kåt), Kuba, Nu-Zeilånd, Urugwai, ets.
8. **Ů, ů:** for dhe reipůlsik **shwa-sond:** bůt, fůrst, fůrther, lův, wůrk.

Figure 12.5 *The General Rules of Kanandan, promulgated by the Internasionål Union for Kånådån (IUK), Toronto, On., Kånådå*

A Plan for the Improvement of English Spelling

For example, in Year 1 that useless letter 'c' would be dropped to be replased either by 'k' or 's', and likewise 'x' would no longer be part of the alphabet. The only kase in which 'c' would be retained would be the 'ch' formation, which will be dealt with later.

Year 2 might reform 'w' spelling, so that 'which' and 'one' would take the same konsonant, wile Year 3 might well abolish 'y' replasing it with 'i' and Iear 4 might fiks the 'g/j' anomali wonse and for all.

Jenerally, then, the improvement would kontinue iear bai iear with Iear 5 doing awai with useless double konsonants, and Iear 6–12 or so modifaiing vowlz and the rimeining voist and unvoist konsonants.

Bai Iear 15 or sou, it wud fainali bi posibl tu meik ius ov thi ridandant letez 'c', 'y' and 'x' – bai now jast a memori in the maindz ov ould doderez – tu riplais 'ch', 'sh', and 'th' rispektivli.

Fainali, xen, aafte sam 20 iers ov orxogrefkl riform, wi wud hev a lojikl, kohirnt speling in ius xrewawt xe Ingliy-spiking world.   Mark Twain

Conclusion

In the long course of its formation over the past five thousand years or so, literate society has imbued language with functions of its own that have no counterpart in non-literate societies. In this chapter we have considered some of the most important ones: introducing literacy as an attribute of social division; engendering a written language which exists not as a representation of, but as a complement to, speech and leads a life *sui generis*; supporting linguistic convergence and standardization, or, conversely, providing the basis for linguistic divergence and secession; binding loyalties and serving as symbols of ethnocultural identity; turning language into a public good that, through schooling, literature in the widest sense, and explicit codification requires government supervision. We have seen that the stigma of illiteracy, rather than being confined to those who cannot read and write, radiates to language. The range of linguistic varieties in literate society includes registers, styles and dialects that are closer to or further divorced from the written standard, the literacy rate being one of the factors that determine the specific arrangement of functionally distributed varieties characteristic of a given society. Diglossia is one of the most conspicuous situations to expose the consequential influence of writing on language and society. Finally, a careful analysis of the phenomenon of digraphia reveals that the script of a language, usually considered an interchangeable exterior form, works as a potential factor in its development, because, like writing system and spelling conventions, it is perceived by the speech community as important. Since language is a mental and a social fact, this in itself causes writing to have an impact on language. In our days, the world is moving in the direction of universal literacy, bringing to a conclusion a development begun five thousand years ago by the first scribes who set out to create written language by way of travelling on mud. It is time to recognize that this journey made a difference not only to society, but to language, too.

Questions for discussion

(1) What does the stigma of illiteracy imply for language varieties in speech communities with restricted and high literacy rates?
(2) Does the notion of 'illiterate speech' make any sense?
(3) How does diglossia differ from a standard/dialects situation, and what does writing have to do with it?
(4) What is an orthography, what are possible reasons to want to change it, and why are orthography reforms difficult to effectuate?
(5) Compare the reform proposals by Mark Twain and Jonathan Keitz and make a better one!

Appendix: Universal Declaration of Human Rights, article 1

Arabic

المادة ١

يولد جميع الناس أحراراً متساوين في الكرام و الحقوق. و قد وهبوا عقلاً و ضميراً و عليهم أن يعامل بعضهم بعضاً بروح الإخاء.

Chinese

第一条
人人生而自由在尊严和权利上一律平等。他们赋有理性和良心并应以兄弟关系的精神相对待。

Chinese pinyin

Rén rén shēng ér zìyú, zài zūnyán hé quánlì shàng yílü pìngděng. Tāmen fùyoǔ lǐxìng hè liángxīn, bīng yìngyǐ xiōng dì guānxi de jǐng shēn xīang dùi dài.

Dutch

Alle mensen worden vrij en gelijk in waardigheid en rechten geboren. Zij zijn begiftigd met verstand en geweten, en behoren zich jegens elkander in een geest van broederschap te gedragen.

English

All human beings are born free and equal in dignity and rights. They are endowed with reason and conscience and should act towards one another in a spirit of brotherhood.

Finnish

Kaikki ihmiset syntyvät vapaina ja tasavertaisina arvoltaan ja oikeuksiltaan. Heille on annettu järki ja omatunto, ja heidän on toimittava toisiaan kohtaan veljeyden hengessä.

Greek

Όλοι οι άνθρωποι γεννιούνται ελεύθεροι και ίσοι στην αξιοπρέπεια και τα δικαιώματα. Είναι προικισμένοι με λογική και συνείδηση, και οφείλουν να συμπεριφέρονται μεταξύ τους με πνεύμα αδελφοσύνης.

Hebrew

סעיף א. כל בני אדם נולדו בני חורין ושווים בערכם ובזכויותיהם. כולם חוננו בתבונה ובמצפון, לפיכך חובה עליהם לנהוג איש ברעהו ברוח של אחוה.

Hindi

अनुच्छेद १.
सभी मनुष्यों को गौरव और अधिकारों क मामले में जन्मजात स्वतन्त्रता और समानता प्राप्त है.
sabhi manusyō ko gaurav aur asikarō ke mamle me janmajat svatantrata aur samanta purapt hai.
उन्हें बुद्धि और अन्तरात्मा की देन प्राप्त है और परस्पर उन्ह भाईचारे क भाव से बर्ताव करना चाचहिए.
unhe buddhi aur antratma ki den prapt hai aur parspar unhe bhaijar ke bhav se bartav karna cahie.

Italian

Tutti gli esseri umani nascono liberi ed eguali in dignità e diritti. Essi sono dotati di ragione e di coscienza e devono agire gli uni verso gli altri in spirito di fratellanza.

Japanese

すべての人間は、生まれながらにして自由であり、かつ、
subete no ningen wa, umarenagarani shite jiyuu deari, katsu,
尊厳と権利とについて平等である。人間は理性と良心よを
songen to kenri to ni tsuite byoudou dearu. Ningen wa, risei to ryoushin to o
授けられており、互いに同胞の精神をもって行動しなければならない。
sakerarete ori, tagai ni douhou no seishin o motte koudou shinakereba naranai.

Kånådån

Al humanes ar bornized friis ånd ekwallik in digniti ånd raittes. Dhei ar endauaized with reizon ånd konsiens, ånd šůd åktaiz twwardikli wůn ånodher in å spiirit ův brodherhůd.

Korean

제1조
je il jo

모든 인간은 태어날때 부터 자유로우며 그 존 엄 과 권리에 있어 동 등 하 다.
modeun inganeun taeeonalttae buteo   jayuroumyeo geu joneomgwa   gwonrie   isseo dongdeunghada.

인간은 천부적으로 이성과 양 심 을 부여 받았으며 서로   형 제 애 의
inganeun cheonbujeoguro iseonggwa yangsimeul buyeo badassumyeo seoro   hyeongjeaeui

정신으로   행 동   하여야 한다.
jeongsineuro haengdong   hayeoya   handa.

Latin

Omnes homines dignitate et iure liberi et pares nascuntur, rationis et conscientiae participes sunt, quibus inter se concordiae studio est agendum.

Malayalam

വകപ്പ് 1.

മനുഷ്യരെല്ലാവരും തുല്യാവകാശത്തോളും അന്തസ്സോടും സ്വാതന്ത്ര്യത്തോടുകൂടി
manusarellavarum   tulyakasrulotam   antassotam   swatantryatukkuti

ജനിച്ചിട്ടുള്ളവരാണ്
janiccittullavarannu.

അന്യോന്യം ഭ്രതൃഭാവത്തോടെ പെരുമാറവാനാണ് മനുഷ്യന്നു വിവേകബുദ്ധിയും മനസ്സാക്ഷിയും
anyenyam   bhrtrbhavattote   perumaravananu   manusynnu vivekabuddhiyum   manassaksiyu

സിദ്ധമായിരിക്കുന്നത്.
siddhamayirikkunnatu

Maltese

Il-bnedmin kollha jitwieldu ħielsa u ugwali fid-dinjità u d-drittijiet. Huma mogħnija bir-raġuni u bil-kuxjenza u għandhom iġibu ruħhom ma' xulxin bi spirtu ta' aħwa.

Mongolian (Kalmyk)

Хүн бүр төрж мэндлэхдд эрх ёөлөөтэй, адилхан нэр төртэй, ижил эрхтэй байдаг. Оюун ухаан, нандин ёанар заяасан хүн гэгё өөр хоорондоо ахан дүүгийн үзэл санаагаар харьцах уёиртай.

Russian

Все люди рождаются свободн ими и равн ими в своем достоинстве и правах. Они наделен разумом и совест ю и должн поступат в отношении друг друга в духе братства.

Spanish

Todos los seres humanos nacen libres e iguales en dignidad y derechos y, dotados como están de razón y conciencia, deben comportarse fraternalmente los unos con los otros.

Tibetan

'gro ba mi'i rigs rgyud yongs la skyes tsam nyid nas che mthongs dang thob thang gi rang
  dbang 'dra mnyam du yod la
khong tshor rang byung gi blo tsal dang bsam tshul bzang po 'don pa' i'os babs kyang yod
de bzhin phan tshun gcig gis gcig la bu spun gyi 'du shes 'dzin pa'i bya spyod kyang lag len
  bstar dgos pa yin

འགྲོ་བ་མིའི་རིགས་རྒྱུད་ཡོངས་ལ་སྐྱེས་ཙམ་ཉིད་ནས་ཆེ་མཐོངས་དང་། ཐོབ་ཐང་། གི་རང་དབང་འདྲ་མཉམ་དུ་ཡོད་ལ།

ཁོང་ཚོར་རང་བྱུང་གི་བློ་རྩལ་དང་བསམ་ཚུལ་བཟང་པོ་འདོན་པའི་འོས་བབས་ཀྱང་ཡོད།

དེ་བཞིན་ཕན་ཚུན་གཅིག་གིས་གཅིག་ལ་བུ་སྤུན་གྱི་འདུ་ཤེས་འཛིན་པའི་བྱ་སྤྱོད་ཀྱང་ལག་ལེན་བསྟར་དགོས་པ་ཡིན།།

Vietnamese

Tất cả mọi người sinh ra đều được tự do và bình đẳng về nhân phẩm và quyền. Mọi con ngườ đều được tạo hoá ban cho lý trí và lượng tâm và cần phải đối xử với nhau trong tình bằng hữu.

Xhosa

Bonke abantu bazalwa bekhululekile belingana ngesidima nangokweemfanelo. Bonke abantu banesiphiwo sesazela nesizathu sokwenza isenzo ongathanda ukuba senziwe kumzalwane wakho.

Bibliography

Abercrombie, David. 1949. What is a 'Letter'. *Lingua* 2, 55–63.
Adams, Marilyn. 1990. *Learning to Read*. Cambridge: Cambridge University Press.
Adiseshiah, M. S. 1990. *Illiteracy and Poverty*. Paris: UNESCO International Bureau of Education.
Ahn Pyong-Hi. 1997. The principles underlying the invention of the Korean alphabet. In: Y.-K. Kim-Renaud (ed.), *The Korean Alphabet: Its History and Structure*. Honolulu: University of Hawaii Press, 89–105.
Albright, William F. 1948. The early alphabetic inscriptions from Sinai and their decipherment. *Bulletin of the American Schools of Oriental Research* 116, 12–14.
Albrow. K. H. 1972. *The English Writing System*. London: Longman.
Anderson, James M. 1988. *Ancient Languages of the Hispanic Peninsula*. Lanham, MD: University Press of America.
Aristotle. 1938. *Peri Hermeneias (De Interpretatione)*. Translated by H. P. Cook. London: Loeb Classical Library.
Aronoff, Mark. 1992. Segmentalism in linguistics. The alphabetic basis of phonological theory. In: P. Downing, S. D. Lima and M. Noonan (eds.), *The Linguistics of Literacy*. Amsterdam: John Benjamins, 71–82.
Assmann, Jan. 1991. *Stein und Zeit: Mensch und Gesellschaft im alten Ägypten*. Munich: Wilhelm Fink Verlag.
Avrin, Leila. 1991. *Scribes, Script and Books*. Chicago: American Library Association.
Battestini, Simon. 1997. *Ecriture et texte: Contribution africaine*. Quebec: Les Presses de l'Université Laval.
Baurain, Claude. 1991. L'écriture syllabique à Chypre. In: C. Baurain, C. Bonnet and V. Krings (eds.), *Phoinikeia grammata: Lire et écrire en Méditerranée*. Actes du Colloque de Liège, 1988. Namur: Société des Etudes Classiques, 389–424.
Bell, Alexander Melville. 1867. *Visible Speech: The Science of Universal Alphabetics; or self-interpreting physiological letters, for writing of all languages in one alphabet*. New York: D. van Nostrand.
Bennet, Jo Anne, and John W. Berry. 1991. Cree literacy in the syllabic script. In: D. R. Olson and N. Torrance (eds.), *Literacy and Orality*. Cambridge: Cambridge University Press, 90–104.
Bennett, Emmett L. 1996. Aegean scripts. In: Peter. T. Daniels and William Bright (eds.), *The World's Writing Systems*. New York: Oxford University Press, 125–33.
Bigelow, Charles. 1992. Typography. In: William Bright (ed.), *International Encyclopedia of Linguistics*. New York: Oxford University Press, IV, 196–9.

Boogert, Nico van den. 1997. Tifinagh. In: P. J. Bearman *et al.* (eds.), *Encyclopedia of Islam.* Leiden: Brill, X, 476–8.

Bradley, David. 2000. Language policy or the Yi. In: Stevan Harrell (ed.), *Perspectives on the Yi in Southwest China.* Berkeley: University of California Press, 195–213.

Bricker, Victoria R. 2000. Bilingualism in the Maya Codices and the Books of Chilam Balam. *Written Language and Literacy* 3(1), 77–115.

Bright, William. 1990. *Language Variation in South Asia.* New York: Oxford University Press.

  1999. A matter of typology. Alphasyllabaries and Abugidas. *Written Language and Literacy* 2(1), 45–55.

Britto, Francis. 1986. *Diglossia: A Study of the Theory with Application to Tamil.* Washington, DC: Georgetown University Press.

Bühler, Georg. 1896. *Indische Palaeographie von circa 350 a. Chr. – circa 1300 p. Chr.* Strassburg: Truebner. Translated as *Indian Palaeography.* New Delhi: Oriental Books Reprint Corporation, 1980.

  1980. *Indian Palaeography.* New Delhi: Oriental Books Reprint Corporation.

Bullough, D. A. 1991. *Carolingian Renewal: Sources and Heritage.* Manchester: Manchester University Press.

Burnaby, Barbara (ed.). 1985. *Promoting Native Writing Systems in Canada.* Toronto: OISE Press.

Butterworth, B., and W. Yin. 1991. The universality of two routines for reading: evidence from Chinese dyslexia. *Proceedings of the Royal Society* B 245, 91–95.

Carl, John W. 1965. American Spelling. In: G. H. Vallins, *Spelling.* London: Andre Deutsch, 184–202.

Carney, Edward. 1994. *A Survey of English Spelling.* London: Routledge.

Catach, Nina. 1978. *L'orthographe.* Paris: Presses Universitaires de France.

  1987. New linguistic approaches to a theory of writing. In: S. Battestini (ed.), *Georgetown University Roundtable on Languages and Linguistics 1986: Developments in Linguistics and Semiotics, Language Teaching and Learning, Communication Across Cultures.* Washington, DC: Georgetown University Press, 161–74.

Cattell, James M. 1886. The time it takes to see and name objects. *Mind* 11, 63–65.

Chafe, Wallace. 1987. Properties of spoken and written language. In: R. Horowitz and S. J. Samuels (eds.), *Comprehending Oral and Written Language.* New York: Academic Press, 83–113.

Chao, Yuan Ren. 1930. A system of tone letters. *Le Maître Phonétique* 30, 24–27.

Chen, Ping. 1996. Toward a phonographic writing system of Chinese: a case study in writing reform. *International Journal of the Sociology of Language* 122, 1–46.

  2001. Functions of phonetic writing in China. In: N. Gottlieb and P. Chen (eds.), *Language Planning and Language Policy: East Asian Perspectives.* Richmond, Surrey: Curzon, 75–94.

Cheng Chao-Ming and Yang Mu-Jang. 1989. Lateralization in the visual perception of Chinese characters and words. *Brain and Language* 36, 669–89.

Chomsky, Noam. 1957. *Syntactic Structures.* The Hague: Mouton.

Chomsky, Noam, and Morris Halle. 1968. *The Sound Pattern of English.* New York: Harper & Row.

Christin, A.-M. (ed.) 2001. *Histoire de l'écriture, de l'idéogramme au multimédia.* Paris: Flammarion.

Civil, Miguel. 1973. The Sumerian writing system: some problems. *Orientalia* NS 42, 21–34.
Clanchy, M. T. 1993. *From Memory to Written Record: England 1066–1307.* Oxford: Blackwell.
Clark, John W. 1965. American spelling. In: G. H. Vallins (ed.), *Spelling.* 2nd rev. edn. London: Andre Deutsch, 184–202.
Coe, Michael. 1992. *Breaking the Maya Code.* London: Thames and Hudson.
Cohen, Jonathan. 1954. The project of a universal character. *Mind* 63, 49–63.
Cohen, Marcel. 1958. *La grande invention de l'écriture et son évolution.* Paris: Imprimerie Nationale. 2 vols.
Cohn, Abigail. 2001. Phonology. In: M. Aronoff and J. Rees-Miller (eds.), *The Handbook of Linguistics.* Oxford: Blackwell, 180–212.
Cook, Vivian. 2002. *The English Writing System.* London: Arnold.
Cooper, Jerrold S. 1996. Sumerian and Akkadian. In: Peter Daniels and William Bright (eds.), *The World's Writing Systems.* New York: Oxford University Press, 37–57.
Coulmas, Florian. 1989. *The Writing Systems of the World.* Oxford: Basil Blackwell.
  1992. *Language and Economy.* Oxford: Blackwell.
  1996. *The Blackwell Encyclopedia of Writing Systems.* Oxford: Blackwell.
  2000. The nationalization of writing. *Studies in the Linguistic Sciences* 30(1), 47–59.
Coulmas, Florian (ed.). 1984. *Linguistic Minorities and Literacy.* Berlin: Mouton.
Cross, Frank Moore. 1989. The invention and development of the alphabet. In: W. M. Senner (ed.), *The Origin of Writing.* Lincoln: University of Nebraska Press, 79–90.
Crystal, David. 1992. *An Encyclopedic Dictionary of Language and Languages.* Oxford: Blackwell.
Cubelli, R. 1991. A selective deficit for writing vowels in acquired dysgraphia. *Nature* 353, 258–60.
Dalby, David. 1967. A survey of the indigenous scripts of Liberia and Sierra Leone: Vai, Mende, Loma, Kpelle and Bassa. African Language Studies 8. London: School of Oriental and African Studies, 1–51.
  1970. The historical problem of the indigenous scripts of West Africa and Surinam. In: D. Dalby (ed.), *Language and History in Africa.* New York: Africana, 109–19.
Damerow, Peter, and Robert Englund. 1989. *The Proto-Elamite Texts from Tepe Yahya.* Cambridge, MA: Harvard University Press.
Daniels, Peter, 1990. Fundamentals of grammatology. *Journal of the American Oriental Society* 110, 727–31.
Daniels, Peter. T., and William Bright (eds.). 1996. *The World's Writing Systems.* New York: Oxford University Press.
Darnell, R., and A. L. Vanek. 1973. The psychological reality of Cree syllabics. In: R. Darnell (ed.), *Canadian Languages in their Social Context.* Edmonton: University of Alberta Press, 171–92.
Daswani, C. J. 1979. Movement for the recognition of Sindhi and for the choice of a script for Sindhi. In: E. Annamalai (ed.), *Language Movements in India.* Mysore: Central Institute of Indian Languages, 60–69.
  2001. Issues of literacy development in the Indian context. In: D. R. Olson and Nancy Torrance (eds.), *The Making of Literate Societies.* Oxford: Blackwell, 284–95.
Davies, W. V. 1987. *Egyptian Hieroglyphs.* London: British Museum.
DeFrancis, John. 1984a. Digraphia. *Word* 35(1), 59–66.
  1984b. *The Chinese Language: Fact and Fantasy.* Honolulu: University of Hawaii Press.

Bibliography

1989. *Visible Speech: The Diverse Oneness of Writing Systems*. Honolulu: University of Hawaii Press.
Deshpande, Madhav M. 1993. *Sanskrit and Prakrit: Sociolinguistic Issues*. Delhi: Motilal Banarsidass Publishers.
Dewey, Godfrey. 1971. *English Spelling: Roadblock to Reading*. New York: Teachers College.
Diller, Anthony. 1992. Thai. In: William Bright (ed.), *International Encyclopedia of Linguistics*. 4 vols. New York: Oxford University Press, 149–56.
Di Sciullo, Anne-Marie, and Edwin Williams. 1987. *On the Definition of Word*. Cambridge, MA: MIT Press.
Diringer, David. 1968 [1948]. *The Alphabet: A Key to the History of Mankind*. 3rd edition, completely revised with the collaboration of Rheinold Regensburger. London: Hutchinson. New York: Philosophical Library. 2 vols.
Downing, Pamela, Susan D. Lima and Michael Noonan (eds.). 1992. *The Linguistics of Literacy*. Typological studies in language 21. Amsterdam: Benjamins.
Driver, Godfrey R. 1976. *Semitic Writing*. Rev. edn. London: Oxford University Press.
Dudley, Homer, and T. H. Tarnoczy. 1950. The speaking machine of Wolfgang von Kempelen. *Journal of the Acoustical Society of America* 22(2), 151–66.
Faber, Alice. 1992. Phonemic segmentation as epiphenomenon: evidence from the history of alphabetic writing. In: P. Downing, S. D. Lima and M. Noonan (eds.), *The Linguistics of Literacy*. Amsterdam: John Benjamins, 111–34.
Ferguson, Charles A. 1959. Diglossia. *Word* (New York) 15, 325–40.
Février, James G. 1948. *Histoire de l'écriture*. Paris: Payot.
Fischer, Henry G. 1989. The origin of Egyptian hieroglyphs. In: Wayne M. Senner (ed.), *The Origins of Writing*. Lincoln: University of Nebraska Press, 59–76.
Fischer, Wolfdietrich. 1992. Arabic. In: William Bright (ed.), *International Encyclopedia of Linguistics*. New York: Oxford University Press, I, 91–7.
Fishman, Joshua A. 1988. Ethnocultural issues in the creation, substitution, and revision of writing systems. In: B. A. Rafoth and D. L. Rubin (eds.). 1988. *The Social Construction of Written Communication*. Norwood, NJ: Ablex, 273–86.
Fodor, Jerry A. 1978. *The Language of Thought*. Hassocks, Sussex: The Harvester Press.
Frith, Uta, and Christopher Frith. 1980. Relationships between reading and spelling. In: J. B. Kavanagh and R. L. Venezky (eds.), *Orthography, Reading and Dyslexia*. Baltimore, MD: University Park Press, 287–95.
Frost, Ram. 1992. Orthography and phonology: the psychological reality of orthographic depth. In: Pamela Downing, Susan D. Lima and Michael Noonan (eds.), *The Linguistics of Literacy*. Amsterdam: John Benjamins, 255–74.
Gair, James W. 1986. Sinhala diglossia revisited *or* Diglossia dies hard. In: Bh. Krishnamurti (ed.), *South Asian Languages: Structure, Convergence and Diglossia*. Delhi: Motilal Banarsidass, 322–36.
Gardiner, Alan. H. 1947. *Ancient Egyptian Onomastica*. I. *Text*. Oxford: Oxford University Press.
Gardiner, Alan H., Thomas E. Peet and J. Černý. 1952. *The Inscriptions of Sinai*. Oxford: Oxford University Press.
Gaur, A. 1985. *A History of Writing*. New York: Charles Scribner's Sons.
Gelb, I. J. 1963. *A Study of Writing*. 2nd edition. Chicago: University of Chicago Press.
Givon, Talmy. 1979. *On Understanding Grammar*. New York: Academic Press.

Goody, Jack. 1986. *The Logic of Writing and the Organization of Society.* Cambridge: Cambridge University Press.
Gray, Bennison. 1981. Parallel structures and 'The Failure of Modern Linguistics'. In: F. Coulmas (ed.), *A Festschrift for Native Speaker.* The Hague: Mouton, 203–20.
Green, Margaret W. 1981. The construction and implementation of the cuneiform writing system. *Visible Language* 15: 345–72.
Grivelet, Stéphane (ed.). 2001. Digraphia: writing system and society. *International Journal of the Sociology of Language* 150.
Gruendler, Beatrice. 1993. *The Development of the Arabic Scripts from the Nabatean Era to the First Islamic Century According to Dated Texts.* Atlanta: Scholars Press.
Günther, Hartmut. 1988. *Schriftliche Sprache: Strukturen geschriebener Wörter und ihrer Verarbeitung beim Lesen.* Tübingen: Niemeyer.
Günther, Hartmut, and Otto Ludwig (eds.). 1994–6. *Writing and its Use/Schrift und Schriftlichkeit: An Interdisciplinary Handbook of International Research.* Berlin: De Gruyter. 2 vols.
Haas, William (ed.). 1969. *Alphabets for English.* Manchester: Manchester University Press.
Haberland, Hartmut. 1994. Danish. In: E. König and J. van der Auwera (eds.), *The Germanic Languages.* London: Routledge, 313–48.
Hall, Robert. 1960. A theory of graphemics. *Acta Linguistica* 8, 13–20.
Hannas, W. C. 1997. *Asia's Orthographic Dilemma.* Honolulu: University of Hawaii Press.
 1999. *Asia's Orthographic Dilemma.* Honolulu: University of Hawaii Press.
Hànyŭ Pīnyīn Lùnwén Xuăn [Collected essays on Chinese phonetic writing]. 1988. Beijing: Writing Reform Committee.
Harris, Roy. 1986. *The Origin of Writing.* London: Duckworth.
 1995. *Signs of Writing.* London: Routledge.
 2000. *Rethinking Writing.* London: The Athlone Press.
Hashimoto Mantarō. 1987. Kokusaigo toshite no kango to kanji [Chinese words and characters as internationalisms]. In: M. Hashimoto, T. Suzuki and H. Yamada, *Kanji minzoku no ketsudan: kanji no mirai-ni mukete* [The kanji people at the crossroad: The future of kanji]. Tokyo: Taishukan, 327–60.
Hayes, John R., and Linda S. Flower. 1980. Identifying the organization of writing processes. In: W. W. Gregg and E. R. Steinberg (eds.), *Cognitive Processes in Writing.* Hillsdale, NJ: Erlbaum, 3–30.
Heath, Shirley B. 1983. *Ways with Words: Language, Life and Work in Communities and Classrooms.* Cambridge: Cambridge University Press.
Henderson, Leslie. 1982. *Orthography and Word Recognition in Reading.* London: Academic Press.
Hofstadter, Douglas R. 1982. Metafont, metamathematics, and metaphysics. *Visible Language* 14(4), 309–38.
Homer, Bruce, and David R. Olson. 1999. Literacy and children's conception of words. *Written Language and Literacy* 2(1), 113–40.
Householder, Fred. 1971. *Linguistic Speculations.* London: Cambridge University Press.
Huang, Jack K. T., and Timothy D. Huang. 1989. *An Introduction to Chinese, Japanese, and Korean Computing.* Singapore: World Scientific.
Hudson, Alan. 1992. Diglossia: a bibliographic review. *Language in Society* 21, 611–74.
 2002. Outline of a theory of diglossia. *International Journal of the Sociology of Language* 157.

Hyman, Larry. 1985. *A Theory of Phonological Weight*. Dordrecht: Reidel.
International Phonetic Association. 1949. *Principles of the International Phonetic Association*. London: University College.
Ives, Josephine P., Laura Z. Bursuk and Sumner A. Ives. 1979. *Word Identification Techniques*. Chicago: Rand McNally College Publishing Co.
Jaffré, Jean-Pierre, and Michel Fayol. 1997. *Orthographes: Des systèmes aux usages*. Paris: Flammarion.
Jensen, Hans. 1969. *Die Schrift in Vergangenheit und Gegenwart*. 3rd. rev. edn. Berlin: Deutscher Verlag der Wissenschaften.
  1970. *Sign, Symbol and Script: An Account of Man's Efforts to Write*. London: George Allen and Unwin.
Jones, Sir William. 1786. *Works*. I. *Discourse on the Hindus*. Edited by Anna Maria Jones (1807). London: Stockdale.
Justeson, John S., and Terrence Kaufmann. 1993. A decipherment of Epi-Olmec hieroglyphic writing. *Science* 159, 1703–11.
Kaiho, H., and Y. Nomura. 1983. *Kanji jōhōshori no shinrigaku* [The psychology of kanji processing]. Tokyo: Kyōiku Shuppan.
Kalmár, I. 1985. Are there really no primitive languages? In: D. R. Olson, N. Torrance and A. Hildyard (eds.), *Literacy, Language and Learning: The Nature and Consequences of Reading and Writing*. Cambridge: Cambridge University Press, 148–66.
Kaplan, Robert K. (ed.). 1995. *The Teaching of Writing in the Pacific Basin*. Clevedon: Multilingual Matters (= *Journal of Asian Pacific Communication* 6(1–2)).
Kavanagh, James B., and Ignatius G. Mattingly (eds.). 1972. *Language by Ear and by Eye*. Cambridge, MA: MIT Press.
Kay, Janice. 1996. Psychological aspects of spelling. In: Hartmut Günther and Otto Ludwig (eds.), *Writing and its Use/Schrift und Schriftlichkeit: An Interdisciplinary Handbook of International Research*. Berlin: de Gruyter, II, 1074–94.
Kaye, Alan S. 2001. Diglossia: the state of the art. *International Journal of the Sociology of Language* 152, 117–29.
Kesavan, B. S. 1997. *History of Printing and Publishing in India: A Story of Cultural Reawakening*. 3 vols. New Delhi: National Book Trust, India.
Kim, Chin W. 1997. The structure of phonological units in Han'gŭl. In: Young-Key Kim-Renaud (ed.), *The Korean Alphabet: Its History and Structure*. Honolulu: The University of Hawaii Press, 145–60.
Kim, C-W., and H. Sohn. 1986. A phonetic model for reading: evidence from Korean. *Studies in the Linguistic Sciences* 16(2), 95–105.
Kim-Renaud, Young-Key. 1997. The phonological analysis reflected in the Korean writing system. In: Young-Key Kim-Renaud (ed.), *The Korean Alphabet: Its History and Structure*. Honolulu: The University of Hawaii Press, 161–92.
King, Christopher R. 2001. The poisonous potency of script: Hindi and Urdu. *International Journal of the Sociology of Language* 150, 43–59.
Klima, Edward S. 1972. How alphabets might reflect language. In: J. F. Kavanagh and I. G. Mattingly (eds.), *Language by Ear and by Eye*. Cambridge, MA: MIT Press, 57–80.
Kohrt, Manfred. 1986. The term 'grapheme' in the history and theory of linguistics. In: Gerhard Augst (ed.), *New Trends in Graphemics and Orthography*. Berlin: de Gruyter, 80–96.

Krebernik, Manfred, and Hans J. Nissen. 1994. Die sumerisch-akkadische Keilschrift. In: Hartmut Günther and Otto Ludwig (eds.). 1994. *Writing and its Use/Schrift und Schriftlichkeit: An Interdisciplinary Handbook of International Research.* Berlin: de Gruyter, I, 274–88.

Laroch, Emmanuel. 1960. *Les hiéroglyphes hittites.* Paris: Centre National de la Recherche Scientifique.

Large, Andrew. 1985. *The Artificial Language Movement.* Oxford: Blackwell.

Ledyard, Gari. 1997. The international linguistic background of The Correct Sounds for the Instruction of the People. In: Y.-K. Kim-Renaud (ed.), *The Korean Alphabet: Its History and Structure.* Honolulu: University of Hawaii Press, 31–87.

Lee Don-Ju. 1990. An explanation on Hunmin-jŏng.ŭm. In: Shin Sang-Soon, Lee Don-Ju and Lee Hwan-Mook (eds.), *Understanding Hunmin-jŏng.ŭm.* Seoul: Hanshin Publishing Co., 37–86.

Leroi-Gourhan, André. 1964. *Le geste et la parole.* Paris: Albin Michel.

Linell, Per. 1982. *The Written Language Bias in Linguistics.* Linköping: Linköping University, Department of Communication Studies.

Liu Hsieh. 1983. *The Literary Mind and the Carving of Dragons.* Translated and annotated by Vincent Yu-chung Shih. Chinese Classics: Chinese-English Series. Hong Kong: The Chinese University of Hong Kong Press.

MacMahon, Michael K. C. 1996. Phonetic Notation. In: Peter T. Daniels and William Bright (eds.), *The World's Writing Systems.* New York: Oxford University Press, 821–44.

Macri, Martha J. 1996. Maya and other Mesoamerican scripts. In: Peter T. Daniels and William Bright (eds.), *The World's Writing Systems.* New York: Oxford University Press, 172–82.

Maddieson, I. 1984. *Patterns of Sounds.* Cambridge: Cambridge University Press.

Magner, T. F. 2001. Digraphia among Croats and Serbs. *International Journal of the Sociology of Language* 150, 11–26.

Mahapatra, B. P., G. D. McConnell, P. Pamanabha and V. S. Verma. 1989. *The Written Languages of the World: A Survey of the Degree and Modes of Use.* II. *India.* Quebec: Les Presses de l'Université Laval.

Mair, Victor. 2001. Notes on the Anau Inscription. *Sino-Platonic Papers* 112, July, 2001. (University of Pennsylvania).

Mallery, Garrick. 1893. *Picture Writing of the American Indians.* Washington, DC: Smithsonian Institution. Repr. 1972, New York: Dover Publications.

  1972. *Sign Language among North American Indians compared with that among Other Peoples and Deaf-Mutes.* Approaches to Semiotics 14. The Hague: Mouton. (First published 1881).

Mallon, Jean. 1982. *De l'écriture: Recueil d'études publiées de 1937 à 1981.* Paris: Editions du centre national de la recherche scientifique.

Man, John. 2000. *Alpha Beta: How 26 Letters Shaped the Western World.* New York: John Wiley & Sons.

Mann, Virginia A. 1986. Phonological awareness: the role of reading experience. *Cognition* 24, 65–92.

  1991. Phonological abilities: effective predictors of future reading ability. In: L. Rieben and C. A. Perfetti (eds.), *Learning to Read: Basic Research and its Implications.* Hillsdale, NJ: Lawrence Erlbaum, 113–29.

Massias, Nicolas de. 1828. *L'influence de l'écriture sur la pensée et sur le langage*. Paris: Firmin Didot.
Michalowski, Piotr. 1996. Mesopotamian cuneiform: origin. In: Peter T. Daniels and William Bright (eds.), *The World's Writing Systems*. New York: Oxford University Press, 33–36.
Morais, José. 1987. Phonetic awareness and reading acquisition. *Psychological Research* 49, 147–52.
Morais, J., L. Cary, J. Algeria and P. Bertelson. 1979. Does awareness of speech as a sequence of phonemes arise spontaneously? *Cognition* 7, 323–31.
Morohashi Tetsuji. 1984–6. *Daikanwa jiten* [Great Chinese-Japanese character dictionary]. 2nd edition. Tokyo: Taishukan.
Murawiec, Laurent. 2001. Géopolitique de l'écrit. *Pour la Science*. Dossier Hors-Série, Octobre/Janvier 2002.
Nagel, Paul. 1930. Chinesisch als Weltschrift? *Ostasiatische Rundschau* 11, 457–9.
Nakanishi, A. 1980. *Writing Systems of the World: Alphabets, Syllabaries, Pictograms*. Rutland, VT: Charles E. Tuttle Co.
Naveh, Joseph. 1987. *Early History of the Alphabet*. Jerusalem: Magnes.
Neurath, Otto. 1980. *International Picture Language: A Facsimile Reprint of the English Edition*. Reading: University of Reading. (First published 1936).
Newell, G. E., and P. Winograd. 1989. The effects of writing on learning from expository text. *Written Communication* 6, 196–217.
Nissen, Hans J. 1996. *Ursprung und frühe Entwicklung der Schrift im alten Orient*. Bad Homburg: Reimersstiftung.
Nissen, Hans J., Peter Damerow and Robert K. Englund. 1990. *Frühe Schrift und Techniken der Wirtschaftsverwaltung im alten Vorderen Orient: Informationsspeicherung und -verarbeitung vor 5000 Jahren*. N.p.: Verlag Franzbecker.
Nyikos, Julius. 1988. A linguistic perspective of illiteracy. In: Sheila Empleton (ed.), *The Fourteenth LACUS Forum 1987*. Lake Bluff, IL: Linguistic Association of Canada and the United States, 146–63.
O'Connor, M. 1996. Epigraphic Semitic scripts. In: Peter T. Daniels and William Bright (eds.), *The World's Writing Systems*. New York: Oxford University Press, 88–107.
OECD (ed.). 1995. *Literacy, Economy and Society: Results of the First International Adult Literacy Survey*. Paris: OECD.
Olson, David. 1994. *The World on Paper*. Cambridge: Cambridge University Press.
Olson, David R., and Nancy Torrance (eds.). 2001. *The Making of Literate Societies*. Oxford: Blackwell.
Ong, Walter S. 1982. *Orality and Literacy: The Technologizing of the Word*. London: Methuen.
Palaima, Thomas G. 1989. Cypro-Minoan scripts: problems of historical context. In: Y. Duhoux, T. G. Palima and J. Bennet (eds.), *Problems in Decipherment*. Louvain: Peeters, 121–87.
Palaima, Thomas G., and Elizabeth Sikkenga. 1999. Linear A> Linear B. *AEGAEUM* 20 (Annales d'archéologie égéenne de l'Université de Liège et UT-PASP), 599–608.
Paradis, Michel, Hiroko Hagiwara and Nancy Hildebrandt. 1985. *Neurolinguistic Aspects of the Japanese Writing System*. Orlando, FL: Academic Press.
Parkinson, Richard. 1999. *Cracking Codes: The Rosetta Stone and Decipherment*. London: The British Museum Press.

Parpola, Asko. 1994. *Deciphering the Indus Script*. Cambridge: Cambridge University Press.
Pattanayak, D. P. 1981. *Language and Politics*. Princess Leelavathi Memorial Lectures. Mysore: University of Mysore.
Pike, Kenneth L. 1947. *Phonemics: A Technique for Reducing Languages to Writing*. Ann Arbor: University of Michigan Press.
Plato. 1990. *Plato: Euthyphro; Apology; Crito; Phaedo; Phaedrus*. Translated by H. N. Fowler. Cambridge, MA: Harvard University Press.
Pollatsek, A., M. Lesch, R. K. Morris and K. Rayner. 1992. Phonological codes are used in integrating information across saccades in word identification and reading. *Journal of Experimental Psychology: Human Perception and Performance* 18, 148–62.
Pollatsek, A., and M. Lesch. 1996. Perception of words and letters. In: Harmut Günther and Otto Ludwig (eds.), *Writing and its Use/Schrift und Schriftlichkeit: An Interdisciplinary Handbook of International Research*. Berlin: de Gruyter, II, 957–71.
Postma, Antoon. 1971. Contemporary Mangyan scripts. *The Philippine Journal of Linguistics* 2: 1–11.
Prince, Alan. 1992. Segments. In: W. Bright (ed.), *International Encyclopedia of Linguistics*. New York: Oxford University Press, III, 384–7.
Pullum, Geoffrey K., and William A. Ladusaw. 1986. *Phonetic Symbol Guide*. Chicago: The University of Chicago Press.
Quine, Willard van Orman. 1960. *Word and Object*. Cambridge, MA: MIT Press.
Rafoth, Bennett A., and Donald L. Rubin (eds.). 1988. *The Social Construction of Written Communication*. Norwood, NJ: Ablex.
Ramsey, S. Robert. 1997. The Korean alphabet. In: Young-Key Kim-Renaud (ed.), *King Sejong the Great: The Light of Fifteenth Century Korea*. Washington, DC: The International Circle of Korean Linguistics, 41–50.
Ratcliffe, Robert R. 2001. What do 'phonemic' writing systems represent? *Written Language and Literacy* 4(1), 1–14.
Reicher, Gerald M. 1969. Perceptual recognition as a function of meaningfullness of stimulus material. *Journal of Experimental Psychology* 81, 275–80.
Ritner, Robert K. 1996. Egyptian Writing. In: Peter T. Daniels and William Bright (eds.), *The World's Writing Systems*. New York: Oxford University Press, 73–87.
Robins, R. H. 1978. *General Linguistics*. London: Longman.
Rubinstein, H., S. S. Lewis and M. H. Rubinstein. 1971. Evidence for phonemic recoding in visual word recognition. *Journal of Verbal Learning and Verbal Behavior* 10, 645–7.
Saenger, Paul. 1991. The separation of words and the physiology of reading. In: David R. Olson and Nancy Torrance (eds.), *Literacy and Orality*. Cambridge: Cambridge University Press, 184–214.
Saint-Jacques, Bernard. 1987. The Roman alphabet in the Japanese writing system. *Visible Language* 21(1), 88–105.
Salomon, Richard. 1995. On the origin of the early Indian scripts. *Journal of the American Oriental Society* 115(2), 271–9.
Sampson, Geoffrey. 1979. The indivisibility of words. *Journal of Linguistics* 15, 39–47.
    1985. *Writing Systems: A Linguistic Introduction*. Stanford, CA: Stanford University Press.

Sanmartín, J. 1988. Silabografías y segmentabilidad fonológica: travestidos grafiáficos en los silabarios antiguos. *Aula Orientalis* (Barcelona) 6(1), 83–98.
Sass, Benjamin. 1988. *The Genesis of the Alphabet and its Development in the Second Millennium B.C.* Wiesbaden: Harrassowitz
  1991. *Studia alphabetica: On the Origin and Early History of the Northwest Semitic, South Semitic and Greek Alphabets.* Göttingen: Vandenhoeck & Ruprecht.
Saussure, Ferdinand de. 1959. *Course in General Linguistics.* Translated by Wade Baskin. New York: The Philosophical Library.
Scancarelli, Janine. 1992. Aspiration and Cherokee orthographies. In: P. Downing, S. D. Lima and M. Noonan (eds.), *The Linguistics of Literacy.* Amsterdam: John Benjamins, 135–52.
Scardamalia, Marlene, and Carl Breiter. 1986. Research on written composition. In: M. Wittrock (ed.), *Handbook on Research on Teaching.* 3rd edition. New York: Macmillan, 778–803.
Schenkel, Wolfgang. 1984. Schrift. In Wolfgang Helck and Wolfhardt Westendorf (eds.), *Lexikon der Ägyptologie.* Wiesbaden: Harrassowitz, II, cols. 1187–9.
  1994. Die ägyptische Hieroglyphenschrift und ihre Weiterentwicklungen. In: H. Günther and O. Ludwig (eds.), *Writing and its Use/Schrift und Schriftlichkeit: An Interdisciplinary Handbook of International Research.* Berlin: de Gruyter, I, 289–96.
Schmandt-Besserat, Denise. 1992. *Before Writing.* 2 vols. Austin: University of Texas Press.
Scholes, Robert J., and Brenda J. Willis. 1991. Linguists, literacy, and the intensionality of Marshall McLuhan's Western man. In: David R. Olson and Nancy Torrance (eds.), *Literacy and Orality.* Cambridge: Cambridge University Press, 215–35.
Scragg, D. G. 1974. *A History of English Spelling.* Manchester: Manchester University Press.
Scribner, Sylvia, and Michael Cole. 1981. *The Psychology of Literacy.* Cambridge, MA: Harvard University Press.
Seeley, Christopher. 1991. *A History of Writing in Japan.* Leiden: E. J. Brill.
Senner, Wayne M. (ed.). 1989. *The Origins of Writing.* Lincoln: University of Nebraska Press.
Shin Sang-Soon, Lee Don-Ju and Lee Hwan-Mook (eds.). 1990. *Understanding Hunminjŏng.ŭm.* Seoul: Hanshin Publishing Co.
Skousen, Royal. 1982. English spelling and phonemic representation. *Visible Language* 14(1), 28–38.
Smith, Philip T. 1996. Research methods in the psychology of reading. In: Hartmut Günther and Otto Ludwig (eds.) *Writing and its Use/Schrift und Schriftlichkeit: An Interdisciplinary Handbook of International Research.* Berlin: de Gruyter, 932–42.
Sohn, Ho-min. 1997. Orthographic divergence in South and North Korea: toward a unified spelling system. In: Y.-K. Kim-Renaud (ed.), *The Korean Alphabet: Its History and Structure.* Honolulu: University of Hawaii Press, 193–217.
Stanovich, K. E. 1993. Does reading make you smarter? Literacy and the development of verbal intelligence. In: H. W. Rees (ed.), *Advances in Child Development and Behavior.* San Diego, CA: Academic Press, 133–80.
Steinberg, Danny D., and Helen Harper. 1983. Teaching written language as a first language to a deaf boy. In: F. Coulmas and K. Ehlich (eds.), *Writing in Focus.* The Hague: Mouton, 327–54.

Steinberg, Danny D., Hiroshi Nagata and David P. Aline. 2001. *Psycholinguistics: Language, Mind and World*. 2nd edition. London: Longman.
Stève, Marie-Joseph. 1992. *Syllabaire élamite: Histoire et paléographie*. Neuchatel: Recherches et Publications.
Street, Brian. 1995. *Social Literacies: Critical Approaches to Literacy in Development, Ethnography, and Education*. London: Longman.
Stroop, J. Ridley. 1935. Studies of interference in serial verbal reactions. *Journal of Experimental Psychology* 18, 643–62.
Stubbs, Michael. 1996. The English writing system. In: H. Günther and O. Ludwig (eds.), *Writing and its Use/Schrift und Schriftlichkeit: An Interdisciplinary Handbook of International Research*. Berlin: Walter de Gruyter, II, 1441–5.
Taft, Marcus. 1982. An alternative to grapheme-phoneme conversion rules? *Memory and Cognition* 10, 465–74.
  1987. Morphographic processing: the BOSS re-emerges. In: Max Coltheart (ed.), *The Psychology of Reading*. Hillsdale, NJ: Erlbaum, 265–80.
Taylor, Insup, and M. Martin Taylor. 1995. *Writing and Literacy in Chinese, Korean and Japanese*. Amsterdam: John Benjamins.
Treiman, Rebecca. 2001. Linguistics and reading. In: Mark Aronoff and Janie Rees-Miller (eds.), *The Handbook of Linguistics*. Oxford: Blackwell, 664–72.
Trigger, B. G. 1998. Writing systems: a case study in cultural evolution. *Norwegian Archaeological Review* 31, 39–62.
Tzeng, Ovid J. L., and Daisy Hung. 1981. Linguistic determinism: a written language perspective. In: O. J. L. Tzeng and H. Singer (eds.), *Perception of Print*. Hillsdale, NJ: Erlbaum, 237–55.
Uhry, Joanna K., and Linnea C. Ehri. 1999. Children's reading acquisition. In: D. A. Wagner, R. L. Venezky and B. V. Street (eds.), *Literacy: An International Handbook*. Boulder, CO: Westview Press, 43–8.
Ullman, B. L. 1989. *Ancient Writing and its Influence*. Toronto: University of Toronto Press.
Unger, John M. 1984. Japanese orthography in the computer age. *Visible Language* 18, 3.
Unger, J. Marshall. 1987. *The Fifth Generation Fallacy*. New York: Oxford University Press.
  1990. The very idea: the notion of ideogram in China and Japan. *Monumenta Nipponica* 45: 391–411.
  2001. Functional digraphia in Japan as revealed in consumer product preferences. *International Journal of the Sociology of Language* 150, 141–52.
Vachek, Josef. 1973. *Written Language: General Problems and Problems of English*. The Hague: Mouton.
Vaiman, A. A. 1974. Über die protosumerische Schrift. *Acta Antiqua Hungarica* (Budapest) 22, 15–27.
van der Molen, W. 1993. *Javaans schrift*. Leiden: Vakgroep Talen en Culturen van Zuidoost-Azi-en Oceani-, Rijksuniversiteit Leiden.
van Sommers, Peter. 1989. Where writing starts: the analysis of action applied to the historical development of writing. Paper presented at the fourth International Graphonomics Society Conference, Trondheim, July 1989.
Venezky, R. L. 1970. *The Structure of English Orthography*. The Hague: Mouton.
Verhoeven, Ludo (ed.). 1994. *Functional Literacy: Theoretical Issues and Educational Implications*. Amsterdam: John Benjamins.

von Soden, Wolfram, and Wolfgang Rölling. 1991. *Das akkadische Syllabar.* Analecta Orientalia 42. Rome: The Pontifical Institute.
Vygotsky, Lev S. 1962. *Thought and Language.* Cambridge, MA: MIT Press. (First published 1934).
Wagner, Daniel. A. 1995. Literacy and development: rationales, myths, innovations, and future directions. *International Journal of Educational Development* 15(4), 341–62.
Wagner, Daniel, Richard L. Venezky and Brian V. Street (eds.). 1999. *Literacy: An International Handbook.* Boulder, CO: Westview Press.
Walker, Willard, and James Sarbough. 1993. The early history of the Cherokee syllabary. *Ethnohistory* 40: 70–94.
Watt, W. C. 1994. Curves and angles. In: W. C. Watt (ed.), *Writing Systems and Cognition.* Dordrecht: Kluwer, 215–46.
   1989. The Ras Shamra matrix. *Semiotica* 74, 61–108.
   1998. The old-fashioned way. *Semiotica* 122(1/2), 99–138.
Webster, Noah. 1992. Declaration of linguistic independence. In: J. Crawford (ed.), *Language Loyalties: A Source Book on the Official English Controversy.* Chicago: The University of Chicago Press, 33–36.
Wells, J. C. 2000. Orthographic diacritics and multilingual computing. *Language Problems and Language Planning*, 249–272.
Wen Hsu. 1995. The first step toward phonological analysis in Chinese: fanqie. *Journal of Chinese Linguistics* 23(1), 137–58.
Widmaier, Rita. 1983. *Die Rolle der chinesischen Schrift in Leibniz Zeichentheorie.* Studia Leibnitiana Supplementa 24. Wiesbaden: Franz Steiner Verlag.
Wilhelm, Gernot. 1983. Reconstructing the phonology of dead languages. In: F. Coulmas and K. Ehlich (eds.), *Writing in Focus.* Berlin: Mouton, 157–66.
Woodard, Roger D. 1997. *Greek Writing from Knossos to Homer: A Linguistic Interpretation of the Origin of the Greek Alphabet and the Continuity of Ancient Greek Literacy.* New York: Oxford University Press.
Wright, Roger. 1991. *Latin and the Romance Languages in the Early Middle Ages.* London: Routledge.
Wurm, Stephen A. 1994. Graphisation and standardisation of languages. In: G. Lüdi (ed.), *Sprachstandardisierung.* Freiburg, Switzerland: Universitätsverlag, 255–72.
Xiàndài hànyǔ cídiǎn [Modern Chinese dictionary]. 1979. Beijing: Commercial Press.
Xīnhuā zìdiǎn [New China character dictionary]. 1992. Beijing: Shangwu.
Yamada, Jun. 1997. *Learning and Information Processing of Kanji and Kana.* Hiroshima: Keisuisha.
Zevit, Ziony. 1980. Matres lectionis *in Ancient Hebrew Epigraphs.* Cambridge, MA: American Schools of Oriental Research.
Zhang Jing. 1986. *Xīnbīan xiàndài hànyǔ* [Practical modern Chinese]. Shanghai: Shanghai Education Press.
Zhōngguó yǔyánxué dàcídiǎn. 1991–2 [Encyclopedic dictionary of Chinese linguistics]. Beijing: Jiangsi Educational Publishers.
Zhōu Yǒuguāng. 1992. *Zhōngguó yǔwén zònghéng tán* [Desultory arguments about Chinese language and writing]. Beijing: Rénmín jiàoyù.
Zima, Petr. 1974. Digraphia: the case of Hausa. *Linguistics* 124, 57–69.
Zipf, George Kingsley. 1949. *Human Behavior and the Principle of Least Effort: An Introduction to Human Ecology.* New York: Hafner.

Index of names

Abercrombie, David 89
Adams, Marilyn 215
Adiseshiah, M. S. 223
Ahn, Pyong-Hi 159
Albright, William F. 194
Albrow, K. H. 183
Alcuin of York 94
Aline, David P. 215
Al-Khatib, Mahmoud xvii
Anderson, James M. 62
Aristotle 2–5, 8
Aronoff, Mark 9, 13
Ashurbanipal 67
Aśoka 132
Assmann, Jan xvii, 8
Atatürk, Mustafa Kemal 238
Augustine 210, 222
Avrin, Leila 117

Bacon, Francis 23
Barthes, Roland 223
Battestini, Simon 15, 22f.
Baurain, Claude 62
Bell, Alexander Melville 28, 30
Bennet, Jo Anne 72
Bennett, Emmett L. 82
Berry, John W. 72
Bigelow, Charles 108
Boogert, Nico van den 201
Bradley, David 83
Breiter, Carl 218
Bricker, Victoria R. 62
Bright, William xvii, 21, 76, 113, 131f., 139
Britto, Francis 229
Bühler, Georg 132, 140
Bullough, D. A. 227
Bulwer, John 89
Burgess, Anthony 62f.
Burnaby, Barbara 62

Bursuk, Laura Z. 92
Butterworth, B. 216

Carney, Edward 183, 185
Carroll, Lewis 109
Catach, Nina 21
Cattell, James M. 213
Caxton, William 101
Chafe, Wallace 220
Champollion, Jean François 9, 170–2
Charlemagne 97, 225
Chen, Ping 86, 236
Cheng Chao-Ming 212
Chomsky, Noam 13, 89f., 183
Christin, A.-M. 191
Cicero 91
Civil, Miguel 177
Clanchy, M. T. 40
Clark, John W. 238
Coe, Michael 2, 62, 196
Cohen, Jonathan 24
Cohen, Marcel 21
Cohn, Abigail 89
Cole, Michael 62, 74
Cook, Vivian 183
Cooper, Jerrold S. 45
Coulmas, Florian 14, 21, 132, 224, 226
Cross, Frank Moore 201
Crystal, David 39
Cubelli, R. 219

Dalby, David 62, 72
Damerow, Peter 41, 44, 192
Daniels, Peter 21, 76, 113
Dante Alighieri 220
Darnell, R. 62
Daswani, C. J. 223, 225, 228, 232
Davies, W. V. 170, 174
DeFrancis, John 21, 55, 57, 93, 165, 233, 236
Deshpande, Madhav M. 132

Index of names

Dewey, Godfrey 183f.
Di Sciullo, Anne-Marie 38
Diller, Anthony 147
Diringer, David 21, 132, 201
Driver, Godfrey R. 126
Du Lun xvii
Dudley, Homer 28

Englund, Robert 41, 44, 192

Faber, Alice 13, 151f.
Fayol, Michel 93
Ferguson, Charles A. 229
Février, James G. 132
Fischer, Wolfdietrich 125, 173, 193
Flower, Linda S. 216
Fodor, Jerry A. 26
Frege, Gottlieb 24f.
Frith, Christoper 219
Frith, Uta 219

Gair, James W. 230
Gardiner, Alan H. 8, 193f.
Gaur, A. 21, 150
Gelb, I. J. 15f., 21, 69, 113f., 131, 197–9
Givon, Talmy 220
Goody, Jack 2, 26, 190f., 224
Gray, Bennison 226
Green, Margaret W. 48
Grivelet, Stéphane 231
Gruendler, Beatrice 122
Günther, Hartmut 21, 90, 214

Haas, William 183, 238
Haberland, Hartmut 106
Hagiwara, Hiroko 211
Halle, Morris 13, 183
Hammurabi 66
Hannas, W. C. 233, 236, 238
Harper, Helen 214
Harris, Roy 15–17, 23, 114, 198
Hasebe, Hiroshi xvii
Hashimoto Mantarō 53
Hayes, John R. 216
Heath, Shirley B. 224
Helmont, Franciscus Mercurius van 26f.
Henderson, Leslie 212
Herodotus 190
Hiebert, Fredrik T. 194
Hildebrandt, Nancy 211

Hofstadter, Douglas R. 204
Holle, K. F. 148f.
Homer, Bruce 220
Householder, Frank 12
Huang, Jack K. T. 54
Huang, Timothy D. 54
Hudson, Alan 229
Hung, Daisy 211
Hyman, Larry 65

Ives, Josephine P. 92
Ives, Sumner A. 92

Jaffré, Jean-Pierre xvii, 93
Jensen, Hans 127, 129, 131f.
Jespersen, Otto 28, 32
Johnson, Samuel 38f., 89, 94
Jones, William 28
Juteson, John S. 196

Kaiho, H. 215
Kalmár, I. 220
Kāngxī 55
Kaufmann, Terrence 196
Kavanagh, James 210
Kay, Janice 219
Kaye, Alan S. 122
Keitz, Jonathan 238, 241
Kesavan, B. S. 136
Kim Hakhyon xvii, 157
Kim, C.-W. 157, 164
Kim-Renaud, Young-Key xvii, 66, 159, 161, 164
King, Christopher R. 232
Klima, Edward S. 183
Kohrt, Manfred 36
Krebernik, Manfred 45, 74, 180
Kubrick, Stanley 1
Kwon Ji-sam 158

Ladusaw, William A. 32
Large, Andrew 23
Laroch, Emmanuel 62
Lee Don-Ju 156f., 159
Lee Hwan-Mook 156
Leibniz, Gottfried Wilhelm 18, 23f., 26, 37
Leroi-Gourhan, André 19
Lesch, M. 214f.
Lewis, S. 214
Liu Hsieh, 4f.
Ludwig, Otto 21

Index of names

Macri, Martha J. 196
Maddieson, I. 91
Magner, T. F. 233
Magritte, René 6
Mahapatra, B. P. 228
Mair, Victor 195
Mallery, Garrick 21f.
Mallon, Jean 94
Man, John 199
Mann, Virginia A. 215, 220
Massias, Nicolas de 9
Mattingly, Ignatius 210
Meillet, Antoine 1
Michalowski, Piotr 41
Morais, José 89, 220
Morohashi Tetsuji 53
Murawiec, Laurent 201

Nagata, Hiroshi 215
Nagel, Paul 26
Nakanishi, A. 21
Natsume Sōseki 182
Neurath, Otto 24f., 168
Newell, G. E. 218
Nissen, Hans J. 41, 44f., 74, 180, 192
Nomura, Y. 215
Nyikos, Julius 101, 184f.

O'Connor, M. 114
Olson, David 13f., 191, 220, 224
Ong, Walter S. 191
Osir, Tsorji 207

Palaima, Thomas G. 62, 192
Paradis, Michel 211
Parkinson, Richard 199, 224
Parpola, Asko 62, 132, 190, 192
Pattanayak, D. P. 232
Pike, Kenneth 97
Plato 5
Pollatsek, A. 214f.
Postma, Antoon 153
Prince, Alan 90
Pullum, Geoffrey K. 32

Quine, Willard van Orman 168

Rafoth, Bennett A. 224
Ramsey, Robert S. 151
Ratcliffe, Robert R. 80

Rawlinson, George 190
Reicher, Gerald M. 213
Ritner, Robert K. 174
Robins, R. H. 113
Rölling, Wolfgang 62
Rubin, Donald L. 224
Rubinstein, H. 214
Rubinstein, M. H. 214

Saenger, Paul 212
Saint-Jacques, Bernard 183
Salomon, Richard 132
Sampson, Geoffrey 38, 157, 168f., 187
Sanmartín, J. 62
Sapir, Edward 13
Sarbough, James 62
Sass, Benjamin 127, 194
Saussure, Ferdinand de 10–13, 16, 38–40
Scancarelli, Janine 70
Scardamalia, Marlene 218
Schenkel, Wolfgang 62, 171
Schmandt-Besserat, Denise 41, 193
Scoles, Robert J. 31
Scribner, Sylvia 62, 74
Seeley, Christopher 78, 181
Sejong 18, 156f., 161, 236
Shimizu, Yoshimi xvii
Shin Sang-Soon 156
Sikkenga, Elizabeth 192
Skousen, Royal 89
Smith, Philip T. 216
Socrates 5f.
Soden, Wolfram von 62
Sohn, H. 164f.
Sohn, Ho-min 233, 236
Steinberg, Danny D. xvii, 214f.
Stève, Marie-Joseph 62
Street, Brian 224
Stroop, J. Ridley 213
Sugita, Yuko xvii
Suzuki, Giri xvii

Taft, Marcus 214
Tamai, Yoko xvii
Tarnoczy, T. H. 28
Taylor, Insup 55, 212
Taylor, M. Martin 55, 212
Torrance, Nancy 224
Treiman, Rebecca 214

Twain, Mark 210, 219, 238, 240f.
Tzeng, Ovid J. L. 211

Ullman, B. L. 132
Unger, John Marshall 57, 182, 233, 236
Uno, Satoko xvii

Vachek, Josef 183
Vaiman, A. A. 49
van Sommers, Peter 200
Vanek, A. L. 62
Venezky, R. L. 183, 187, 224
Verhoeven, Ludo 224
Vygotsky, Lev S. 210, 220f.

Wagner, Daniel 224f.
Walker, Willard 62
Wang, Shuming 50
Watanabe, Makoto xvii
Watt, W. C. 113, 203
Webster, Noah 238
Wells, J. C. 102
Wen Hsu 86

Widmaier, Rita 24
Wilhelm, Gernot 62
Wilkins, John 28f.
Williams, Edwin 38
Willis, Brenda J. 31
Winograd, P. 218
Woodard, Roger D. 190, 207
Wright, Roger 228
Wurm, Stephen A. 228

Xǔ Shèn 55

Yamada, Jun 212
Yang Mu-Jang 212
Yin, W. 216
Yuan Ren Chao 106

Zhai Jiaxiong 86
Zhang Gonghui 86
Zhou Minglang xvii
Zhōu Yǒuguāng 55
Zima, Petr 233
Zipf, George Kingsley 54f., 199

Index of subjects

abjad 113
accent marks 235
acrophony 126, 194
Africa 23
Africa alphabet 102
Akkadian 21, 49, 67, 74f., 77f., 82, 112, 169, 178f., 188f., 207
  cuneiform 62
  interpretation 180
  writing 176f.
akṣara 135f., 138, 142
alphabet of human thought 24
alphabetic letter 89, 183
alphabetic literacy 9
alphabetic notation 107, 138
alphabetic orthography 91f., 94, 101, 107, 214
alphabetic words, pronounceability of 91
alphabetic writing 9, 13, 90, 97, 199f., 220
alphabetography 197, 199
alphabets 201
alphasyllabary 132, 152
American English 233
Amharic 112, 154
Arabic 35, 64, 231
  alphabet 73, 122f., 201f.
  orthography 125
  script 73, 116
  writing system 126
Aramaic 112, 120
  alphabet 116, 122
  script 115f., 132, 203, 206
  script, dissemination of 203
Armenian alphabet 201
articulation 26, 28, 63, 157, 159, 161
  manner of 28, 139
  organs of 26, 33, 157, 160
  places of 28
articulatory phonetics 160, 217

Assyrian 131
  cuneiform 209
autonomy 136, 184

Babylonian 67, 169
Begriffsschrift 24
Bengali 140, 228
book-keeping 225
Brāhmī 132–5, 139f., 143, 150
Brāhmī-derived scripts 148, 150
Burmese 65
bustrophedon 128

calligraphy 6, 158, 218
Cambodian 35
Canaanite alphabet 207
capitalization 31, 218
Carolingian reform 227
Castilian 229f.
Catalan 229f.
categories 7, 9, 53, 56
categorization 160
Cherokee 31f., 62, 69f.
Chinese xviii, 23, 36, 38, 40, 49, 63, 65f., 74, 82, 179, 196, 215
  characters 18, 24, 36f., 50f., 53f., 57, 60, 67, 74f., 78, 86, 152, 156f., 163, 169, 178f., 183, 188, 198, 200, 208, 215, 237
  graphic complexity of 157
  dictionaries 58
  interpretation 179
  language 53
  phonetics 156
  script 26, 190, 202
  origin of the 194
  syllables 67
  texts 59, 67
  word 58, 152, 161
  writing 50, 178, 195
  writing system 24, 56–8, 152

Chinese (cont.)
  written language 181
  reform of 236
Classical Arabic 111, 122, 229
Classical Greek 82
classical languages 299
classifications 212
clay 41, 43, 191, 208
clay tablets 1
clay tokens 41, 193
code 21f.
collective memory 22
communication 16, 19
  international 23, 26
  system of 15
complementary distribution 159
complex syllable 164
composition 218
conjunct consonant signs 136
consonant 28, 63, 87, 109f., 114, 125, 129, 154
  alphabet 113, 122, 126f., 172, 190
  cluster 71, 134, 136, 145
  length 100
  letters 118, 159
  palatalized 78
consonantal roots 110
consonantal writing 118
consonants, geminated 77
context 39, 47, 215, 218
contrastive tone 145
Coptic 201
copyright 225
count stones 41
Cree 62, 69f., 72
Croatian 35, 233
cuneiform 43, 46, 66, 77, 82, 131, 169, 172, 207
  direction of 48
  logograms 180
  origin of 192
  signs 55, 74, 188, 193
  syllabary 77
  syllabic signary 67
  syllabographic writing 78
  text 67
  writing 191, 200
cursive script 170
Cypriot 62, 69, 82
Cyrillic 115, 140, 201, 232
  alphabet 232, 235

Dakota winter count 22
Danish 102, 106, 111
Dead Sea scrolls 116

decipherment 2, 21, 192, 209
decoding 200
deep systems 214
deficiencies in writing vowels 219
determinative 47f., 67, 173, 175f., 178, 189, 198
Devanagari 35, 136–40, 142, 152, 232
diachronic linguistics 10
diacritic 72, 81, 102f., 111, 120, 121, 136, 138, 143–5, 153, 234
  vowel indication 134, 136
diacritical tone marks 106
dictionary 13, 39, 46, 54f., 101, 86, 214
diglossia 122, 229–31
digraphia 231, 233–5
digraphs 99f., 188
diphthong 110, 123, 128, 134, 139, 145
direction 48, 128
disambiguation 47
discourse 5
double articulation 53
duration 118
Dutch 98, 100, 102, 204

Egyptian 21, 62, 169, 189, 193, 196
  'alphabet' 173
  hieroglyphs xviii, 8, 23, 60, 188, 193
  letters, history of 198
  text 7
  writing 8, 170, 178, 188, 200
  writing system 198
  writing, origin of 193
Ethiopic syllabic alphabet 154f.
Elamite 62, 67, 78, 208
encoding 200
English 63f., 66, 87, 95, 97, 111, 169, 199, 204
  alphabet 36
  lexicon 188
  orthography 152, 183, 185, 187, 200
    complexity of 152
  spelling 89, 200, 214
    reform proposals for 238
  vowel system 185
    word 58, 101
      phonetic interpretation of 99
  writing 32
  writing system 183f.
Etruscan 202
etymology, principle of 186
evolutionism 16

faculty of language 10f., 34
fanqie 86f.

feature 162
Finnish 169, 213, 233
font 204
foreign names 194
foreign spelling 98
French 36, 64, 111, 169, 204, 228–31
function of writing 3, 5, 15f., 22

Ge'ez 154, 228
Georgian alphabet 201
German 66, 98, 100, 102, 111, 204, 230
   spelling 233
Glagolitic alphabet 232
Graeco-Latin alphabet 111
grammar 13, 31
grammatical relations 39
grammatical theory 11
grammatical unit 38
grammatical words 187
grapheme 36, 74, 70, 72f., 80, 82, 93, 98–101, 103, 217, 219
grapheme–phoneme correspondence 99, 101, 184, 213–15
graphemic words 220
graphic 136
   signs 19
   syllable 62, 136, 145
   word 98, 101, 213
graphization 227, 232
graphotactics 217
Greek xviii, 3f., 8, 30, 36, 40, 82, 90, 127, 190, 196, 204, 207, 233
   alphabet 4, 31, 109, 122, 126, 128f., 131f., 170, 199, 201, 209
   orthography 235
   spelling 128
   writing 3, 126
Gujarati 228
Gupta script 143
Gurmukhi 140

Haitian Creole 231
handwriting 203
Han'gŭl 156–63, 165–9, 233, 237
   orthography 163
heavy syllable 80
Hebrew 36, 64, 112
   alphabet 26, 116, 121
   consonantal alphabet 118
   Square script 116, 122, 203
hieroglyph 60, 170, 173, 175, 194
Hindi 136, 232, 288
hiragana 69, 78, 81

historical linguistics 34
historicity 197
   principle 184
history of civilization 191
Hittite 208
   cuneiform 62
   hieroglyphic xviii, 67, 209
   signary 67
homonyms 46
homophone differentiation 60, 184
homophony 52, 55, 60, 187, 197
Hurrian 62, 78
hyphenation 31, 218

iconicity 8, 157, 167
ideogram 57, 59
ideographic 40f.
ideographs 51
ideography 57
illiteracy 221, 223, 225f., 238, 241
Indian
   scripts 142, 144, 151, 153f., 156, 208
   writing systems 131
indicators 47
Indus script xviii, 132
inner writing 8
inscriptions 50
internal code 26
international communication 23, 26
International Phonetic Association 28
Internet 1
interpretation 17, 32, 40, 46, 52, 75, 78, 94, 118, 160, 165, 168, 177, 182
   Akkadian 180
   Chinese 179
   consonantal 127
   contextual 78
   Japanese 179, 181, 183
   lexical 177, 179
   linguistic 48, 60, 101, 169, 179, 190, 192, 196–8, 200, 203f.
   phonetic 15, 31, 33, 35, 80, 82, 91, 95–7, 100, 107, 118, 125, 129, 136, 152, 154, 163, 165, 175–7, 179, 181, 204–6, 208
   of characters 58
   semantic 33, 35
   Semitic 194
   sound 57
   Sumerian 180
   syllabic 86
   unit of 152, 164f.
Inuktitut 220
IPA 28, 30–2, 103, 107, 145

Index of subjects

Iranian languages 115
Italian 228–30

Japanese 36, 39, 67, 74f., 62, 82, 169, 179–81, 188f., 208
  interpretation 179, 181, 183
  syllabaries 69, 75
  words 180
  writing 178, 233
  writing system 169, 182

kana 62, 68, 79, 81, 87, 163, 179, 183, 220, 233
kana syllabaries 78, 80
Kannada 142
Kashmiri 140
katakana 69, 78, 81
Kharoṣṭī 132
kokuji 180
Korean 35–7, 66f., 203, 208
  alphabet 151
  language 156
  script 26, 156
  syllable structure 164
  syllables 164f.
  words 161
  writing system 165, 237

Lahu 106
language 10, 16, 53
  agglutinative 48, 59
  conception of 12f.
  contact 208
  cultivation 227
  identity 230f.
  isolating 59
  nature of 7
  of thought 26
  processing 211
languages, inflecting 59
Latin 38, 40, 91f., 95, 227–30
  alphabet 15f., 30–2, 35, 62, 73, 90, 93–7, 100, 102f., 107f., 111, 184, 189, 199, 201, 233
  archaic 204
  death of 229
  spelling 93, 186
letter 2f., 7, 12, 14, 28, 30f., 90, 95, 98, 188, 214
lexical access 215
lexical segmentation 60
lexicography 38, 54
lexicon 13
ligature 93, 136, 138, 140, 142f.

Linear B xviii, 62, 69, 82, 209
linear order 152
linearity 3, 151, 154, 170
  syllabic 155
linguistic
  analysis 139, 151
  change 208
  communication 17
  evolution 11
  knowledge 40
  orthodoxy 10
  sign 12
lishū 50
list 39, 48
literacy 3, 13f., 191, 220, 224, 226f., 236, 238, 240
  alphabetic 9
  restricted 230
literal meanings 14
literary variety 230
literate
  culture 6, 10, 16
  society 14, 221, 223, 225, 240
liù shū 55
loanword 101, 177, 181f., 186, 208
logical thinking 3
logogram 46–9, 55, 59, 67, 77f., 169f., 173, 176–8, 198
logographic
  system 47
  writing 40, 180, 187
logography 62, 74, 197, 199
Lolo 82
Loma 72f.

Malayalam 142
Mandaic 116
Mangyan
  language 154
  syllabic alphabet 153
Manichean script 202
Manyōgana 67f.
Marathi 136, 228
mathematics 18
matres lectionis 118, 120, 122, 126f., 131
Maya 2, 21, 62, 196, 209
  calendar 196
meaning 11, 14, 18, 24, 31, 41, 46, 58, 63, 91, 215
memory support 20
Mende 72f.

Index of subjects

Mesoamerican scripts, origin of 196
Middle French 97
minimal pairs 64
mnemonic devices 20f.
Mongolian 203, 233
   alphabet 204–6
mora 65, 80f., 88
morpheme 31, 38, 48, 53, 57f., 72, 101, 182f., 188, 212, 216
   constancy 184
morphology 13, 31, 38, 67, 75, 216
   effects of 217
   grammatical 67
morphophonemic orthography 183
morphophonology 188
morphosyllabic writing 69

Nabataean script 116, 122, 201
Nepali 136
Nestorian 201
norms 229
Norwegian 100
notation 15, 24, 188
   alphabetic 107, 138
   mathematical 15
   musical 15
number signs 41f.
numerals 52

Old Church Slavonic 228
Old French 96
Old Hebrew 204–6
Old Persian cuneiform 169
Olmec 196
oracle bone inscription 50, 195
organs of speech 139
origins of writing 192, 196
Oriya 140, 228
orthographic
   standard 233, 238
   word 39f.
orthographies 101
   alphabetic 91, 101
   deep 108
   shallow 102f, 108, 213
   surface 102
orthography 35, 80, 93, 100, 231, 241
   alphabetic 92, 94, 214
   English 183
   morphophonemic 183
   reforms 241

Paleo-Hebrew script 116
Pali script 203
Palmyran 116
Persian 203
Perso-Arabic script 232
Phoenician 112
   alphabet 113, 116, 129, 132
   letters 128
phoneme 14, 30f., 36, 63, 91, 93f., 97, 99, 107, 109, 188, 212, 217, 219
   constancy 184
   of English 184
phoneme–grapheme correspondence 101, 107, 234
phonemic 70
   segment 89
   writing 93f., 99, 101, 107
phonetic 52, 56, 58, 136
   complement 47, 60
   features 90, 157
   indicator 48f.
   transcription 28, 32
   values 74
   words 101
   writing 173
phonetics 11, 28, 31, 60, 139
phonetization 198
phonics 214f.
phonogram 86, 170, 173, 176, 198
phonographic
   texts 122
   writing 111
phonography 18, 33, 37
phonological
   awareness 220
   form of words 214
   interpretation 214
   recoding 91, 213f., 216
   segment 153
   word 39, 214, 216
phonology 11, 13, 31, 87, 106, 188, 216, 231
   Western 159f.
physiological alphabet 28f.
pictograms 43, 51f.
pictographic icons 24
pictographs 21
pictorial signs 192f., 196
pictures 19, 21, 41, 192, 196
Pinyin 36, 106, 204, 233, 236
pitch 65, 70, 103, 109
plene writing 77, 118

polyfunctionality 188
polyvalence 94, 98, 101, 143, 180, 185, 199
Portuguese 100, 229f.
Prakrits 228
principle of autonomy 33f.
principle of economy 200
principle of etymology 186
principle of historicity 33f., 168
principle of interpretation 33f.
principle of least effort 199
pronunciation 227
    competence 219
proposition 3f.
Proto-Sinaitic 194f., 209
pseudo-etymological spelling 96
pseudoword 213
punctuation 218

quipu 20

radical 55–8, 60
reading 210, 215, 221f.
    disorders 211
    research 91, 216f.
    social aspects of 224
    teaching of 215
real time 7
rebus writing 46, 52, 74f., 197
recording system 20, 197
religion 201, 232
rhythmical time 65
Roman 35, 140
roman
    alphabet 197, 208, 211
    letters 28, 30, 32, 36, 188
Romanian 203
romanization 36, 106, 234, 236
Rosetta Stone 170
Russian 64

sandhi 140
Sanskrit 132, 136, 143, 228
    writing 140
schooling 225, 240
script reform 235
scriptism 14
scriptura continua 128, 130, 212
segment 53, 87, 90f., 93, 98, 106, 154, 162
    phonemic 89
segmental
    analysis 155

script 169
    writing 87
segmentation 107, 220
semantic
    categories 57
    classifier 47, 52, 56, 175
    determinative 55, 60, 176
    extension 177
    primitives 24, 26
    script 24
semiography 18, 33, 37
Semitic
    alphabet 115, 123, 126f., 129f., 173, 193, 207
    interpretation 194
    languages 74, 110, 126, 171
    scripts 114
    writing 111–15, 126, 154
sentence 2, 13f., 24, 31
Serbian 233
    writing 35
Serbo-Croatian 233
Serto 201
Shuō wén jiě zì 50
silent letters 96
silent reading 212
Sindhi 136, 140
Sinhala 230
social control 20
Somali 154
sound 11f., 18, 26, 28, 31, 33, 41, 46, 58, 91, 184, 208, 214
    change 30, 109
    continuum 11
    images 12
    interpretation 57
    pattern of English 183
    segment 107, 161
sound–letter correspondence 97, 184, 187
Spanish 169, 204, 213
speech syllable 62, 136
spelling 35, 58, 147, 183f., 208, 218f., 222
    competence 219
    convention 186
    conventions 101, 184, 188
    disorders 219
    etymological 145, 165
    historical 96, 98
    pronunciation 97, 208
    pseudo-etymological 96
    reform 234f.
    system 236

Index of subjects

spelling-pronunciation 147
standardization 97, 182, 203, 208, 225–7, 229, 240
stimulus diffusion 193
stress 64, 103, 109
Sumerian 40, 46, 49, 59, 74, 178f., 207
   cuneiform 47, 55, 75, 176, 178f.
   interpretation 180
   language 47, 59
   script 43
   signs 60
   word 46, 77
   writing 41f., 48f., 76, 177, 193
Sumerograms 180, 208
Summer Institute of Linguistics 201
suprasegmentals 106f., 145
surface 213
Swahili 233
Swiss-German 230
syllabary 57, 66, 69–71, 77f., 81, 83f., 87, 93, 114, 153, 199
syllabic
   alphabet 132, 140, 148
   interpretation 86
   linearity 155
   writing 69, 78, 82, 164
   writing system 62, 66, 69
syllabification 64
syllable 7, 31, 57f., 62–4, 70, 72, 74, 84, 86–8, 114, 131, 136f., 138f., 145, 154, 156f., 159, 162, 182f., 212
   atonal 148
   blocks 161f., 164
   complex 164
   duration of 65
   heavy 80
   Korean 164
   light 80
   long 80
   notions of the 63
   structure 63, 67f.
   type 66
   writing 75
syllabogram 67, 76, 83, 169f., 177–9
syllabography 74f., 197, 199

tally sticks 20
Tamil 139–42, 145, 231
teaching of reading 215
Telugu 142
temporal duration 33, 90, 137, 152

temporal sequence 136
text 5, 14, 40, 45
Thai 65f., 139, 152
   orthography 145
   syllabic alphabet 146
   writing 145, 148
Tiberian pointing 120f.
Tibetan 139, 152
   alphabet 35
   script 203
   syllabic alphabet 144
   writing 143
Tifinagh script 201
Tigrinia 154
time 32, 90
tone 65, 83, 86, 106, 109, 143, 145, 148
   diacritic 107, 148
   language 65, 68, 106
   marks 145, 148, 161
   syllable 57, 148
transcription 30–3, 36, 67, 101, 214
transliteration 36
triconsonantal root 111, 171, 173
trigraphs 99f., 188
Turkish 203, 238
Tyrrhenian alphabets 201

Universal Alphabet 28, 30
universal
   character 33, 41, 168
   code 23
   literacy 223, 225f., 240
   script 23f.
Uratian 78
Urdu 232, 288

Vai syllabary 62, 69, 72f.
Vietnamese 38, 66f., 106, 203, 208, 234
visible speech 18, 28
visual perception 19
vowel 28, 63, 77, 87, 109f., 120, 125, 129, 154, 185, 219
   indication 111, 121, 172
   'inherent' 134, 140
   length 64f.
   letter 160f., 198
   long 124, 145
   short 123

Wei 82
West African scripts 62

Index of subjects

West Semitic 194
Western phonology 159f.
word 7f., 13f., 31, 38f., 53, 59f., 91, 98, 101, 123, 175f., 212f., 220
  boundary 175
  concept of 13, 40
  interpretations 77
  lists 98f.
  orthographic 39f.
  phonological 39, 214, 216
  recognition 212–14
  separation 39f., 128
  spacing 31, 40
  superiority effect 212
world script 26
writing 21, 210, 221
  acquisition of 224
  authority of 225
  autonomy of 16, 136, 145, 184
  cognitive consequences of 220
  definition of 2, 4, 15
  evolution of 198
  function of 15
  history of 1, 191, 193, 196, 200, 203, 208f.
  paradoxical character of 7
  social aspects of 224
  social value of 225
  theories of 2
writing group 123
writing process 211, 218
writing reform 84, 86, 234, 237
writing systems 188
  development of 191
  dissemination of 203
written communication 49
written language 9, 12–14, 16f., 35, 39, 43, 118, 211, 223, 226, 228, 230, 236
  mastery of 221
written text 31, 99
written word 182, 213

Yi 35, 82, 87
  characters 83
  script 84
  syllabary 85f.

Zapotec 196
zero letter 159f.